RAY WINSTONE

THE BIOGRAPHY

THE STORY OF THE ULTIMATE SCREEN HARDMAN

NIGEL GOODALL

JOHN BLAKE

Published by John Blake Publishing Ltd,
3 Bramber Court, 2 Bramber Road,
London W14 9PB, England

www.johnblakepublishing.co.uk

First published in paperback in 2008

ISBN: 978-1-84454-659 -6

British Library Cataloguing-in-Publication Data:

A catalogue record for this book is available from the British Library.

Design by www.envydesign.co.uk

Printed and bound in Great Britain by Creative Print and Design, Blaina, Wales

3 5 7 9 10 8 6 4 2

Papers used by John Blake Publishing are natural, recyclable products
made from wood grown in sustainable forests. The manufacturing processes
conform to the environmental regulations of the country of origin.

Every attempt has been made to contact the relevant copyright-holders,
but some were unobtainable. We would be grateful if the appropriate
people could contact us.

This book is dedicated to the memory of Nellie Mercer, my childhood mentor at the Essoldo Theatre in Tunbridge Wells, who instilled in me a keen love and appreciation for cinema and film.

ALSO BY NIGEL GOODALL

David Tennant: A Life in Time and Space

Fearne Cotton: The Biography

The Secret World of Johnny Depp

Being Davina

Christian Slater: Back From The Edge

What's Eating Johnny Depp: An Intimate Biography

Kylie Naked: A Biography
(with Jenny Stanley-Clarke)

Demi Moore: The Most Powerful Woman in Hollywood

The Ultimate Queen
(with Peter Lewry)

Winona Ryder: The Biography

The Ultimate Cliff
(with Peter Lewry)

Jump Up: The Rise of the Rolling Stones

George Michael In His Own Words

The Complete Cliff Richard Chronicle
(with Peter Lewry)

Elton John: A Visual Documentary

Cher In Her Own Words

Cliff Richard: The Complete Recording Sessions
(with Peter Lewry)

www.nigelgoodall.co.uk

About The Author

NIGEL GOODALL has been a highly respected music and film journalist for almost twenty years and now has over two dozen books to his credit, including *Being Davina* and the bestselling Kylie Minogue biography, *Kylie Naked*. He has written about some of the biggest names in show business including Elton John, George Michael, David Tennant, Johnny Depp and Winona Ryder, which, combined, have sold over a million copies and won him a literary prize nomination. Formerly a graphic designer with over 300 record sleeves to his name, a pop manager, a voice-over artist and disc jockey, and the co-producer of the syndicated 1978 *Elvis Gospel* radio special, he has also contributed to various album, video and television projects for over a decade, including, most recently, the A&E biography of Demi Moore. He lives in Sussex, England, from where he travels occasionally to New York, San Francisco and Los Angeles for research and author interviews.

www.nigelgoodall.co.uk

'The greatest dramas in the world are
about sex, violence and death.'
Ray Winstone

CONTENTS

Acknowledgements

Writing this book has been both an intriguing and rewarding experience. I want to thank everyone who has made it possible; my editor Mark Hanks and the team at John Blake Publishing; Keith Hayward for his tireless effort in searching for names, people and places and asking for nothing in return; Charlotte Rasmussen, another good friend, whose film glossary at the end of the book offers one of the best understandings for film language and speak; Sean Delaney and his staff at the library of the British Film Institute in London for the articles, production notes and other materials; John Popely for sharing with me his recollection of London's East End in the 1950s and for his efforts to track down friends and colleagues of the Winstones; Jayne Knight for her memories of Ray at London's Corona Stage School and for the school's family history. Thanks also to Simon W. Golding, an early believer in this book, for his wonderful foreword, and his endless help with theatre and filmography matters as well as everything else, especially for putting me in touch with Philip Jackson who was happy to reflect with me on his memories on making the theatrical version of *Scum*, until Ray was told that he had spoken to me. Although Ray was happy for me to use what Philip had told me in our first telephone interview, he was not very keen on the idea of this book, and therefore, out of respect to both Philip and Ray, I decided not to include any material Philip had given. I feel I would be remiss not to mention how grateful I am for his time. I would also like to thank the picture agencies for the permission to use their images; Edmonton County School in Enfield for clarifying some factual information and the information from their website. For their help with production notes and DVDs, thanks go to Kate Birch at Entertainment Films, Diane Bartholomew at Granada Ventures, Karen Williams at the ITV press office, Chinapa Aguh at Media Communications and Paul Hembury at 2entertain. Thanks are also due to Philip Sprinks for the loan of his film collection, the Brian Glover Estate for the *Theatre Box* tape, Jeff Piccinini for his chapter suggestions, and Alison Carter, the webmistress of *About Ray Winstone* for her invaluable critique, help, guidance and information. Her collection of online materials went a long way to improving the accuracy of this work. But, above all, I want to thank my son Adam (who like Ray is a West Ham football supporter) and my daughter Kim, for their support every time I write a book and, on this occasion, for calling me up, or sending me a text, every time Ray was in the tabloids, on television or in a film at the local multiplex.

Foreword

When Nigel Goodall told me he was writing this book, I have to admit that I was slightly green with envy, not because I didn't think Nigel could tell the story with his usual balanced approach, but, if there was one book I would have loved to have written myself, it is this one. So you can imagine that, when I was asked to pen a foreword for it, I was simply delighted and thrilled for two reasons. Firstly, I adore Nigel's unique style of writing biography and, secondly, because of Ray's growing cannon of work.

Before taking this on, however, I read some of Nigel's previous volumes on such wonderful film talents as Winona Ryder, Johnny Depp and Demi Moore, and what I liked about each one of them was his sympathetic and affectionate style of writing. I immediately knew, if there was anyone who could do justice to Ray Winstone's story, then it was Nigel. Secondly, there is simply no one in British film today that excites me more than Winstone, so the combination of writer and subject I feel will distinguish this book above any others that follow.

I have to say that nearly almost all of Ray's performances on both the small and big screen have left me enthralled every time I watch them and, in doing so, he and his films have also made an indelible imprint on my memory. As one journalist correctly noted, he is the ultimate personification of 'rock-hardness', and probably one of film's few tough guys to portray violence as it really is, to emphasise that violence of any kind is not pleasant.

One also cannot help but admire how Ray has attracted some of the finest film directors to add their seal of approval to his work by offering him roles in their films. People like Anthony Minghella, Martin Scorsese and, one of his own personal favourites, Gary Oldman. The way in which he succeeded in playing alongside some of his own childhood heroes, such as Michael Caine, Tom Courtenay and David Hemmings, is enough, I imagine, to fill any other actor from his generation with envy.

Ray Winstone: The Biography is soaked in nostalgia of places, people, crime, race, events and memoirs of a young boy who loved football, boxing and cinema. The love of cinema is something Nigel shares with Ray, which places him, I believe, in a unique position to write this book. Most of Nigel's childhood was spent hanging out at the Essoldo Theatre in Tunbridge Wells, where he befriended management and staff and was given posters, stills, lobby cards and complimentary tickets each week. He grew up surrounded by film and cinema from an early age. He even lists the same favourite movies as Ray does from that period of time in the early to mid-sixties.

What I like so much about the book is how Nigel appears to place himself squarely in the midst of Ray's life and career with an intriguing run of surprising behind-the-scene glimpses of Ray both on and off screen, and his portrayal of the Ray Winstone whom readers will certainly recognise from the celebrated public image. From his humble beginnings stalking the notorious streets of the East End of London to strolling down the red carpet at any number of award shows and celebrity party bashes, it is a nuanced portrait sharply drawn, and closely observed, from a wealth of sources and material, that are never presented with anything less than admiration for one of Nigel's favourite actors – and mine – ever since we both watched *Scum* in 1979.

At the centre of it, of course, are the films and television, for which Ray so far has notched up more than a hundred appearances. Every one is as impressive as the last. Whether a bit part, a cameo, a supporting or lead role, or simply advertising a healthy breakfast cereal, it is an impressive count that any actor would be proud of.

Certainly, the way the book flits between the Moors Murders and the Krays (both illuminating in Ray's childhood) is very rewarding. There are also tales of some of the sparkling things that happened to Ray in his early life, and so often with celebrity biographies this is not the case. It can be a bit of a tyranny when reading someone's early years in a biography. This is a syndrome Frank Skinner summed up by commenting, 'Hurry up and get famous, you bastard!' Crude, but true. The opening chapters in this tome, however, are an insight into the richness of London's East End – a part of England's capital that is notoriously connected with the criminal underworld. A piece of turf you get the feeling Ray, in his early years, was very comfortable prowling. Throughout, Nigel's narrative is drenched in Ray's gritty cockney dialogue, both real and humorous. You can actually hear him saying the words. After reading this book, there can be no doubt that you will have what I believe is a truly accurate account of Ray's life and career so far and, most intriguing of all, some illuminating insights to what his rise, fall and rise again must have looked like from his side of the screen.

Simon W. Golding
Novelist, scriptwriter and playwright

CHAPTER 1

In The End

Ray Winstone is gutted. It was 1 July 2006, the day England blew their chance to win the World Cup, and, like every other supporter, he couldn't get over how on earth they had been knocked out of the most important football competition of all. Was it really possible that England, the favourite team to win in many people's eyes, had just lost out to Portugal in the quarter-finals with a 3–1 defeat in a simple penalty shootout? It seemed it was.

In the lead-up to the match, not surprisingly, Ray, like most English fans, had been feeling very confident of victory over Portugal. 'They have got a great footballing side but we have a team to match and better them. We will beat them comfortably enough. Sometimes you get a little feeling. The players have no fear. I was impressed with the way the training went, the way Steve McClaren coached the boys, the respect they clearly have for Sven. We have been scraping

1

through but doing a job. The Italians have been doing the same thing for years – not been playing that well but getting results – that is what wins a World Cup.'

Three months earlier, Ray had rolled into his agent's office in Soho to meet *Observer* journalist Lynn Barber with his friend, the writer Tony Grounds. They claimed they had been working in the dubbing suite, but Barber was not so sure. She thought that they had been having one of their 'jolly' lunches instead. She had just watched Ray playing a terrifying football manager in a preview of his latest Channel 4 telefilm *All in the Game*. Like most others who get to interview him, Barber was kind of expecting to find him quite intimidating, all bulging eyes and bursting violence, but actually, she wrote, 'he is a polite and thoughtful interviewee'. Even so, she still had the impression his heart wasn't in it. 'He tends to gabble and half-tell anecdotes without ever finishing them. He doesn't seem to have the self-obsession you can usually rely on with actors. He'd much rather be in the pub with Tony and his mates, talking about football.'

On top of that, Barber thought it quite ironic that Ray had just been appointed spokesman for the Football Association's anti-hooliganism campaign. Ironic that is, when you consider that *All in the Game* was days away from being screened in the Thursday-night peak-hour viewing slot.

According to the *Guardian*, Ray was heading up the *Alltogethernow 2006* campaign, to build on the impressive behaviour of the England fans at the World Cup 2002 and Euro 2004. And that, he explained, was what it is all about. 'I am proud to be an England fan and enjoy nothing more than joining in with the crowd to get behind the team, but, let's get this straight, causing trouble at a football tournament is unacceptable. I'm as passionate about being an England fan as the next man, but the moment you get involved in violence you let down the team and the country.'

Run by England fans and the Football Association, the campaign was aimed at showing a positive image of England fans to people in Germany and around the world, demonstrating that the stereotyped image of anti-social and violent behaviour is not a true reflection of genuine England supporters. Before and during the World Cup, a range of initiatives took place around England and in Germany, organised primarily by the fans for the fans and supported by the FA. They included road shows, regional competitions, player messages, ambassador visits to Germany and a variety of media events.

And it couldn't have been better timed as *All In The Game* premiered on the small screen at around the same time. Written by Tony Grounds, the telefilm portrayed the very worst side of Premiership football. Not bad behaviour by the fans, but by the management, agents and players. All up to their necks in dodgy deals, bungs and betting scams. Although Grounds insisted that it wasn't based on any particular club or individual, it certainly had the feel of insider know-how.

Both Grounds and Ray claim they taught each other all there is to know about football, having met as teenage West Ham supporters. Despite Ray bailing Grounds out when he was arrested for causing a nuisance, they both still support West Ham. 'The way we look at football, people my age,' says Ray, 'is, if you came from West Ham, you supported West Ham, and you probably grew up with some of the players. But today kids who come from London support Manchester United or Liverpool and I can't understand that. Football's moved on – I haven't.'

As if to prove the point, he set aside the whole of June to go to Germany with his mates, as he put it, to watch England win the World Cup, make a video diary of his trip, and talk to all kinds of people to find out what they really think about the English, rather than how stereotypes are portrayed in the media. It seemed, by all accounts, he had the time of his life. 'We have done some camping, gone back to our roots. We have had a blinding time and meeting the players has been the icing on the cake.' But there was a downside during the second week. 'My mate's partner he works with was taken very ill while he was away and he had to come back early, so I made a different kind of film really, just a film about the World Cup. It isn't the film I wanted to make, but we got enough for the kids to see their two dads out and about and misbehaving and all that sort of stuff.'

If nothing else, *All in the Game* was remarkable for having the highest count of abusive language that one could ever imagine would be allowed on television. Asked if all the 'fucks' and 'fuckings' were in the script, Grounds claims they were. 'Ray's very good. He plays every word as written. But we had a meeting with the Channel 4 producer about a week before we started shooting and he had the script and there were about a thousand stickers in it – blue, yellow, green, pink – and I said "What's all that?", and he said, green is fucking, yellow is cunt, blue is racial abuse or whatever, and he said, "We should have a cunt reduction." But it's part of the culture, part of the natural flow of the language. And Ray knows how to swear.'

In short, it was the story of Ray's character Frankie, who, in his words, 'is old-style, he comes from football when it was a "sport". When it was great to play football, when there was no money in the game, but you played for the love of the game. And that was Frankie's dream, but his world has changed. He's ended up in a world of corporations and is now surrounded by young kids who earn a lot of money.

'For Frankie, football has become a game of money, it's all money. He's ended up in a sport that's not a sport any more but a business run by the people who sit upstairs and the TV moguls. I guess that's where a kind of bitterness sets in for Frankie. They're all earning money out of it, so he might as well earn money out of it too. Frankie's put enough years into it. That kind of grief comes from the destruction of the game as he knows it, but that's the beast that the sport has become. He wants nice things for his family too. He's got the big house and all the trappings – he wants to live the life and for his family to have the things that he never had. But Frankie has created a monster in his son Martin (played by Danny Dyer). By sending his boy to a posh school and getting him an education, he has created his own Frankenstein. It is the downfall of Frankie, a moralistic man. But he's ripped his morals out and has forgotten what the game is all about.'

Not everyone, however, liked the sound of it. One of those was the *Radio Times* critic David Butcher. 'If any youngsters tug your sleeve and ask if they can stay up to watch this football drama starring Ray Winstone, on no account let them. Apart from the fact that Winstone swears like a rabid docker throughout, it's a very long way from *Roy of the Rovers* territory. Winstone plays Frankie, a blood-and-guts manager of the old school and hero to his club's fans. But behind the scenes, he and his son Martin, a player's agent, are bung junkies, feathering their own nest at the expense of the club and its beleaguered chairman. The plot doesn't so much progress as unravel via various betrayals that leave each character more or less wrecked. It's not easy to watch, but its portrait of football as a giant pigs' trough is horribly powerful. By the end, Winstone's fevered performance as the tormented anti-hero reaches an intensity that feels more RSC than ITV. And boy, can he swear.'

In fact, it was the concern over the bad language that seemed to be at the top of every critic's list for disapproval. Andrew Anthony's review in the *Observer* certainly echoed that sentiment. 'Winstone is a blinding actor but here he was mostly just effin – though, to be fair, the "c"-word also got a rare double-airing. He swore at everyone and anyone, including his chairman. It was a grotesque performance completely out of scale with the rest of the production. It was as if his character from *Nil By Mouth* had turned up in an episode of *Dream Team*.'

There were, however, a handful of reviewers that were a lot more favourable to Ray's performance than to his scripted dialogue. The general consensus was weighed up pretty accurately and fairly by Ray Bennett writing in the *Hollywood Reporter*. 'Ray Winstone at full throttle is like a force of nature, and he's firing on all cylinders as a passionate but corrupt English Premier League soccer manager in this scalding sports drama. It's Winstone's show, however, making the manager swaggeringly, charmingly and obnoxiously unforgettable.' But again there were references to the dialogue. 'Granada International is handling international sales, and it might need subtitles for some of his authentic Cockney slang. Crude, uncouth, and bitter, Frankie talks and begs in order to get his way, with every second word having four letters. It's a blistering performance.'

But, as *The Sunday Times* correctly noted, perhaps there is an intrinsic design flaw in being Ray Winstone, which is that nobody else is Ray Winstone. 'It's very, very difficult for anyone else to act on the same small screen as him. The hugely popular persona has grown so manically into an operatic cockney Abanazer that he sucks up all the available atmosphere, completely overwhelming the rest of the cast, who, in this case, tiptoed around him as if he were a bee-stung boar in a farrowing pen. The dialogue was all written for Winstone's benefit. He didn't just get the best lines, he got them in rhyming slang. And it was bravura stuff, but it played the rest of the production to a standstill. This was a drama of two halves, both being played simultaneously. One was a Winstone masterclass in baroque-ney; the other was with everybody else. The grand comeuppance finale was weirdly like *Don Giovanni* meets *EastEnders*.

'Winstone is a big draw, one of the few actors who can guarantee to deliver a primetime audience. But he can also almost promise to squash every other performance in the same frame. When he does play it sotto voce, we feel sort of cheated. I think the answer is that he should only be cast alongside actors who are as generous with their personalities as he is.'

But, then again, it should not be *that* surprising that Grounds had come up with the script he did, especially when you consider that it was Ray he had in mind for the role ever since he thought of the idea. 'I've always loved Ray. He was around 21, 22 when he did *Scum* and he was always a hero and a figure to emulate for a lot of us growing up. He done something that we were all so proud of – and all my friends still feel the same. So, as soon as I could, I wrote something I could put him in.' That 'something' turned out to be *The Ghostbusters of East Finchley* for the BBC in 1995. It probably worked so well because, 'I understand what Ray likes to do, and he understands my writing.'

Ray agrees. 'He's got a great ear, he gets the speech patterns and the way people talk, and if you don't know that, and you change the words round, it don't sound right. It's almost Shakespearean in a way – it's got that rhythm about it, it's like poetry.'

Ray and Tony share far more than just a working relationship. As Ray points out, 'We knock about together, me and Tony, he doesn't live far from me and I understand his dialogue. He understands the way I think and I understand the way he thinks. Although he is completely off his trolley, we have the same passion about football. We both support West Ham as that's where we're both from, so it's part of our identity and culture. It's funny, mostly when you make films about sport, the good ones, you don't actually see the sport – it's what's going on behind the scenes. This drama is like that. It's like making a film about a painter; you don't want to see him paint a picture, you know what a picture is. You want to know what he was all about. *All in the Game* has its funny moments and humour in very dark and black times. I think it will keep you glued.'

But he laughs at the suggestion that one journalist made that he would make a good football manager. 'I would shoot them. I would be the worst fucking football manager. If my lot hadn't done what they were supposed to have done and lost, then I would line up those prime bits of beef running about and shoot them, but I'd probably regret it the next week.'

Although he enjoyed playing the character, he still reckons the real job is much harder than it looks. 'I think every football supporter thinks he's a manager. I think I know everything about football but, when it comes down to it, none of us could. Yeah, I'd love to be a football manager but I'd love to be a player more than anything else.'

Even if Ray had got a taste for being a football manager, then it would have surely been the scene he filmed before a real live match at the then all-new 32,000-seat Ricoh Arena at the Coventry City Football Club. Certainly, walking out on to the pitch to a full stadium was something he wasn't going to forget in a hurry. 'The big thing is when you look down that tunnel and you get in the stadium, which is banged out with people, the atmosphere there is unbelievable. For a minute you have to hold your buttocks very firmly together because if you farted you'd follow right through! Then you go, "Right, you've really got to go for this, Ray." Either you're going to go out all sheepish and get it – you expect a load of people to go "ahh, you cockney bastard" – or you've got to just go for it. And I did.

'I went for it and you know what? I wanted to do it again! It's the only time I've wanted to do a take again. I had to come out as Frankie literally just before the real match. The fans were fantastic because they all went with it and they were cheering and screaming, it was fantastic. I actually thought I was a football manager for a day. You know I came back in off the pitch and went in the home dressing room and saw the Coventry team (it was Wisey's first game for Coventry) and I said, "Stuff it right up them, I fancy your mob today." He got booked within two minutes, but they won 6–1. So maybe they should have me back there every week!'

It was while the finishing touches were being put to the filming at Coventry City's new Ricoh Arena in April 2006 that Grounds, sitting in the empty stands, while Ray ranted through a scene behind him, explained to journalist Jim White what had motivated him to write such 'a dyspeptic assault' on something he and Ray have been in love with all their lives.

'It's been simmering in my mind for years. Being a fan and seeing the changes in the game I just got more angry. I know the world has to move on, we can't go back to Bovril and rattles, but there was a time it was rooted into a community. It felt like the clubs were ours then. I love the game, but I'm not sure I recognise it now. If you go to football, you meet people; Ray's character in the film is a bit of all those old-style managers. I think it's better if the research isn't precise; 51 per cent of what Ray does comes from my imagination. It's a sad indictment of the state of the game that it's from the wilder stretches of your imagination and everyone thinks it's the truth.

'And yeah, the language is very strong. That's important. These days football is presented as so happy clappy, foam hands and Sky TV, yet everyone knows that, in the stands and in the dugout, everyone's screaming, "He's playing like a cunt." Set among this splendour of lovely facilities and canapes and poshness, there's someone effing and blinding. That jarring of the worlds is football. If you were writing a play about the army or the City, it's the same, it's all a group of men together, the language is ripe. For me, too, it's important that it's Frankie who does most of the swearing. He swans into corporate hospitality, swearing like a trooper, embarrassing his chairman, embarrassing his son. He's a dinosaur in this nice air-brushed world.'

At the heart of the piece, noted White, 'is the tension between this dinosaur's natural competitiveness and his love of cash'. When the film opens, Frankie is keen on any little deal that might buff up his current account. As it progresses, his corruption compromises his ability to do his job properly and keep the club he loves in the Premiership. When he realises what he has done, it cuts him to the quick. In short, it is not Frankie that Grounds portrays as his real villain. It is money.'

Grounds agrees. 'One of the lines that Frankie says is, "How come every bugger on that pitch is on ten times more than I am?" That's why he falls for the temptation. People don't want to sell their soul, but they're prepared to lease it out, put it on a mortgage. They hope to get it back, but it doesn't work like that. I mean take the way players these days behave. They've got no reason to be that swanky, roasting these girls, driving these cars. Wouldn't it be great to have a real humility back in the game? Money corrupts at every single level. Speak to a 16-year-old who's just signed and they're full of optimism. Two years later, they're behaving like Hollywood. So where does that corruption came from? The trouble is it's like global warming – have we gone too far now, is there anything we can do about it?

'Of course not,' he continues. 'Look, Arsenal got fined over some £30 million tax dodge and nobody cares because they've got to the Champions League final. I shouldn't think anyone will be remotely bothered by me and my little film. Mind you, I'm glad we got it made. And I'm glad we did it as a drama.'

And again, he is right. As most reviewers said at the time it was shown on Channel 4 in May 2006, 'There is no way anyone could make a documentary like this. There are far too many truths in it.'

What is perhaps strange when you consider Ray's love for football is that he believes that there is something rotten in the state of it today. 'It's been corrupted because of money,' he sighs. 'When pound notes are involved, there will always be corruption. An agent might say to a manager, "I've got this player valued at £25 million, but, if you pay £28m for him, we'll have a drink with the rest." I don't mind people earning a living by ducking and diving a bit. But they have to put something back – they shouldn't be allowed just to rip the heart out of the game. People like us, who go to the matches week in, week out, are getting shafted. Football is not really just a sport any more, it's a business, and the people behind the scenes are now running it. They're taking our clubs away from us.'

Although he agrees with Grounds that *All In The Game* is fiction that is based on a little bit of fact, because 'if we actually made a film [purely] about fact, we would probably get sued! So I hope it shakes people up. In fact, I want people to complain about it, because that's what makes great drama. Can this film change anything? Well, I hope it might make some of the people [responsible for] this skulduggery shit themselves!'

In the film, Ray's character reserves particular disgust for the 'parasites' who attach themselves to Premiership players and suck cash out of the game. When he spies a dodgy agent circling one of his star players at the training ground, he rants, 'It's people like him who are killing the game I love. Sky and all their money and all the shit that goes with it – face painting and big foam hands and silly kick-off times.' He even goes on to rally against the pasta bars that are springing up at football grounds: 'What's wrong with a pie all of a sudden?'

As journalist James Rampton says, Ray fires with both barrels in his performance as Frankie. He clearly feels so passionately about the subject of television that he thinks he would be compromised if he reined himself in. 'You can only go by what you feel. If you hold back, you're not telling the story. If you're making a film about a subject and you don't tell it how it is, you're belittling it. Censoring a drama is like taking a painting by Constable and rubbing out half of it. I'm a viewer, too, and I like to watch things that hit me between the eyes. I want still to be talking about a film when I come out of the cinema. Good God! We're given bland stuff all the time. Television commissioners say: "That last thing was a success, let's do something else like it." They're obsessed with formats. They should allow writers to write what they like and take a few risks.'

Another drama that was sure to hit viewers between the eyes was *Sweeney Todd*, with Ray in the title role. This gruesome melodrama was shown in January 2006 on the BBC, during the same period Ray was filming *All In The Game* in Coventry for Channel 4, , just two months before Ray's 34th film, *The Proposition*, was on nationwide release in Britain.

According to the film's production notes, it was a visually stunning tale of loyalty, betrayal and retribution set in the frontier of 1880s Australia, where in the harsh, unforgiving landscape of the outback, Charlie Burns is presented with an impossible proposition by Ray's character, local law enforcer, Captain Stanley. Stanley tells Charlie that the only way to save his younger brother Mike from the gallows is to track down and kill Arthur, his psychotic older brother. Meanwhile, Stanley has other problems to contend with. Having given up their comfortable life in England, he is desperate to shield his innocent wife Martha from the brutalities of their new surroundings. He also faces mounting pressure from renegade Aborigines and his superior Eden Fletcher to bring order to the region. An uneasy sense of foreboding grows as events close in and each character faces a punishing moral dilemma that leads inexorably to a devastating climax.

Ray had made the film in the Australian outback two years before its release. It was his first visit to Australia, but he had no idea what to expect. 'I landed in Brisbane, stayed there one night, then got a plane the next day straight out to the bush. It was fantastic. That's the only way to go to Australia, to go straight out into the bush before I went to any cities. It's just such a magical place, a spiritual place. I think it's something to do with the water going down the plughole the wrong way – no, seriously, I think all the water in your body must go the opposite way as well. You get off the plane and it's like you've been at sea for four years.' Shot in extreme conditions, with temperatures pushing 50 degrees centigrade, *The Proposition* was an uncomfortable shoot for cast and crew alike. Ray flew in via Dubai in a vain hope of becoming gradually acclimatised, but the jump to sauna-like conditions still left him frazzled and dazzled. 'It was my 25th anniversary just before, so my wife took me to Dubai,' he recalls. 'But forget the desert in Dubai – the desert in Australia is real heat. There were days where you were cooking from the inside out. There was one scene where I'm on the horse. I've got to ride between two hills, and I just blanked – I didn't know what I was doing, I went off to somewhere else. And that was from the heat.'

Despite the heat, and Ray not knowing what he was doing during some of the filming, most critics agreed that he gave an extremely nuanced performance in a script that had been written by rock musician Nick Cave, who to this day is probably still well remembered for his duet with Ray's *Magic Roundabout* voiceover cohort, Kylie Minogue. *Where The Wild Roses Grow* was a murderous love song culminating in Cave's character beating Kylie's to death with a rock. Despite the unlikely pairing of Cave and Kylie, the track and the video that went with it received widespread critical acclaim on its release as well as winning Cave numerous awards. Just the same as Kylie was when duetting with Cave on that hit song, and playing Cave's victim in the video, Ray was very proud to be working in a movie written by Cave. As far as he was concerned, Cave's script offered him another great opportunity for him to play a hard man with a dangerous soft side.

As he saw it, 'Stanley went out to Australia on a high, looking forward to the challenge. Thinking he could change the place, civilise the place and the people with the British Empire behind him. But of course, the reality was somewhat different.'

Although Ray's character was the bad guy of the piece, it was also a very interesting role to play, Ray explains. 'We see him being very brutal to a young boy and then he makes a completely immoral suggestion, asking a man to kill his own brother. But then, in contrast, you see this man at home with his wife, loving his wife and being a normal human being. He has a very strong belief in what to him is right and wrong and believes his actions are completely justified. I thought he was very cleverly formed.'

Aside from his enthusiasm for playing Stanley, Ray was simply thrilled to be working on the film, although he did wonder how Cave had moved from working in one medium to another with such ease. 'Nick has probably always written songs on his own, but with this he had to deal with a bunch of actors who like to talk about things, ask questions and mark changes. I was surprised how well he relaxed into that process and how well he collaborated with us. He was really keen to hear our comments and ideas and change things around accordingly. I think he really enjoyed the process.

'And I can't praise John Hillcoat enough. He's a wonderful

director – very visual, very artistic. But he's also wonderful drawing out the best performances from his cast and it's rare to have both those things. It was an absolute privilege to work with him and I really enjoyed making this film.' He had enjoyed it as much as he said he did making *Sweeney Todd*, which going by the advance reports at the time, would prove as gripping as *The Proposition* was compelling.

It was the first adaptation of the story for the small screen since Ben Kingsley and Joanna Lumley starred in John Schlesinger's *The Tale of Sweeney Todd*, a television movie made for the Sky cable channel in 1998, and for which Kingsley received a Screen Actors Guild Best Actor nomination.

Although Ray won no such nominations, his portrayal did receive a fair and by then (for anything with Ray in it) almost predictable number of accolades and praise. According to most critics, his performance was second to none. What is so good about Ray is that he always plays the villain as the good guy. But, as Ray says, 'If you make him more of a man, you make him more of a monster.'

With shaven head and eyebrows, his inspiration for the role came from a Hogarth painting. 'There's a guy laying on the floor with his wig off and he's bald, so I used the wig as my hat. Having no hair changes your face completely.' He remembers meeting his daughter Ellie Rae at the airport. 'She came running out, saw me standing there, then looked both ways and ran back in. She was quite freaked.'

As was Tom Howard with Ray's transformation. Writing in London's *Time Out* magazine he raved that Ray was simply excellent, 'giving a restrained performance, but conveying Todd's inner turmoil perfectly'.

The Herald's Ian Bell said much the same, describing Ray's performance as huge. 'He took the old rule that says screen-acting must be underplayed to its absolute limits. His demon barber was so reticent he was almost inarticulate. Winstone's Todd was a man of grunts and half-finished sentences, a gentle soul who could hardly bear the world's injustices.'

Elsewhere, Ray was credited as giving a performance of rare subtlety as the murderous barber who, because he was an abused child, grows up with a confused sexuality. 'It's that thing of feeling dirty about sex,' confirms Ray. 'Wanting to be loved but not knowing how to go about being loved.' Unable to consummate a relationship with his neighbour, played by what most critics shouted was a splendidly vampish Essie Davis, he spies on her and her lovers. 'He's very mixed up, not because he might be gay but because he's killing people. There are still people who disappear off the face of the earth. We hear about some when their killers are found, but there are many more we have no idea about.'

Certainly, continues Ray, it was a gruesome tale, and one he reckons would have viewers ending up feeling slightly sorry for him. 'He's a man who's profoundly tortured. He spent 20 years in jail for a crime he didn't commit. His brother was hung and he was raped, and so Sweeney comes out completely tormented. I'm not asking anyone to sympathise with him. But, like the men I played in *Nil By Mouth* and *The War Zone,* he's a character you may find yourself feeling sorry for. Men like that are interesting emotionally.

'The great thing about these men is finding the weakness in them. The weakness, not the strength, is the most interesting side to any person because that's the one they try to hide. I can't remember Sweeney's story being told in its entirety in a drama before. There is the Stephen Sondheim musical, which is lovely and jubbly, but this is a much darker and more compelling version. We're not glorifying murder. These sorts of things happen. We show it, and it isn't nice.'

Even though playing Sweeney Todd may be gory, Ray still argues that it could not be done authentically in any other way. Anyway, he says there is a strong British tradition of unflinchingly portraying violence in drama. 'What did Shakespeare write about? That's right, the same subjects that are covered in this drama. All the great Shakespeare plays are about killing. Alas, poor Yorick – that's about death. And in *Romeo and Juliet* everyone ends up dying. The greatest dramas in the world are about sex, violence and death.'

If there was any criticism that *Sweeney Todd* was another example of Ray playing a hard man, he himself was not concerned. Why should he be? After all, 'I haven't got the sort of face where I could ever be a heartthrob, and I've never thought I'd like to play Hamlet. Shakespeare didn't write for chappies like me. I get cast as thugs and I enjoy playing them. I understand that's the way it works. But it's not a question of being typecast because there's a million ways to play it. I'm not always just the bloke with the gun in his hand.' If anything, he confesses, 'The whole thing makes me laugh. I sometimes watch myself and get the giggles. I think, "What a ridiculous way to earn a living. Dressing up and pretending you're someone else. Get a proper job, son."'

The idea of making a television version of *Sweeney Todd* was the brainchild of Joshua St Johnston, a producer-turned-writer, and also one-third of Ray's production company, Size 9, who had suddenly realised what a great part it would be for Ray to play. Although, says Ray, 'I wanted to make a film like *Tin Drum*. You know, that metaphor of the person who stops growing when Germany succumbs to Hitler, we didn't have time to do it. I love that film. I've got it at home and even watch it in German.'

In the initial stages of St Johnston's idea, though, he couldn't help wondering what the real story was. And it was the real story that he really wanted to tell. 'Researching on the internet was very confusing, some sites said Sweeney Todd was a real character and others said he was entirely fictional. In the end it was only by visiting St Dunstan's Church in London's Fleet Street, where Todd was meant to have hidden the bits of the bodies that didn't go into pies, that I realised he probably didn't exist, as there was nothing there referring to it.'

It turned out, St Johnston continues, 'that the character was originally created in 1846 in a story called *The String of Pearls* that ran in instalments in *The People's Periodical*. It was so popular that, before the serial had even petered out some six months later, there was a play of *Sweeney Todd* being performed at the Britannia Theatre in London's East End. In fact, throughout the 19th century new dramatic versions were regularly churned out to great success, but they are high melodrama of a sort that would seem very creaky to today's audiences.

'The Sondheim musical is the version that many people are familiar with these days, but it was only invented in the early 70s by Christopher Bond, who decided to splice together the stories of *The Count of Monte Cristo* with *The Revenger's Tragedy* and put *Sweeney Todd* at its heart. It's a brilliant story, but still very melodramatic, and I decided I wanted to try and write something that felt more like it could be the true story. It's an attempt to apply a 21st-century understanding of criminal psychology to an 18th-century serial killer.'

Attempting to find a new angle for his retelling, St Johnston decided to set his story of the Sweeney Todd myth in the 18th century because, as he explains, 'the original story takes place when George III was a young man, which I reckoned would be the 1760s, and also it was a way of differentiating it from other versions, which all feel very Victorian.'

Visiting the Museum of London, examining Georgian medical implements at the Royal College of Surgeons, going to the Foundling Museum to study Hogarth's prints, as well as reading literary material by Vanbrugh, Gay, Fielding and Defoe, confirmed to St Johnston that London of the 1760s was indeed a filthy and terrifying place.

'The streets would have been filled with shit, gin addicts, beggars, animal torture passing for entertainment, dead babies, it's not a version of Georgian England that we're often exposed to. From reading the histories, I learned that in the 1760s the Bow Street Runners were in their infancy. It's a fascinating time, because the notion of a police force was unpopular for reasons of civil liberty (much like identity cards today) but the Fielding brothers had seen the need and were trying to introduce a force on the sly. I thought it would be interesting to introduce the historical figure of Sir John Fielding into my story.'

But, asked to sum up the time in which the drama is set, he says, 'It was a brutal and brutalising world, and that we don't know of any real serial killers from that time might be more to do with the fact that murder was so easy to get away with, rather than that there weren't any. Maybe there really was a Sweeney Todd after all, and he just never got caught.'

Once St Johnston knew he had something that would make a good script, he was determined to find someone to make it with. That someone turned out to be Gub Neal, the founder of the internationally successful Box TV production outfit. 'As the prospective producer, I felt, perhaps for the first time in my life, that I had fallen into a field of clover. A great title, a great star, it was as if the package had been assembled in heaven,' enthuses Neal.

'But, as the script unfolded, it became clear that this was no burlesque musical horror story. Sweeney was to be portrayed as a real man, someone whose own history was full of suffering and whose life would become a kind of paradigm for the darkness of his age.'

Not only that, but Neal was pleased that his star could sum up the piece so succinctly. 'Ray put it very clearly when he said, "Sweeney is London. He's this man whose very life becomes a response to the inhumanity of the city." Not since I had been involved with *Cracker* – over ten years ago – had I felt that here was a chance to tell a story that got right into the mind of character and the motivation of the killer.'

Co-producer Caroline Hewitt agrees. She is equally enthusiastic about St Johnson's multi-layered story, and still praises Ray's performance. She explains that there is an understated emotional intensity running through Sweeney's character. 'Ray is brilliant at showing us Sweeney's gentle and kind side, in spite of his emotional inarticulacy. He makes Sweeney totally compelling and believable. Watching Ray's performance, we gradually understand how this shy and self-effacing barber has been rendered impotent by his background and see that, when the past revisits him, he is capable of committing acts of terrible savagery. His killing is a kind of warped cathartic purging for him. Yet, despite these heinous deeds, Ray manages to keep Sweeney sympathetic. The audience will gradually learn how Sweeney was brutalised by a wrongful imprisonment in Newgate gaol when just a mere boy. The abuse he suffered there has left him unable to love or form close relationships. This damage is brought to a head when he meets and falls deeply in love with Mrs Lovett, but cannot love her in a conventional way.'

Neal also makes the point that it's not often that writer, producer and director can all grapple with the idea that only bad and not good people can do bad things, and argues that such universal truths that reflect real life greatly enrich drama. 'Josh has portrayed Sweeney as a man capable of great compassion and love, but whose only ability to exert power over the world was to murder.'

Although making a film that promised so much would, under normal circumstances, take far longer than the four weeks it actually took, Ray's schedule was at a premium. He had already agreed to appear in Martin Scorsese's *The Departed* and, before that, in Robert Zemeckis's *Beowulf*, in which he had been signed for the title role, and was due to start shooting during the last week of September 2005, just a month after production on *Sweeney Todd* started.

Under the watchful stewardship of Box, the production company and a team of adventurous BBC executives, the production moved east to Romania's Media Pro studios near Bucharest, where other Box dramas have been successfully made. 'Luckily, both the director, David Moore and our production designer, Michael Pickwoad, signed up to the project,' recalls Neal, and in less than six weeks the film was cast, sets under construction and a crew assembled. 'One of the advantages of shooting everything in a studio is that you get to construct what you want.'

Fleet Street, a key location in the story, where both Sweeney's and Mrs Lovett's shops are set, was adapted from the remains of a French street left over after the filming of

Andy Garcia's *Modigliani*. The speed at which the design, the costuming and wigs were assembled was remarkable. Complex prosthetics were made, not just for the murders but also for Mrs Lovett's progressive affliction from that scourge of 18th-century life, the pox.

'Fortunately, we had a top make-up designer, Penny Smith,' continues Neal. 'Her deftness with plastic skin-boils and wigs astounded everyone – not least our beautiful leading lady, actress Essie Davis, who was bowled over by the veracity of her pox-laden period-piece make-over.'

Despite the pressures placed on everyone, there was plenty of good humour to alleviate the underlying anxieties about the schedule and telling the story of a serial killer. As Neal explains, 'In this respect, Ray was a great asset. His escape from Sweeney on set was to shower those around him with jokes, usually of the rudest kind. But it's the test of a great actor that he can step out of part, land a punchline on an unsuspecting electrician, and jump back in the rhythm of the scene as if he never left it.'

Ray's scenes were shot in just three weeks before Ray had to leave for Los Angeles. But then, reported Neal at the time, 'With one week to go, the scorching sunshine vanished and a storm of rain swept down from the Carpathian Mountains. Drenched by precipitous flooding, our Fleet Street no longer looked like London but a Canaletto impression of Venice! Supporting artists literally waded through rivers of rain as the production managers pumped, dredged and swept water away. But somehow the wrath of the weather was no match for the determination and madness of our collective will to complete *Sweeney Todd*.'

If there was a downside to it all, it was the fact that the film had to be shot in Romania because of a tax ruling made by the British Government, which, as Ray has rightly said, is killing off the film industry in Britain. He said then Chancellor and now Prime Minister Gordon Brown's decision to close tax loopholes on British-made films the year before *Sweeney Todd* went into production has had a disastrous effect. 'Our TV is the best in the world but thanks to the Government we have to make films in other countries. Each time a film doesn't get made here, four to five hundred people are out of work, people who pay their taxes. I don't see the logic in that.' As far as he was concerned, there was only one proper place to film *Sweeney Todd* and that was London. 'It's about London and I want to make it here, but it would cost two or three times more to make it here. It actually starts to dishearten you. It breaks your heart a little bit.'

But there was an even bigger disappointment in store when he arrived on the set of *Beowulf*. It was here that he would supposedly encounter a fall out with co-star Angelina Jolie, even though, according to Ray, she hadn't yet arrived on the set.

CHAPTER 2

A Boy From Plaistow

To a first-time visitor, Plaistow, in the East of London, is not a picture postcard of British charm and character, but a poor and crime-affected area. Some may have wondered why the Winstone family, originally from Cirencester, the picturesque town in the heart of the Cotswolds moved here in the 1950s. It was from there that half the family moved to Wales and the other half to London. Which is how Raymond, Ray's father, ended up running a string of fruit and veg stalls across the London markets. These markets were in places like Poplar, Roman Road, St Albans, Enfield and Hertford. His wife, Margaret, emptied fruit machines in the local pubs. To all intents and purposes, they were grafters. It was from their home in Plaistow that the couple travelled to Hackney Hospital for Margaret to give birth to their son, Raymond Andrew Winstone, on 19 February 1957. This was the boy who would become the ultimate screen hard man.

Life in the 1950s was very different to today. Harold MacMillan was Britain's Prime Minister, the first manned spacecraft was nearly three years away, the farthing was still legal tender, Elvis Presley was about to be inducted into the US Army, and there was no such thing as video recorders to liberate viewers from the tyranny of television programming schedules.

Back then, Plaistow was also different. It was a mainly residential area, with several council estates, one of which was where the Winstones lived. The main road through the town was known by several different names, including Plaistow Road, High Street, Broadway and Greengate Street. It contained relatively few shops and amenities, but did boast the historic Black Lion public house, said to have links to the infamous 18th-century highwayman Dick Turpin. It was probably the Winstones' local as well, and may have been one of the many pubs in which Margaret emptied fruits machines. The pub was also interesting if you were a sports star-spotter, as it was the regular haunt of legendary West Ham United players, including Bobby Moore, during the same period.

Despite this, 'We had a community of people where it was fucking hard,' says Ray. 'I was born 12 years after the Second World War, and there were still bombed houses round where I lived, and it wasn't till the 1960s that they moved us all out and built those shit holes they call flats. It was just after rationing, the black market and all that. People want what they can't have, and the only way to get it is on the black market, which creates villains.'

Not that villains were strangers to him. In a photograph from 1984 published in the *News of the World*, Ray was surrounded by a gang of jailbirds, who all seemed to be his best mates. One of them, Joey Pyle, who had done six years for cocaine dealing, but was acquitted of murder, told the tabloid that he would like to think that Ray 'got a lot out of being out and about with us. He never seemed uncomfortable with what some of us had been up to.'

But did he really mix with all those gangsters? Although Ray objects to the word 'gangsters', yes he did. 'I went to school with criminals or people who turned out to be criminals. People you've liked don't always do the things in life that you agree with. It's a funny old world out there, you know? And I still know them or I know their sons. A lot of their sons have gone on to do their business. I mean they were different times for that generation I guess. It's more white-collar villains now, you know? I was always treated very nicely and I learned a lot.'

One of the other things Ray learned was how, as a youngster, he was surrounded by violence. 'Everywhere you looked – in pubs, clubs, streets, markets – there were women standing there, telling each other how their husbands had beaten them up the previous night, so it was nothing out of the ordinary. And they'd be talking to each other. "He's given me a hander this week, that bastard." And her mate gets the same, and their mate gets the same. Their mum got the same, their grandmother got the same. It's almost like a part of life. I've seen women with eyes out here.'

But as Ray points out, it was sort of acceptable because it was familiar to them. And that's why some of them stayed. Not even the social worker telling them they must leave their fella or husband seemed to help. 'They just think, "Well, it may not be like this for you, but this is the way we live." These people actually do love one another. But there's a frustration in not being able to express themselves. Dad liked a drink but more the partying kind, so ours wasn't a violent house. And, anyway, I don't think booze is to blame. If a man is going to hit his wife, he'll hit his wife. The booze is just an excuse.'

Indeed, the Winstone household, like most families from the East End, trapped living on a poor estate, was like most others, but without the violence. 'Very, very loud and lots of screaming and shouting. No one lives in a perfect world where there are no arguments and there were definitely arguments in our house about things that I can't even remember. But we'd all be shouting one minute and then everything would be fine. There wasn't any sulking, but there was always something going on. Sunday mornings, for instance, Judy Garland and Frank Sinatra would probably be on the record player.'

There was one argument, however, he *does* remember. 'We was sitting all round the dinner table and me and my sister Laura was arguing and she threw a knife on the table, and it bounced on the table and it struck me in me sternum. Whoooiinngg! It fell out and there was a trickle of blood going down my shirt and I went berserk and dived across the table. I'm strangling her, my dad was strangling me and my mum was strangling my dad. And me foot went through the French window. It was like a nuthouse. But 20 minutes later we were all sitting down after Sunday dinner, what was left of it, watching *The Champ*, and we were all crying.'

Outside of the family home, Ray spent much of his time, he recalls, roaming bomb sites with friends. In those days, especially in the East End, bomb sites were common place. Factories and houses that once stood were still derelict from Hitler's bombs. They were the children's playgrounds, and shrapnel their toys and treasure. But all that stopped the day

'Moors Murderers' Ian Brady and Myra Hindley were arrested after preying on children, and their confessions were heard and made public. Up to that time, Ray recalls, no one ever heard about kids going missing. 'It wasn't, after all, reported like it is now. That didn't mean it wasn't happening, but the first big case, yes, was the Moors murders. I can remember how it really changed things overnight. Of course, people are right to want to know it's going on but it means every parent is now terrified of something happening to their kids. You don't take your eyes off them for a second these days.'

Ray can still recall the sheer terror he and his wife, Elaine, felt when one of their girls went missing. 'She hadn't really been gone for that long, but we had the police out and we were searching everywhere. I was going out of my mind. One of us had to stay by the phone while the other one was out looking, and that waiting indoors is the worst feeling in the world. It turned out that she had a new mate over the road and had been there all the time.

'The first thing a parent does in that situation is pick their kid up and tell them how much they love them, then you go completely insane. You probably end up frightening the life out of them but only because they've frightened it out of you.'

And, on another occasion, Ray remembers how he had to rugby tackle his eldest daughter, Lois, to stop her running into a busy road. 'She was terrible for running off when she was little, and how I managed to catch her that day before it was too late I'll never know. I went mad. That's when they find out just how much you love them, but I must have looked like the beast who'd just rode in from hell!'

And, of course, he is right, just as he was in remembering

how the Moors murders changed things when he was growing up. It changed, because parents became more vigilant in the safety for their own children and the children of others when he was a child. Especially in such a close-knit community as Plaistow, where everyone looked out for everyone else. Even today, the case is fixed in the mind of anyone old enough to remember the terrible search on Saddleworth Moor by police officers, with spades, looking for the graves of missing children.

Television drama *See No Evil: The Story of the Moors Murders* threw new light on the case when it was aired in 2006 on the 40th anniversary of Ian Brady and Myra Hindley's conviction. The two-part programme reinforced why, to this day, Brady and Hindley remain two of the most reviled people in Britain. Hindley in particular provokes the strongest emotions, because people find it difficult to understand how any woman could be involved in such dreadful crimes against children. As much as she tried to minimise her involvement in the murders, the fact is that, without her, the crimes may not have been committed. It was Hindley, after all, who helped to entice the four children into her car, and then drove them on to the moors to be tortured and killed.

Hindley was imprisoned in 1966. Over 20 years later, she claimed she was a completely reformed character who did not pose a threat to children or society in general. But the relatives of her victims actively lobbied against her release from prison and there remained genuine fears that, if she was freed, her life would be in danger, such is the hatred which her name generated.

A lot of people, including Ray, shared the rage. 'She's an animal. She tortured children on the moors. Tortured them.

She sat there and watched kids and then raped them on a moor and buried them, and won't tell the parents where their kids are, so she ain't changed. Top her. Put her out of her misery and our misery. Gone. I'd have no qualms in pushing the button. Get rid.'

In the end, no one had to push the button where Hindley was concerned. She died in November 2002 from a chest infection following a heart attack. Ian Brady, on the other hand, remains in a mental institution.

Far less harrowing than the news of the Moors murders were Ray's trips to the cinema with his father. 'As far back as I can remember. From five or six years old, my dad would pick me up from school on a Wednesday and take me to the pictures. Jimmy Cagney, John Wayne, Edward G. Robinson and all that. I fuckin' loved it. Then we had films like *This Sporting Life* and *Saturday Night and Sunday Morning*.' That's when the acting bug bit for the first time. 'You'd have these normal working-class blokes playing the parts. And I thought, "Blimey! I could do that, I could be that geezer." All of a sudden it wasn't John Mills, who I love to bits, playing a cheeky cockney. They were people like me. I thought all these people that come from where I come from, they're actors.'

Perhaps one of his most memorable trips to the cinema, though, was the first time he ever went to see a film, when he was just five years old. He and his dad had gone to Disney's *101 Dalmatians*, and 'I went down the front shouting at the screen. Cruella de Vil was beating the doggies up.'

He also loved epic films. 'My dad took me up the West End once a month.' This was, as far as he was concerned, the real treat, the real magic. It was 'Cinemascope, you see. We saw *Zulu* there, *Becket*, *Lawrence of Arabia*, *How the West Was*

Won, 633 Squadron... and, when the film finished, my dad would say, "D'you want to see it again?" so we'd just stay where we were. One time, we went to see *Jason and the Argonauts*, and he fell asleep, so I sat through it again, and he woke up in the same place he fell asleep. When we got out, it was dark. He went, "You bastard!"'

Even though he liked the epics and a good war film, like most other kids born in the fifties, he also loved Cagney when he was a kid. 'I thought he was a great actor. He was proper. You believed him, you believed everything he said and done. I really fancied it. What a life that must be, being a kid all your life, making out you're somebody else, dressing up as cowboys.'

But, above all else, he had a particular fascination for English actors. 'I loved *The Loneliness of the Long Distance Runner* with Tom Courtenay,' and anything with Albert Finney in. 'When I was at college, I got a job in the wardrobe department at the National Theatre and dressed him for two weeks. Blinding man!'

In fact, it was Finney's early films that inspired Ray to take to the stage himself in a school production of *Emil and The Detectives*. He even borrowed some extra tuition money from his friend's mother, interestingly enough, a drama teacher, to make sure he would get cast as a cockney newspaper-seller in the play.

Away from the stage and the pictures, Ray's other big childhood passion was sport, both football and boxing. Footy he probably ranked as his number-one favourite, much the same as he does today. His first memory of the beautiful game, as he calls it, was as a young kid, and he was, he recalls, 'standing at the bottom of my street blowing bubbles as the West Ham team came along on a coach.

They'd just won the 1964 FA Cup final against Preston North End. The coach didn't even have an upstairs to it, they were just sitting on the roof. Bobby Moore, Martin Peters, they were all there. The first game that I actually went to see was with my uncle Len. It was Southend playing Scunthorpe or Stockport down at Southend's ground because my nan lived in Shoeburyness. I went to all the 1966 World Cup England games with my dad when I was nine – and I went to West Ham games obviously.'

Not so good, he remembers, again when he was a kid, was 'coming back from an England international at Wembley and sitting on a church wall in Edmonton, North London and getting pulled in by the police, accused of wrecking gravestones and urinating in the churchyard. My dad had to come and sort things out at the police station.' He was totally innocent. By the time he got to his teens, however, such dramas were less frequent. Or at least when it came to football, they were. Then it was a case of simply spending every Saturday afternoon with his dad standing on the terraces watching West Ham play.

Although he enjoyed watching football as much as he did playing it with his mates and probably trying to emulate his West Ham heroes, he was also a huge fan of boxing, but what drove him to actually step inside the ring for the real thing rather than just be a spectator may now be a curiosity to most. But then again, it wasn't regarded as the barbaric sport it is today. Although the way Ray explains one fight he had, it was pretty rough!

'I boxed a kid down Canterbury, and I had a lovely pair of velvet shorts on, green velvet shorts, and in the first round I boxed really well. He never laid a glove on me, and this kid had a pair of old shorts on and pumps, no front teeth and a broken nose. So he was easy to hit. And the second round I put him on the floor. And he went berserk. He went absolutely totally berserk. And he bit me, kicked me and everything. I won the fight on points, but I couldn't get out of bed for two days.'

The secret of winning, of course, he continues, is knowing how to deliver a knockout punch. He makes a fist, raises it to head height and flicks it forward a few inches. 'And very short distance. You only need to travel that far.' Again, he flicks the fist a few inches forward. 'It's timing and then coming on to your punch,' he says. 'Bang. Just drop it. You just do that. If your timing's right. It's not nice, actually. I was quite shocked the first time I done it. You're more worried about them than you are about yourself. You're meeting a kid you've never met before, and, yes, there's something quite barbaric about the whole thing.'

But then again, he explains, 'My dad (nicknamed Sugar, after world welterweight champion Sugar Ray Robinson) and my granddad both boxed, and so did most of the kids in our street. It was the thing to do; a way of keeping kids off the streets.' He trained at Repton Boys Club, the oldest boxing gym in London, where the notorious Kray Twins also boxed as kids. Interestingly enough, just nine years before Ray arrived in the world, Reggie Kray was the Schoolboy Champion of Hackney and went on to win the London Schoolboy Boxing Championships as well as being a finalist for the Great Britain Schoolboys Championship. Just eight years after Ray was born, the Krays were arrested for murder, among other things, by Inspector 'Nipper' Read in Old Street, not that far from Repton. Perhaps like the Krays, though, Ray considered boxing an essential part of growing up, learning discipline, good defence and helping to achieve personal goals, which for Ray meant acting. Certainly, he says, 'It was good training.'

But nowadays, he continues, 'Heavyweight boxing is not based on skill. It's all about big powerful guys and I don't like the way they talk. I may be old-fashioned but it's lovely to hear fighters say, "He's a great boxer," rather than "I'm going to kill him."

'If you can get in a ring with 2,000 people watching and be smacked around by another guy, then walking on stage isn't hard. It taught me a lot about the job I do today. The worst that can happen is you're booed. Every time I went in the ring I wondered why I was putting myself through it, but it was quite intellectual really, like a chess game.'

The Kray Twins, of course, were a different matter entirely. Best known and remembered as Britain's most brutal and notorious criminals of the 1960s, the Krays were also held, strangely enough, in high esteem by many of their neighbouring communities. But one cannot help wonder why their array of organised crimes would attract anyone to hold them in any kind of regard. They were, after all, involved in everything from protection rackets and illegal gambling to drug trafficking and murder. And all in a period of little over a decade. Like those involved with the 1963 Great Train Robbery, the Krays gained notable status and popularity, for some reason, when captured, arrested and finally imprisoned. It seemed to some they were simply champions of the poor rather than the vicious thugs they had been labelled, as if they were some kind of modern-day Robin Hoods. But were they?

Throughout the 1960s, the Krays were redolent of that decade for their illegal activities, making a name for themselves as the worst of the most insalubrious members of the London underworld. In 1966, for instance, Ronnie Kray shot a man who had called him fat. And, in the following year, Reggie stabbed another to death.

Indeed, their trial was one of London's most sensational. They each received life sentences with eligibility for parole after 30 years. Ronnie was eventually sent to a prison for the criminally insane, where he died in 1995 of a heart attack. Reggie, terminally ill with cancer, was released from prison in the summer of 2000. He died that October while on a long-delayed honeymoon trip with his wife, who had married him while he was incarcerated. Many East Enders, as well as others from all around Britain, continue to see the Krays as folk heroes, noting that they never harmed women or children, only fellow criminals. Many more, however, saw them as nothing more than villains, thugs and gangsters. Interestingly enough, there was once talk of Ray playing both the twins in a new British film that promised to reveal the unvarnished truth about their so-called reign of terror. It would, say some, have given Ray the roles 'he was born to play' and won him equal or even greater acclaim than Martin and Gary Kemp did for their performances in the 1990 movie.

If what the Krays got up to didn't make the world stand still, it did force people to look at the world a little more closely and, although they were locked up by the time Ray was old enough to understand why they were so notorious, he did kind of follow suit, so to speak, when it came to boxing.

Ray was known to his schoolfriends as Winnie, and, at home, Little Sugs, because of his father's nickname, Sugar. His mother called him Ray-Ray. He reckons he wasn't a very good boxer despite winning 80 fights and only losing eight. At welterweight, and following in Reggie Kray's boxing footsteps, he was London Schoolboy Champion, only for Ray, unlike Kray, he was champion three times, and again, going one better than Kray, he competed for England twice. Even though it was only at novice level, it is still something he is proud of to this day.

But, if he reckons he wasn't very good at it, one cannot help wondering how he managed to do so well. 'Knowing how to get out of the way,' he jokes. 'I used to fall asleep before a fight. But that was nerves.' As soon as the bell rang, he was awake. 'I'm lucky because I've still got a straight nose. I always had a fear when I went into the ring but knew I had to overcome it; to bring something out, to win. I had mates that used to get sick, but, as soon as the bell rings, you're awake.'

It was that knowledge that helped him with his acting career. 'With every part, it's like facing a new opponent and you can't let it beat you. You have to pull something out of the bag, and that's what I try to do.'

He continues. 'I think something of that mentality remains with me. You walk into a ring, look across it, and you know instantly whether you can beat up the man in front of you. It's like walking on stage. If you think, "I can't do this," well, you have to. That's where the boxer's training comes in. You might have to change your plan, pull something out of the bag. Overcoming that fear is probably the best buzz I know.'

It's probably why he still thinks boxing and movies go hand in glove. 'There is something special about boxing movies. Even those people who think the sport barbaric and would like to see it banned seem to find them fascinating.' But other films about sport, he says, 'especially football, are naff. Just think of *Escape To Victory* and *Yesterday's Hero*. Not only are the actors unconvincing as players, but the stories aren't really about anything. Team games can't have the emotional depth.

'Boxing is different; the last of the gladiators, one on one, two fighters baring their souls. In fact, the best boxing films aren't really about boxing at all; they're about survival, ideals, corruption, life. Then there is the beauty of boxing – two men perfectly toned, at their physical peak. And [playing] the mind games, the game of chess. You stare your opponent in the eyes and know you only have to hit him once and stop him hitting you to win.

'Think of a typical boxing movie and you're bound to think of *Rocky*. For me, though, the *Rocky* series is just entertainment, a soppy comic strip, miles removed from the real thing. No one could take the amount of punishment Sly Stallone does. And the way both boxers always fall down at the end, with everyone going mad round the ring, that's just fantasy boxing. But, when you see a film like *Raging Bull*, you know you've come across the truth. Again, *Raging Bull*, isn't really about boxing, it's about a man struggling with demons. What makes it a great film, a real film, is that it's also about the way people live and the language they use. I saw it on Channel 4 once and they'd cut out the swearing and it became a lesser film.

'I've always thought there's a relationship between acting and boxing. It taught me how to control and use my body, but it also made me fearless. Once you've boxed in front of thousands of people, you're not going to be frightened of walking out on stage – the worst that can happen is you get booed.

'*Raging Bull*, *Somebody Up There Likes Me* [based on the life of Rocky Graziano and the film that made Paul Newman famous] and *On The Waterfront* are also about little men pitted against big men, only the big men are the local mafia.

On The Waterfront is perhaps the perfect non-boxing boxing story. It's the oldest tale in the book, repeated as much in politics or business as in the ring. People start out wanting to improve the world, and become corrupted in the process of achieving their aims. Brando has to throw a fight to appease his brother who is in tow to the union bosses who, in turn, are in tow to the mafia.

'Boxing reflects life; life reflects boxing. Everyone, even politicians, starts out with good intentions, but, once they've got to the position where they can change the world, it's too late for them – they've sold their souls. There's the heartbreaking speech when Rod Steiger has just pulled a gun on his brother, Brando, who says, "Ever since I threw that fight at Madison Square Garden, I was never the same fighter. It was you, Charlie, you, you was my brother; I could have been a contender. This guy gets a shot at a title and I get a one-way ticket to palookaville." Brando has just begun to see. He was destroyed as a fighter but more painfully he was destroyed as a man. That scene makes me cry even now.'

The Boxer was another to rank high in his iconography of boxing movies. As was *Twenty Four-Seven*, which he declared he had more than just a passing interest in. 'It was down to me and Bob Hoskins for the main part. Bob got the nod, and it's perfect for him. The film is about a former boxer desperate to put something back into the community and keep the kids off the streets. That's another thing I love about boxing – it's a working-class sport. Most of the films are about young men trying to box their way out of poverty into a better life.'

After winning 80 trophies and medals himself over the ten years he was boxing, he finally packed it in when he was 19. 'My last fight was in the Tate & Lyle factory in Silvertown

[East London]. They had a gym upstairs. I won, but I couldn't get out of bed for a week. I was good at getting out the way. I always concentrated on defence, because, if they can't hit you and you hit them once, you've won. We had some world champions from our club. John H. Stracey, he's still a mate. I love John. Maurice Hope. And Audley Harrison comes from our club. I think he's all right, just needs to fight better opponents. Boxing's like acting; to improve you've got to be in classy company.' But, as one journalist noted, the danger of that tactic is that you can quickly look outclassed, out of your depth.

And perhaps that is what Ray felt about starting out in London's East End where, growing up, he was faced with the choice of the usual escape routes for working-class boys. 'Boxing, football and villainy – those were the ways out. I was a decent boxer and could play a bit of football. But I knew I was never going to be good enough to crack a living at them. And I knew I'd be totally fucking hopeless as a villain. I could never have been a thief, 'cos I knew that I'd be the one who always got caught.'

The East End, he says, 'is a funny place. 'Cos in the East End, people think of the way they look before they buy food. Which they never seem to get right on TV, by the way. You never see anybody in the East End pull up in a Ferrari, or in a nice Armani or Gucci suit on TV. Where I come from, fashion is nine-tenths of the law.'

CHAPTER 3

Dangerous Student

In 1964, when Ray was seven, Raymond and Margaret moved their family north to Enfield from where Raymond continued to run his fruit and veg stalls across the London City markets, Margaret carried on emptying fruit machines and their two children, Ray and Laura, were sent to new schools.

If Enfield is famous for one thing today, it is probably for having the world's first ever cash machine installed at a branch of Barclays Bank in the Summer of Love, 1967, ten years after Ray was born. It was also the first place in the world to manufacture the colour television set.

The surroundings in Enfield were probably not that far removed from those the Winstone family had been familiar with in Hackney. Council flats were four or five storeys high and made of red brick. Entry to each front door was accessed by walking along the balconies on the outside of the building.

41

Laundries and public baths would have also been commonplace. Perhaps one of the reasons why more and more people began to move to the suburbs, to avoid the daily hassle of living in the city, was because train fares were now more affordable.

If you asked Ray what Enfield is best known for, considering his love of football, he would probably tell you, for its sporting associations. Enfield FC was, after all, one of the best football clubs between the 1960s and 1980s and, to this day, is still regarded as the most successful non-League club ever. Various cricket clubs in the borough have also achieved success over the years. Much of the local sporting success has been attributed to the local schools and their sports activities for pupils.

By the time Ray was 11, he was enrolled at Edmonton County, a successful and mixed multicultural school for over 1,600 students. It had an excellent reputation for providing the best learning opportunities for pupils of all abilities, and helping them achieve the best they could by developing their own individual talents.

But Ray simply loathed it. For a start, he swears, 'There were two teachers who were complete, unbelievable, outrageous bullies. They were the sort of guys who pinched your face to get hold of you. One was a Welshman who was into rugby, except we didn't play it at our school, so he always had the hump. I've never forgiven the other one because he gave me detention and wouldn't let me play in a cup final. I've seen him since and, although it all happened years ago, the first thing I thought was, "You bastard!" I was only a little kid.'

With or without those two teachers, Ray still ended up with the record for most detentions at the school. And, on one occasion, he even got himself suspended. Or rather his father did. That was because he took Ray out of school to take him to the Derby. 'Yeah. That was my dad's idea. He got hold of all these umbrellas. So he thought it'd be a good idea to take me off school for the day and take me to the races to see if we could sell these brollies. It was a bright, sunny day and we had all these umbrellas to shift. It looked like we were on a hiding to nothing. Then, just before the big race, it started pissing down. So we got a result. The next day, I told the headmaster why I'd been absent and he sent me home for a week. My dad was fucking livid.

'As far as he was concerned, going to the Derby was a great education for me. He couldn't see the problem at all.' Basically, Ray had been suspended for telling the truth. His father, who to this day Ray describes as 'a blinding dad, a good dad' and who now works as a London cabbie, had thought it would be an educational experience. It was not the first time, though, Ray had been reprimanded for what the school termed bad behaviour. No stranger to punishment, Ray was frequently caned across the hand or slippered across his backside. It was not an uncommon way of enforcing discipline in education during the 1960s. But the day he got caned 'six of the best across me arse', when he was just six years old, his father decided to take action, and stormed into the school and complained bitterly. 'It looked like there was going to be a war.'

Even if he doesn't bear a grudge about it now, he would still argue that his upbringing gave him an extra shot of ambition that has transcended his life from child to adult. 'Oh yeah,' he once explained. 'Because I just don't give a fuck. I just do what I want to do, I enjoy myself, and I don't really take a lot of notice what other people think. It kind of drives you on a little bit I guess. But I've never really put myself in a class. I go to work, I've got a family. I'm family class, if you like – and by that, I mean me, my family, my mates. We're our own little mob, you know? And fuck everyone else!'

Perhaps that's why some say he was something of a tearaway during his youth. Not that Ray would agree. 'Nah,' he laughs, 'that's just newspaper talk. They always call me "a crafty Cockney chappie" or "a former East End tearaway". But I was never really a tearaway as such. I got up to my fair share of mischief, like most kids. I had the odd skirmish. But I was never the sort of kid who hung around in a gang and got into trouble. I'd set fire to stuff occasionally. As you do. But nothing too serious. When I was about seven, I set light to this chair on a dump and ran away. For months afterwards, I believed the rozzers were after me. Frightened the fucking life out of me. But that's the sort of thing you do when you're a nipper. Your mum tells you not to play with matches. So your first thought is, "What can I set fire to?" It's just a giggle, innit? It's just part of growing up.'

Overall, though, despite the difficulty he encountered fitting in with school authority and discipline, and the fact that his heart wasn't into anything academic, he reckons he had a very happy childhood. 'I was lucky. I had parents that loved me and I had good mates. I always thought that I was a nice kid but, when I ask around, everyone seems to think I wasn't so nice.'

Nice or not, Ray was like his parents. Grafters who weren't afraid of work. Standing on soap boxes, attempting to convince punters they couldn't live without the particular items that had fallen his way in sizeable bulk, he worked with his father on the market stalls. 'I was helping him out at weekends from the age of 13. Working on a market stall is a great education. You meet people from all walks of life –

every character in the book. And there's nothing quite like the banter and the sense of humour. Even ranting becomes an art form. Screaming out "Cauliflowers" and, you know, "Mushrooms", and stuff like that, you have to have plenty of front. The skill was knowing how much to buy. It's like if you're a football manager, knowing when your players are on song and when they're not. It's the same with your punters.'

But the hardest thing he says he ever had to try to sell was ladies non-reusable underwear. 'You couldn't reuse them 'cos they were made out of cheap paper. Fucking horrible. Not surprisingly, no one wanted them. In the end we sold them as a job lot by taking out an advert in the *Evening Standard*.'

When he was 13, Ray acted in a school play of *Emil and the Detectives* and 'had a laugh doing it'. It was then perhaps that he became more interested in acting. Perhaps it was that feeling that many actors are said to have when they act for the first time. That sort of 'Yeah!' feeling. Whatever it was, it was around this time that he first thought that being an actor could be a possible career for him.

While he was helping his father out around the markets, and while he was still at school in Edmonton he first attended drama classes and elocution lessons with the mother of a schoolmate. By the time he left school, he would best be described as a skinhead who liked Ska music and would wear two-tone mohair suits with the tie and pin and hankie. It was very stylish and polished or, as Ray describes it, very mint. It was not, as some have suggested, fascist. How could it be fascist? he once retorted when asked. 'It's West Indian music, so it ain't going to be fascist. That's just bollocks.'

Apart from listening to the Ska and punk bands of the day, he also listened to bands like Roxy Music and anything by Bryan Ferry. He loved Bryan Ferry simply because he was very

English and, if there is one thing that Ray adores, it's England.

He also adored shoes, and still does. They were very important to him. 'Shoes say it all. We had shoes from Church's when we were kids, good leather shoes. And I rarely bought shoes from a high-street store as they fell apart. Even as a kid, before Christmas, we'd go and have trousers and a jacket made. Our overcoats made. We'd always be sharp, I've got pictures of the whole family – and we're not talking about wealthy people – where everyone is looking immaculate.'

Although Ray could never be described as academic, and he left school with only one qualification, a grade-2 CSE in drama, it was enough to win him a place at the Corona stage school in Chiswick, West London, which, at the time, seemed the perfect place to pursue his interest in drama.

What is perhaps quite amazing is how his parents, who were probably strapped for cash more often than not, found the money to send him there. 'They probably looked at me and thought, "What else is he going to do?" Because I was pretty lazy at school. I'd done boxing and that kept me off the street corners and they probably felt it's another way out. My mum and dad were not backward in the way of looking to the past, so I was pretty lucky in that way. My parents paid £900 a term for me to go to drama school – which was a hell of a lot of money in those days – because they saw that maybe it was a chance for me to do something different.' But, just as he had been with most things at school, 'I was lazy and didn't take it seriously, despite the fact that they had made enormous sacrifices.'

Interestingly enough, the school had started out as a troupe of 12 children called the Corona Babes, run by their founder Miss Rona Knight and assisted by her sisters Hazel and

Muriel, performing in music halls all over the country in the 1920s. By the 1930s it had grown into two troupes of 24 girls. After World War II, during which Rona Knight had her own career under the name of Rona Brandon and had worked for ENSA (Entertainments National Service Association), she opened her first full-time school in Chiswick in West London. This was so successful that the school later moved, and was housed, during the 1950s, in larger premises in Ravenscourt Park, where it remains to this day. By the time Knight retired in 1989, such former pupils as Richard O'Sullivan, Dennis Waterman, Francesca Annis, Judy Geeson, Nicholas Lyndhurst and, of course, Ray, had become well known in their own respective fields of theatre, film and television.

But not all was well with Ray. Even with the full academic studies in the morning and the vocational training in the afternoon, it was not what he expected of a drama school.

'Seventy-five per cent of the boys in my class were gay. No one would ever admit they were gay where I came from so it was a real eye-opener. I met people from all over the place, so, if I'd never become an actor, it would have been an education in itself.' Ray was also subjected to ballet classes where, as he puts it, 'you had to get into all this leotard gear so you could learn movement. I was a terrible dancer; I'm like a lump of wood. The only thing I can do is the pogo – where you jump and spit [so] I just turned up with a pair of huge steel-capped Doc Martens. I was a silly boy and sent out. I thought I fitted into the school and maybe I am being paranoid or an inverted snob, but it was just the accent that the teachers held against me.'

Not that Jayne Knight would agree. She was the niece of the headmistress Ray came to loathe so much. Jayne was a teacher herself at the same time Ray was a student. 'There are quite a few actors who had similar accents to Ray, like Dennis Waterman. No actor is singled out because of the way they talk. And, although I would have probably taken classes with Ray, quite frankly, I can't remember him that well, so he didn't probably strike me as someone who stood out.'

Certainly, Ray didn't see the point of the ballet classes. Sure, he had already admitted to being able to do the pogo, but that was about all he could do when it came to that sort of thing. To Ray it was no better than getting all dolled up to go out, and then flogging yourself to death dancing in a club. 'By the end of the night you're sweating your nuts off trying to pull a girl, but chucking your guts up with these huge sweat patches under your arms.'

Matters didn't improve when he got a zero in his LAMDA (London Academy of Music and Dramatic Art) exam after he recited the tribune's "Wherefore rejoice?" speech from Shakespeare's *Julius Caesar* in cockney and got admonished for it. 'Everyone else did it German. I thought I've got to do it a bit different. Everyone's doing the same thing. I played it like a geezer who's just gone in the pub and having a go at everyone who's changed colours. And I got nought. I never even got one for information. I thought if this is what it's about I've obviously got it wrong. But I thought, "Fuck 'em," I'm gonna just keep doing what I do. You gotta be different. You don't copy people. You do your thing your way.'

And of course, he was right. But, even today, his understated, naturalistic style of acting can lead to criticism. 'I don't want to show that I'm performing, but some people in the business don't like what I do. They like to see obvious performances, but that ain't me. When I do something, I don't want to see the cracks.' And he still believes that 'there's a class thing in this business. A lot of actors say, if it wasn't for acting I'd be in prison, but that's bollocks. It ain't the case for me, I was brought up well. We weren't thieves. Dad went to work to get me things, so I didn't have to go down that road. I have mates who have been in trouble – kids who I went to school with. That's the path they took, but it doesn't mean they are any less of a friend. I didn't go down that road, but I can play those types, I've seen them enough."

But, as far as drama went, and as if to almost prove that, when it rains it pours, when he made his professional acting debut at 17, in a play called *What A Crazy World We're Living In* at the Theatre Royal Stratford East, he remembers his dad coming to watch him. 'I danced the wrong way. I sang out of tune. I told jokes that nobody laughed at. I went up to my dad afterwards and said, "What do you reckon?" And he just took a sip of his gin, looked up, sniffed and said, "Bit of advice, son. Give up while you're in front." He's very straightforward, my dad. So it dawned on me that I wasn't quite right for acting. But I wasn't going to be put off so easily. I thought, "Fuck it, I'll give it another go."'

Despite his father's counsel that he may not have had what it took to be a burgeoning actor, Ray was determined to give it another go. His mother agreed. She encouraged him to stick at it, no matter what. After all, 'what else was he going to do?' It was probably equally concerning to his parents that Ray didn't settle that well into the regime of drama school either. Although he has said himself that he only spent one year at Corona, and much the same has been written elsewhere, whenever journalists have dug up his past, he was, interestingly enough, on their books for three years between 1973 and 1977.

Whether or not Ray actually attended the school for the duration of those three years doesn't really matter. What mattered was his final year. That's when all hell let loose and he was expelled for puncturing the principal's car tyres in anger after he was not invited to the school's Christmas party. In fact, he was the only one not invited. 'Yeah,' he tells most that ask him about it, 'I sabotaged the headmistress's car. This old bird, Mrs Knight, was a nasty old bitch to me, she was always having a pop at me, because I was the toe-rag from up the road. So I put tacks under her tyres and I got expelled, and was asked to leave the premises.'

Looking back now, the only thing Ray says he picked up at drama school was how to conduct himself at parties. But he also acknowledges that he himself may have been the problem. 'As an adult, you wipe out all you did as a kid, and I don't remember going through puberty, or being a pest to Mum and Dad.'

At drama school, though, it seemed to be a different matter entirely. According to Ray, and supporting his class-distinction theory that he was considered a disruption, and maybe he was, his classmates were told 'I was a danger to them because of my cockney accent, and that I would hold them back, but I think we should be judged on what we say, not how we say it.' Perhaps it was because of the way he thought he was being singled out that also got him thinking he would take revenge on the principal's decision to bar him from the Christmas party. And what better than to hammer some tacks through a piece of wood, place it under the wheel of her car and blow the tyre out. What he hadn't expected, however, was for one of the other kids to grass him up. That's when I was asked to go. But I was always getting in trouble, so perhaps I deserved to get thrown out.'

Even if he was right that he deserved to get kicked out, he does admit to having two very good teachers at Corona whom he still remembers with gratitude, because, as he confesses, 'I was a handful, you know, but they persevered with me.' In hindsight though, according to Ray, perhaps he *was* a disruptive influence, but once again, he is convinced it had something to do with his working-class background. But did it? Or was it just Ray being assailed with self-doubt? Whatever it was, perhaps it has something to do with the fact that he chose to become an actor in the first place. Back then, the East End wasn't exactly the hotbed of dramatic talent it has since become. If anything, as one journalist put it, he came from a family of kitchen thespians.

Many actors at the time spoke with received pronunciation, and perhaps that is what made Ray so convinced that his tough working-class roots and the way he spoke was in some way intoxicating and dangerous. 'I was always treated as a bit of a danger at drama school.'

Not that his accent should have made a difference and it probably didn't. What may have had an effect was the fact that he swore like a trooper. If that was so, then was it any surprise that he was perhaps made to feel like an outsider or someone from another world? One of the times when he felt particularly angry was when he went for an audition as an extra. 'This director picked me up and moved me. I said, "Excuse me. Don't pick me up. If you want me to move, ask me and I'll move." He said, "You'll do as you're told," so I head butted him.'

On another occasion while he was still a drama student, he even had a go at the director Ken Russell. It happened when he was walking along the line of extras at a casting call with a woman with blue hair. 'We had long hair at the time,' Ray explains. 'And, as he was walking along, he was going, "Yes, yes, yes, haircut, haircut." I felt like a cow standing at the market. I said, "Excuse me, do you want me to get my hair cut, do I get paid extra for that?" He told me I wouldn't get paid extra, so I told him I didn't want to do it. And he retorts by saying, "You'll never get anywhere like that." I said, "You're telling me to get my hair cut and she's got blue hair. Who do you think you are?"'

Not that he had to worry. On the day after he left Corona, he auditioned, almost by accident, for a part in *Scum*, a film about young Borstal offenders that was then about to be made for the BBC by director Alan Clarke. What is perhaps ironic about how Ray ended up in the television drama is that he had gone along to the casting call simply because some of his mates were auditioning. 'I didn't go in there for a job, so I was pretty relaxed about it all. I was only going up with all the boys, who were going to the audition, so I could have a drink with them after and say ta-ta.'

It has been said that Ray was only auditioned himself because of his flirtatious advances on an attractive receptionist, although this does not appear to be entirely true. 'Sure,' says Ray, 'I got talking to the receptionist and she said, "You wanna go in and meet the director?" And I said, "Nah, not really, I'm off for a drink with the boys," I was flirting with her really, showing off, but I went in and met Clarkey. And I got the job! I didn't have a clue what it was, hadn't seen the script, and I didn't really care. I thought, "Yeah, I'll do it, bit of a laugh." It was written for a Scotsman originally, he was a Glaswegian in the script.' But apparently he got the part because, like, in most true romantic showbiz lore Clarke spotted him walking down the corridor of the BBC – and liked what he saw. Even though Ray had been kicked out of drama school the day before, and didn't really have a clue about what he was going to do next, it was something as simple as his walk and the way he held himself that altered the course of his life – and career – forever.

CHAPTER 4

From Stage School To Borstal

Two weeks before *Scum* was scheduled to air on BBC Television in 1977, in the *Play for Today* slot, the BBC powers-that-be deemed it too controversial and far too brutal for broadcast and, so, they effectively banned their own programme from being shown, which Ray remembers, caused one 'hell of a controversy'. It would not be seen for another 14 years, when, in July 1991, exactly one year after director Alan Clarke's premature death from cancer, it was finally aired, for the first time on British television, on BBC2. The same network that had banned it in the first place.

Clarke was in many quarters regarded as the greatest British director since Alfred Hitchcock. By the time he had discovered Ray, and put him on the path to greater things, Clarkey, as he was known to industry insiders, had directed some of the best and most provocative television plays of the 1970s by always working with the best TV drama writers. It is probably true to say that his collaboration with Roy Minton on *Scum* proved to be one of his most fruitful.

Even so, the decision to ban *Scum* from being shown on television was perhaps not that surprising, when you consider, as Ray puts it, 'The government ran the BBC, and the government also ran Borstals. So it was like sending up their own system.' And there was no way on earth they were going to do that.

It seemed the problem lay in the brutality of the film, which seems rather strange today, considering that it was 'the brutality' that would end up giving the film its notoriety and, at the same time, established writer Ray Minton and Clarke's trademark approach to tackling contentious social issues without wrapping them up in cotton wool. Censorship in those days was a lot tougher than today, and that alone could have been reason enough to have the film taken off the air before the television-viewing public had the chance to see it and make up their own minds. For those critics who did eventually get to see it at a screening in January 1978, most agreed that, whereas the bullying, rioting, rape and suicide scenes featured in the play were more likely than not to have taken place at one time or another in the real-life institutions of the day, as far as the BBC were concerned, the events in the film were all shown happening within a unrealistically short space of time. This left it wide open to critical accusations of melodrama.

Interestingly enough, the 75-minute play had been shot using 16mm film at a time when most television productions were made on videotape. The use of film was probably deliberate though. Film, like cinema, can be far more realistic than video. But then again, that was another complaint about the production. It looked too much like a documentary and could therefore confuse the television-viewing public. This had been a common objection since Ken Loach and others had started using real locations and documentary film techniques in their drama productions a decade earlier. Watching *Scum* today, it looks, as you would expect, slightly softer and grainier than the now more commonly used 35mm cinema film. Perhaps that is part of its appeal. Unlike the widescreen formats of today, and because it was shot in the then normal 4.3 screen ratio for television, it carries a certain edge of cold bleakness to it. Perhaps this was the whole point.

One of the biggest problems for *Scum*, though, was that, by the time it was ready for broadcast, violence and censorship had become a hot topic for debate, to be analysed, picked on and picked over, discussed, dissected, distorted and dismissed. More intriguing then is how some very strong material was available in cinemas from major distributors back then. There was, for instance, the graphic rape in *Lipstick*, violence as catharsis in *Taxi Driver* and, in the same year that *Scum* was scheduled for transmission, another BBC drama to be dogged by censorship was the crime series *Target* starring Patrick Mower, and produced by a post-*Doctor Who* producer Philip Hinchcliffe. Partway through its run on BBC1, it was pulled off the air over concerns about its violent content. More or less in the same fashion, the *Scum* banning was just one of several BBC vetos at the time. As if to prove the point, in the previous year, *Brimstone and Treacle* by Dennis Potter had been produced but not shown. Even worse was when the pre-production on Howard Schuman's scripted *Censored Scenes from King Kong* and Ian McEwan's *Solid Geometry* was halted altogether. So it was hardly surprising that, when

Scum was pulled from the television schedules, it made national headlines. Ban something and, rest assured, it will attract attention, like bees to a honey pot.

But that wasn't the only thing at stake. It was, after all, 1977, the year when punk, the music that Ray had embraced as one of his favourites as a teenager, had reached new heights of antisocial and violent behaviour. In fact, it was in the same month that punk reached its outrage in Britain that, at the other end of the spectrum, Elvis Presley's death would be as controversial as the Sex Pistols were shocking. It seemed impossible, but, at the age of forty-two, it was true, Elvis was dead. The loss seemed to affect people everywhere. It was like those who can still vividly remember the day John F Kennedy was assassinated down to the last detail of what they were doing and where they were when they heard the news. The loss then, as now with Elvis, seemed on a very personal level. Whether people liked the man and his music or not, they couldn't deny the affect his death had on them.

The swearing on live early morning television by the Pistols didn't have the same impact the world over as Presley's untimely death. They probably wish it had. But instead, they were, perhaps unsurprisingly, thrown off the EMI record label because of the controversy and uproar they were causing. If there were two polar opposites in the public eye in 1977 it would have to be Elvis and Pistols frontman Johnny Rotten who, despite picking up some popularity in the celebrity jungle in 2006, had, in the same year that *Scum* was banned and Elvis died, projected an arrogant petulance which gave the impression he didn't care about anything in the world.

It was also the year, probably unbeknown to the general public, in which Margaret Matheson had been appointed the new producer of the BBC *Play for Today* strand, for which the general idea was to offer up new drama that was both typical and provocative. A natural progression, some would say, from the 1960s *Wednesday Play* which had nurtured such talents as Dennis Potter and David Mercer, best known for *Morgan: A Suitable Case for Treatment* in 1966.

One of the provocative dramas that Matheson commissioned was *Scum*. Based on extensive research that writer Roy Minton carried out at several real-life Borstals, and with Alan Clarke in the director's seat, how could it go wrong? Certainly, both Minton and Clarke could be relied on to deliver what was needed. After all, they were both established veterans of film and television and had earned themselves quite a reputation in their own respective fields.

The first indication of trouble with *Scum*, however, came from the BBC board of directors, who asked for cuts. The suicide of a boy named Davis towards the end of the film was removed, which left the final scene in an odd kind of limbo, and the scene showing the screw looking in at the rape in the greenhouse, which was the catalyst for the suicide, was shortened, to make it less complicit. Certainly, the complicity of the scene would have provoked a nation of television viewers into jamming the switchboards at the BBC, simply for how shocking it was.

When Matheson was told that the play would not be broadcast on television, she could not believe it. Nor could she believe the demand not to show it to the press. The BBC's reason for the ban was quite simple. In their eyes, it was unrepresentative to have all the incidents that happened in the film happening in the same Borstal in a short period of time. The answer to that, as Matheson and others have since pointed out, is that, selection, heightening and emphasis is the nature of drama. The ban was undeniably political, a reflection of the BBC's relationship with the government of the day. In the end, they were nervous about such a negative vision of an aspect of the British prison system in which the screws were equally brutalised and institutionalised as the boys they were meant to be looking after. It was simply a no-no to put it out on national television to an audience of millions. So perhaps it wasn't that surprising when it was remade into a vehicle for theatrical release two years later.

Both the television and film version of *Scum* centre on life in a contemporary institution run by violence and brutality, rather than reason, and where a boy who can fight his way to the top of the heap and reign as 'the Daddy' will gain the respect of both his fellow inmates and prison officers.

The principal character is Carlin, played by Ray, who has been transferred from another Borstal for having retaliated against violence from officers, and, even though he insists it was self-defence against 'two of them kicking the shit out of me', he has been tagged a hard case by one and all. Needless to say, he is roughed up, more or less, from his arrival, first by the officers, who are determined to beat any resistance out of him, and secondly by Banks, the reigning 'Daddy' played by John Blundell, who among other things runs a vicious protection racket aided by his sidekicks played by Ray Burdis and Phil Daniels, who, interestingly enough, would soon feature in another two Winstone movies, and now, of course, a regular in *EastEnders* playing Kevin Wicks.

About 15 minutes into the film version, after Ray's on-screen debut with the opening credits, he is befriended by another principal character, Archer, played in the film by Mick Ford, an older inmate, who has his own methods of bucking the system, and who, above all else, is determined to survive his sentence on his own terms and cause as much bother to the authorities as he possibly can. He refuses to wear leather shoes as he claims to be vegetarian, requests the literary work of Russian writer Dostoevsky for the library, and opts out of attending church services on the grounds that he is an atheist. Later, he finds himself strongly drawn towards the Islamic faith of Mecca, much to the warden's religious disapproval.

The character of Archer was based on a man Minton had met who'd had a similar experience to Archer. 'In fact, he should have been sent to prison,' said Minton. But instead, 'he was put into Borstal, was a total misfit, and appeared to me to invent his own persona to survive in an environment which he loathed. He was an intelligent man and he ended up as I had Archer, I believe, doing his full time.'

In fact, nowhere is the character of Archer better demonstrated than in one of the later scenes of the movie when Archer, instead of attending church, is left with Mr Duke, a veteran officer. It is where Archer explains that, contrary to Duke's belief, Borstal cannot build character, as it is an institution based on degradation. 'I don't want to underestimate your lifetime's work,' he tells Duke, 'but the punitive system does not work. In my experience of Borstal, it convinces me that more criminal acts are imposed on prisoners than by criminals on society.'

Banks, the reigning 'Daddy', is not so easy for Carlin to befriend. Not that he particularly wants to. Despite Minton's basing Archer on a real-life 'total misfit', it shows something of his character when he warns Carlin that Banks would be seeking him out to establish his supremacy over Carlin with a series of violent attacks. With a deliberate decision by warders to put Carlin in a dormitory with Banks and his honchos, rather than in a single cell, the bullies are able to give Carlin a thorough late-night beating, for which Carlin is, shortly afterwards, put into solitary confinement after being accused of fighting. Cleverly, he endears himself to the highly religious governor by referring to his comfort in being Church of England, being polite and courteous – while denying a fight – and not even questioning his punishment.

After a fair amount of abuse and provocation from Banks and his toadies that gets Carlin into even more trouble with the warders, he decides to take over through a mixture of violence and force of character. In a graphically violent sequence, and probably Ray's finest moment in the movie, he proceeds first to beat Phil Daniels's Richards, one of the Daddy's toadies, with a cosh consisting of a long sock containing two snooker balls taken from a game going on in the recreation room. The scene in the film version is shocking because it is more realistic than the version filmed for television. It was the first time that Ray played the kind of character which has defined his career – the movie hard man.

In the television version, the snooker scene is slightly different as Carlin places the socked snooker balls in his pocket. For the film version, the scene was filmed in one continuous take, as Ray carries the sock down by his side and an assistant to the director had to lie on the floor and hand Ray another sock, containing something less lethal, out of shot. But as well as the violence that lay at the heart of the scene, it was a telling point in the relationship between Carlin and Archer.

The impact of Carlin's actions scares Eckersley, the other toady in the room, who obeys when Carlin tells him to get back when he tries to escape and warn Banks of the incident. Carlin then replaces the balls on the table. 'Yeah, well, carry on!' he tells the two lads who are still playing the same game as before he snatched the balls off the table. He then heads to the dormitory area where, having established that inmate Jackson was still in the dormitory, for alibi purposes, he goes to find Banks in the bathroom, where, again for the film version, and far more graphically than was evident in the television play, he administers a frenetic beating and kicking. 'Right, Banks, you bastard, I'm the Daddy now – next time I'll fucking kill you!'

He leaves Banks bleeding on the floor where Sands, the warder, finds him and further assaults him. The badly injured Banks is not seen again until the riot scene in the dining room towards the end of the film.

Somewhat surprising, though, in the television version, but cut from the film, was the suggestion of a homosexual relationship between Carlin and a young new inmate called Rhodes. As Minton explains, 'Carlin wasn't homosexual, it was distinctly established that during the time in there – and that came out of research met a career criminal who had been through Borstal and prison and I met him about six times and got quite pally with him and he told me about these cavortings, very much on a public-school basis. He would have a missus inside, he called him his missus just for the time inside, and it was "I'm no fucking poofter, but you're my missus." That I felt was rather sad because it extended Carlin's character quite a lot for me. Made him vulnerable in an area were he couldn't afford to be vulnerable, just showed a flaw. In his own terms, he was flawed because he had this sexual lead in those circumstances.'

A particularly controversial part of the film features a suicide. Throughout the film, the character of Davis constantly looks disheartened and terrified of his surroundings and is noticeably weaker than the other inmates. His misery grows to its limit when he is raped in a graphic scene by three older and stronger boys while on greenhouse duty. One of the warders, Mr Sands, witnesses the rape from afar, but takes no action, highlighting the utter immorality and corruption of the system. Highly distressed by the incident, Davis is further disturbed while hearing a conversation between other boys at his table in the mess hall in which they imply that they will repeat the act the following day. In the middle of the night, he uses his cell's alert buzzer to call the night-duty warder. The warder dismisses him as a time waster and orders him back to bed, despite Davis's obvious distressed state. Davis then cuts his wrists with a razor blade while in bed, but seems to change his mind, perhaps due to the unexpected pain. The warder ignores his repeated presses on the alarm bell. As one would expect, he loses a lot of blood, which soaks through his bed sheets, turning them bright red, and he is found dead the next morning.

Davis's suicide naturally causes a stir and upset among the inmates – including those who had raped him and the toadies of Banks who had previously bullied him – and they go on a hunger strike and start a riot in the mess hall, which leads to the final scenes of the film. The ringleaders of the riot, one of whom is Ray's character, Carlin, are badly beaten by the warders and thrown into solitary confinement. The film ends on a very sober note with the overtly religious governor addressing an assembly of the other inmates, warning them that the damage to the mess hall will have to be repaid through loss of earnings. He then, without any feeling or emotion whatsoever, orders a moment of silence for Davis.

The television-play version of the film featured less graphic rape and suicide scenes than the later cinema version. An additional scene, cut from the final print of the film version, shows Davis trying to talk to Carlin about the incident. But Carlin dismisses him when he refuses to talk in front of his so-called 'missus'. He then commits suicide. In the later version, released in cinemas, although the relationship between Carlin and his 'missus' doesn't feature, Davis looks up at Carlin from the dining table as if about to confide in him, but Carlin, not realising, chooses to get up and leave at that point.

Despite the furore over the television banning, the film version couldn't have done better. As the trade journal of the day *Screen International* noted, it was 'Strong meat, but never gratuitously shocking, this is a feather in the British film industry's cap to be worn with pride but with humility rather than arrogance... *Scum* is powerful, disturbing and moving; it is also absorbing, exciting entertainment with inbuilt suspense and paced to allow for the nervous relief of laughter. The performances of the young actors are impressively convincing... Clarke directs Roy Minton's crusading screenplay with a controlled ferocity that makes no compromises. He shows us a hell in which the inmates and the screws are equally damned but the absolute power of the officers ensures their absolute damnation.'

The *Sun* agreed. 'It is an important film and one which should be seen.'

And as if to prove the point, the review in *Now* magazine said much the same. 'It is brilliantly made, anger vibrating through every moment... it is a remarkably courageous film with outstanding performances.'

Even the *Sunday Telegraph* couldn't ignore it. 'A scorchingly fine film: I cannot remember the last time I saw a British picture so confident in the courage of its convictions.'

What is perhaps interesting is that at the preview screening in 1978 all the journalists screamed the same message. One of those was Stephen Gilbert, who wrote in the *Observer*, 'Within the naturalistic framework there's a rattling good tale in the staunch tradition of Hollywood liberalism. The hero, a clear victim of injustice, overcomes the system, holds to his integrity, vanquishes the villains and establishes a new and, it's implied, more principled order... Another obvious parallel is the Warner Bros cycle of the Thirties. Carlin is no more heroicized than the figures Cagney played in, say, *Angels with Dirty Faces* or *Each Dawn I Die*, movies which, like *If...* the BBC is content to screen.'

Gilbert's review could not have been better timed for producers Clive Parsons and Davina Belling. They were, according to Parsons, seeking a film project at the time they read Gilbert's review. 'We were looking for something that would be intrinsically about life but of universal appeal without being parochial, something that had real guts and substance rather than a piece of candy floss.' So, after watching the banned television film, Parsons and Belling bought the screen rights and made the screen version, and to all intents and purposes, along with executive producer Dan Boyd, who insisted that Ray must be in the film, no matter what, rescued *Scum* from television obscurity by retaining much of the original cast, director Clarke and writer Minton to produce a feature film that was, as one critic said, 'bristling with anger and realism'. It perhaps says something of Ray's presence on screen at that time that Boyd really wasn't interested in bankrolling the film unless Ray resumed his role as Carlin.

However, when the television version was pulled from the schedules, even after it had already been listed in the *Radio Times*, it seemed, from where Ray was standing, as if the setback was permanent. 'I said, "That's the final straw. I've been fired from drama school, the main lead I've got in a film, out of luck, got banned, so I'll go out and get a proper living.'

Even though Ray thought landing the part was something of a doddle, one cannot help wondering how his career might have panned out without it. But it is also interesting to speculate whether, if the television film had not been banned and no cinema version made, he would have ended up the star he is today. Even without the cinema version, making the television film must have been an ideal opportunity for Ray to familiarise himself with such things as film language, like rolling, speed, slate and action. After all, filming was not like drama school and, although the Corona stage school would have probably taught him how to get into character, getting into the story was perhaps a different matter entirely, especially if the film was shot out of sequence, as most are, he must have wondered, like any newcomer does, how on earth he was going to get into the story when the plot, continuous on paper, was suddenly flying to all points of the compass to be reassembled later on the cutting-room table.

But, according to Parsons, 'It was fascinating to watch Alan direct because a lot of the time he was directing untrained actors. They were not people who had been to drama schools and he just had the ability to, to almost threaten the performers in a way. He'd get up really close to an actor and just the way he did it was fascinating drawing a performance out of these actors. He really was – I mean we work with all sorts of directors – and some directors you find spend very little time with the actors, which is really crazy. That's where they ought to spend their time, but they're much more concerned with the camera and the angles, you know, all that sort of thing. Alan was very much an actor's director and I think that he did get wonderful performances out of the mainly young actors.'

Not that there were many offers lurking in the wings for Ray after the television version was banned. 'I got no work, other than lots of parts that were just rubbish, so I decided I'd had enough and binned it.' Even though he is said to have quit acting at that point, or, as he says, binned it, and returned to work with his father on the market stalls for the next two years, it was less than a year after the television version of *Scum* had been completed and was subsequently banned that he got a phone call from Belling asking him if he would like to be in the feature-film version of *Scum*.

Ray, of course, jumped at the chance. And, as if to suggest that he already had box-office clout, and perhaps to satisfy Boyd's demands that Ray *must* resume his role for the big-screen version of *Scum*, Ray was offered the principal role in another one of the film projects that Belling and Parsons were making that spring in Torquay, Devon. Although one of Ray's least-seen films, and even if it didn't, as some critics warned, sound all that promising, *That Summer*, a kind of punky coming-of-age flick set by the seaside, won Ray a BAFTA nomination for the most promising newcomer in a leading film role.

In many ways, *That Summer* picks up where *Scum* could have left off. It was the story of two girls who travel to Torquay in Devon from the North of England to work as chambermaids for the summer. They meet two boys, also in Torquay for the summer, one of whom is Ray's character, Steve, fresh out of Borstal who enters himself in the 'round the bay' swimming race. They have a run-in with a gang of Scottish lads, one of whom is played by Jon Morrison, who is also entered in the swimming race. Various confrontations ensue with Morrison and his friends framing Ray for a robbery in a chemist's shop. Winstone is arrested just as he is about to start the race. He escapes from the police and follows Morrison into the water, catches him up, and forces him to confess to framing him and then goes on to win the race.

Even if it was typical and predictable late 1970s cinema fare, making the film did offer Ray something else that not even he had expected. It was while he was on location that he would meet his wife-to-be Elaine McCausland, a graphic designer and ex-Bunny girl, who, on holiday with her parents, was in a telephone box by the beach when Ray opened the door and struck up a conversation. 'I had to do a bit of work to get her to go out with me, but she did and we've been together ever since. It's been like a holiday romance that has lasted a lifetime.' And, if you ask him if it was love at first sight, he'll tell you, without any hesitation, yes it was. 'She's got really great eyes, and a really great bum, a blinding bubble. I noticed the bum first, but she's got terrific green Irish eyes and it was bada-bing bada-boom.'

They got married in 1979, the same year that *Scum* was released into cinemas on the ABC circuit, then one of the largest cinema franchises and exhibitors in Britain.

As journalist Brian Viner remembers, 'I first set eyes on Ray Winstone when, aged 15 or so, my friends Billy Birtles, Rob Waggett and I managed to bluster our way into the ABC cinema in Southport to see the X-rated *Scum*. Winstone played a vicious Borstal boy called Carlin, whose weapon of choice was a sock filled with snooker balls. We did not see the film as a profound comment on the psychosis of violence, we were just impressed by how hard he was. We were at a boys' school, where hardness counted for a lot. Tony Rodwell? Rock-hard. Mo Thabet? Rock-hard. But Ray's Carlin? In our adolescent minds, he became the ultimate personification of rock-hardness, and, whenever I see Winstone on screen, it is an image I still find hard to shake.'

As if to support Viner's impression, Ray himself would later tell journalists that he used to get a lot of looks on trains shortly after he played the lead in *Scum*. Travellers would spend the whole journey sizing him up, and only smile weakly or offer a compliment when it was their stop. Ask him today about it, and he will most probably joke with you. He is often reported to imagine himself in a Merchant-Ivory production of *Scum*, purely for his own amusement. 'Can you imagine it? I say, dear boy, where's your farking tool?' And it wasn't just on the trains he was getting attention. 'I did once get a very strange fan letter from a Glaswegian psychopathic homosexual who wrote to me after watching *Scum*. I remember thinking at the time, "I don't want any more like that." He was bang in love with me. I never replied to him. My bottle went.'

All the same, Ray continues, 'I was suddenly in a film that everyone was talking about. I walked around like Jack the Biscuit,' which, according to *The Times* magazine in September 2004, alienated him from casting directors all over town, and the work dried up almost completely. So, 'Thank God,' Ray says, 'I had mates who'd give me a clump and tell me to behave if I got above myself.'

But it wasn't just the attention that was paid to Ray that had him buzzing. The release of the film, once again, attracted much the same controversies as the banned television play had. As Clive Parsons confirms, when the theatrical version was eventually shown on the small screen in 1983 (by which time, incidentally, the Borstal system had been abolished), the British public-morality campaigner Mary Whitehouse had won a court case against Channel 4 for showing the film. It was judged that the Independent Broadcasting Authority had made a 'grave error of judgement' in allowing it to be screened. But the IBA won an appeal in the House of Lords which turned the Whitehouse verdict upside down. Never before or since has a movie that started out as a television drama stirred up so much trouble, and probably, in some quarters, still does to this day. Like Clive Parsons, Ray simply thought that, 'if *Scum* stopped one kid from going to Borstal, then the film has done its job.'

If there was one thing that did concern Clarke and Boyd, it would have been the cheering from audiences at the London premiere at the Prince of Wales cinema when Carlin in the film beats up the black 'Daddy' and calls him a black bastard. The film was never intended to have racial undertones, or anything that could be even closely regarded as racist. It was just written that way, because that is how some people talked at that time and, of course, it was in keeping with the way Ray's character spoke.

But, as Boyd says, 'What I couldn't have predicted was that not only would the film change the penal system for young offenders in Britain but it would be the inspiration for a vibrant generation of audiences hungry to see characters they could identify with portrayed truthfully on the screen. These audiences were the catalyst for a revival in British cinema that still continues to astonish audiences all over the world with its ability to tell stories which are as moving as they are shocking. The fact that this subversive masterpiece was finally shown on television the night Margaret Thatcher became Britain's prime minister and garnered a vast audience late at night continues to provide me with an ironic smile.'

CHAPTER 5

The Quiet Rocker

No sooner was his work on the *Scum* set complete than Ray was starting work on yet another movie, and one that probably reminded him of how, when age seven, he stood on a street corner in Plaistow waiting for the Mods and Rockers to come back from Margate. Joining his old *Scum* ally Phil Daniels and an array of other names that were still newly emergent in British film, including Leslie Ash, Mark Wingett and Phil Davis, Ray headed down to the south coast of England to film *Quadrophenia*. This was Franc Roddam's opus of The Who's 1973 rock opera and based on real-life events that took place in August 1964.

Produced by Roy Baird, Bill Curbishley and members of the band for their own production company, The Who Films, and written by Roddam, *Quadrophenia* was based on the album Pete Townsend had conceived six years earlier. The general consensus was that the movie had a much more naturalistic style than The Who's previous cinematic outing *Tommy*, directed by Ken Russell, the same director that Ray had argued with at an earlier audition. Perhaps the reason *Quadrophenia* worked better than *Tommy* was down to the producers giving director Roddam an unprecedented amount of directorial freedom to create the authentic experience of being a working-class boy in changing times. 'The important thing for me,' he reflects, 'was I was making a film about teenage angst and youthful emotions.'

Perhaps another reason *Quadrophenia* worked so well is that Roddam decided to use the same 18 and 25mm lenses that turned Orson Welles into a master filmmaker. Together with the Eastman colour stock, and the use of a hand-held camera for many of the scenes, this gave the film a sense of realism. Another bonus, perhaps, was the idea of bringing the ensemble together a month before shooting began so the actors could be encouraged to give their characters histories and future relationships which, in turn, built a naturalistic 'gang' feel into the film.

Shot in five weeks with a script that evolved with the casting, *Quadrophenia*'s youthful stars and timeless theme of rebellion struck a chord with most audiences when it went on release in November 1979, just two months after *Scum*. But, as Roddam again reflects, it was two years before punk when 'we were shooting the film, a movement with a very strong attitude about what things should be left behind and what things move forward. I didn't want to make a film that was set in an era that current youth were abusive towards. I felt that I made a very emotionally honest film, so it didn't matter what period it was set in.'

He need not have worried though. *Quadrophenia* arrived with immaculate timing into a Britain that was already re-

Modifying with the re-emergence of Ska and Two-Tone music through various London and Coventry clubs and bands. With the soundtrack album and the roar of scooters up and down the seaside promenades again, how could anyone fail to get an impression of what the sixties must have been like at the height of the Mod era. Today, the film still retains its iconic resonance, dealing as it does with the timeless themes of rebellion and conformity. Named as the 35th greatest British film of all time by *Total Film* magazine in 2004, *Quadrophenia* rightly takes its place in the canon of great coming-of-age movies, dealing, as it does, with the road journey we all have to take to find our true selves, and the wrong turns we may take along the way.

Like Roddam, the Mods were very slick and mostly kitted out in Parka coats and rode either Lambretta or Vespa scooters, many modified with elaborate customisations, paintwork and mirrors. They were into what was then being called the new rhythm and blues and Ska music aligned to such bands as The Who, The Yardbirds and The Small Faces. The Rockers, on the other hand, were a throwback to the old Teddy Boys of the 1950s. They wore jeans and leather jackets often adorned with studs, patches and pins, rode British motorcycles and were into rock'n'roll. As far as they were concerned, the musical genius of legends like Elvis Presley, Gene Vincent and Eddie Cochran still ruled. As one Australian Mod, nicknamed True Blue, still remembers, 'You had to be one or the other, otherwise you would get a hiding from both groups.'

The clashes of the Mods and Rockers on the beaches of Margate, Bournemouth and Brighton on the Whitsun May bank holiday of 1964 certainly sparked off a moral panic about British youth. Many ended up with prison sentences following the violent clashes between the two gangs. In one incident, in Margate, two youths were taken to hospital with knife wounds and 51 were arrested after hundreds of teenagers converged on the town. The *Daily Mirror* dubbed it 'the second Battle of Hastings'. Dr George Simpson, then the chairman of Margate magistrates, imposed fines totalling £1,900 on 36 people. Three offenders were jailed for three months each and five more were sent to detention centres for up to six months.

Three months later, during the August bank holiday weekend in Brighton, on which the disturbances in *Quadrophenia* were based, the riots got even worse. Two youths were jailed for three months and a record number of others were fined. More than 1,000 teenagers were involved in skirmishes on the beach and along the promenade. Never before had anyone witnessed such behaviour. Deckchairs were used for bonfires, obscenities shouted at passers-by, holidaymakers jostled and elderly residents terrified for their safety. When the two rival groups gathered at the now famous Palace Pier, they continued to chant and jeer at each other and, when they weren't doing that, they were showering the police with stones and anything else they had to hand.

There were also running battles on the beaches which resulted in major casualties to both sides, including the police. Elsewhere, further damage occurred when gangs smashed council-flat windows and vandalised pubs and hardware shops. By the evening, hundreds of young men and women were still wandering around the resort long after the last train. At this time police stepped in to prevent further violence and dispersed about 30 Rockers marching up and down the promenade shouting 'Up the Rockers!'

Two years after the seaside riots, much of the furore over the Mods and the Rockers had faded into oblivion as a new burgeoning counterculture scene was gathering momentum. Although the Mods and the Rockers will always be associated with the sixties, the decade is also remembered as the one in which many came of age. One when free thinking, free love and free drugs became the buzz words of a generation. And one in which it seemed the entire world felt the need to go to San Francisco and put flowers it its hair, and embrace a 'brave new world' through the musical likes of Scott MacKenzie, Donovan and the Byrds.

Just as Woodstock defined the hippie era, so *Quadrophenia* defined the period of the Mods and Rockers. By the late sixties, things had changed dramatically, especially for the Mods. Their beloved Friday-night television show *Ready Steady Go* (or *RSG* for short) – far more youth oriented and informal than any other on the box at the time – was taken off the air. Interestingly enough, it was the only pop programme that had allowed artists to perform full versions of their songs rather than the short versions demanded by the other pop shows of the day, such as *Thank Your Lucky Stars* and *Top of the Pops*.

The Mods had also become bored with rioting and their once-exclusive fashionable Carnaby Street had gone commercial. The conditions for everything 'Mod' had altered. Radio, which in those days was dominated by offshore broadcasting from such ships as Radio London and Caroline, was playing the things kids wanted to hear and shops were selling the stuff kids wanted to wear. But, as one reviewer correctly pointed out, the film perfectly captured the teenage need to belong and to identify with their peers.

Quadrophenia was the story of Jimmy Cooper, played by

Phil Daniels, who divides his time between hanging out with Mod friends and slaving in the post-room of an advertising firm. He doesn't work there because he wants to or has any great desire to further a career. Quite the opposite, in fact, if anything, all Jimmy is bothered about is having enough cash in his pocket to keep his scooter running and his custom-made suits trim, and leaving a little time and money for the music he loves.

But, come Saturday, Jimmy's down the sauna getting scrubbed down for a weekend of mayhem. Unfortunately someone in the next cubicle is singing, off-key, the sort of tunes that really bug Jimmy. Gene Vincent's *Be-Bop-A Lula*. When he doesn't stop, but sings even louder, Jimmy sticks his head over the partition, looking for trouble, only to find Kevin (played by Ray) an old schoolfriend. Warmed with memories of some good times, Jimmy meets Kevin in a nearby cafe for a sit-down breakfast. It's only then that Jimmy realises that Kevin is a Rocker, the sworn mortal enemy of the Mods, forcing him to make an excuse and leave.

But Kevin doesn't give 'a monkey's arsehole' about the Mods and the Rockers. As far as he's concerned, everyone is the same underneath, no matter what they wear or ride. Slightly shocked and surprised by Jimmy's disapproval, Kevin snaps back, 'What, am I black or something?'

Jimmy is adamant. 'Well, you ain't exactly white in that sort of get-up, are you.'

The episode is soon forgotten, though, for Jimmy is looking to have some success with women that evening. He's had his eye on the lithe Steph, played by a very young and attractive Leslie Ash, whom every Mod seems to want to shag, even though she's currently hitched up to Pete. After procuring a few pills from their supplier Ferdy, the gang rolls around looking for a party to gatecrash. Out in the suburbs, the opportunity arises and soon everyone is swaying to the 'top sounds of the day.' The problem for Jimmy is that Steph is all caught up with Pete, leaving him to the tender mercies of Monkey played by Toyah Willcox whose band at the time was gaining critical success with their debut single 'Victims of the Riddle'. Unlike the real Willcox, her character was out for a good time, a typical 1960s man-eater, who it seems has Jimmy in her sights. Not surprisingly, it all goes pear-shaped, especially when Jimmy finds that everyone apart from him has found a partner for a bout of sweaty, consensual sex. Luckily, the following weekend is a Bank Holiday and they are all off to Brighton for some fun. However, from the press clippings pinned to Jimmy's bedroom wall, it's clear that he's expecting something a little more exciting.

Not helping matters are Jimmy's uncomprehending, but loving parents, played by established actors Michael Elphick and Kate Williams. What they don't know is that all Jimmy is interested in is the London Mod scene and how he can get into the midst of the longstanding Mod vs. Rocker conflict. To Jimmy, being a Mod is everything; a way of life, a community and a chance to be special. As he explains to Kevin, he wants to be different, to stand apart from others. But it's kind of ironic how he achieves it. Joining a herd of Mods is one way, simply for the appeal of it all. It's an appeal that seems perfect for Jimmy who is portrayed as nothing more complicated than a vulnerable, impressionable and confused teenager who above all else is trying to get to grips with life. It is fascinating to watch how the film almost lovingly recreates both the period detail and the sense of alienation that many teenagers suffer, and none more so than Jimmy.

Somewhere around the mid-point of the film, long after Ray's character is beaten up by a group of Mods – a scene that was filmed in Shepherds Bush Market where Ray's father at one time had his fruit and vegetable stall – the beach-front of Brighton explodes into a pitched battle between the Mods and the Rockers. From a small punch-up in a cafe, thousands of excited teenagers look for any excuse to fight, in what quickly turns into a riot. However, while the action on the screen has dissolved into chaos, according to most of the film's supporters, director Roddam keeps a firm hand on the proceedings, orchestrating the violence beautifully. So, while the riot is both nasty and quite scary, the film never loses sight of the principal figures (Jimmy and Steph), who during the riots slip into a back alley where Jimmy finally gets to shag her in an almost 'wham bam thank you ma'am' fashion while they are still both on their feet.

As most reviewers agreed, Daniels was absolutely excellent as a kid chasing dreams in a haze of tiny blue pills, rapidly succumbing to drug-fuelled paranoia, and the fact that, at the end of the day, it's all smoke and mirrors. All this becomes rapidly obvious as the story unfolds.

Despite some positive views, the film was, on the whole, received negatively by critics and panned for its large amounts of sex, violence, profanity and drug use, which at the time was fairly uncommon. It did, however, pick up a large word-of-mouth following among teenagers who were too young to go and see it because of its 'adults only' over-18 'X' certificate rating. Today, it is considered a cult classic and is recognised as one of the best and most realistic reflections of youth culture in the 1960s. Many have praised Phil Daniels's intense performance. Not only that, but the film also proved a major influence on the short-lived Mod revival in music and fashion which provided a launching pad for the careers of bands such as Secret Affair, The Chords and The Lambrettas while boosting the popularity of The Jam, who had previously been perceived as a punk act. It is also said that Sting's appearance as the 'Ace Face' Mod in *Quadrophenia* benefited his band, The Police, no end, despite their music, unlike The Who, being wholly incongruous with traditional mod tastes.

Even though, on the whole, filming went well, there is still talk about how it almost got halted and postponed indefinitely when the band's drummer, Keith Moon, suddenly and tragically died during the latter stages of filming, on 7 September 1978, at the age of 32. It happened after Moon had attended a preview of *The Buddy Holly Story*. After dining with Paul and Linda McCartney, Moon and his girlfriend, Annette Walter-Lax, returned to a flat on loan from singer Harry Nilsson in Curzon Place, London. He died having overdosed on medication taken as part of a programme to wean him off alcohol. When the police investigated the cause of his death they determined that there were about 32 pills in his system, some of which were still undissolved.

In fact, filming went so well that only one scene in the entire film was shot in the studio. All the others were filmed on location. One of those locations was Beachy Head, where Jimmy may or may not try to kill himself at the end of the film. It was the location of a real-life suicide that influenced the soundtrack and film adaptation, and still today remains a popular spot for suicides. It was while shooting the final scenes of the movie that things could have gone wrong. The stunt co-ordinators had somehow underestimated the length that the scooter would fly through the air after being driven off the cliff top just outside Eastbourne in Sussex. Perhaps even worse for Roddam, who shot the scene from a helicopter, was that he was almost hit and could have ended up with the scooter at the bottom of the cliff.

There wasn't much critical opinion made of Ray's role in the movie, but, then again, not many considered it a Ray Winstone movie as such, which was quite understandable, as his role in the film was relatively small. He appears in just four scenes and, too often, his character seems almost like an afterthought, trailing after an old friendship, neither catalysing nor complementing the storyline.

Strangely enough, it was after *Quadrophenia* that everything seemed to go quiet for Ray, a case of feared today, gone tomorrow, or, as he recalls, the time when 'I became a really bad actor, and I got bored and lazy,' which in itself was strange seeing he was still being hailed as one of the new faces of British youth, earning himself comparisons with James Cagney and the adoration of boys whose nearest brush with violence was when they got a nick from their first Bic razor.

It was around this time that Ray ran out of money and was unable to meet a tax demand. But perhaps that wasn't surprising when you consider he received £365 for the television version of *Scum*, and only £1,800 for the film. 'It was the normal thing,' he told journalists later. 'I spent the money from *Scum* and assumed I'd pay tax from the next job. I was irresponsible and was sure something would turn up. Perhaps I'm being flippant but I do believe the more you worry, the more you get yourself into trouble. I always thought everything would be all right, mate, every cloud has its silver lining, what will be will be, *que sera sera*.'

But there was no work, no parts. There was nothing. 'Not

In his early career, in 1986, Ray appeared in the ITV television series *Robin of Sherwood*. He is shown here *(above, far left)* with the cast *(left to right)* Phil Rose, Judi Trott, Jason Connery, Clive Mantle and Peter Llewellyn Williams.

Below: An action shot depicting his character Will Scarlet, Robin's rebellious brother.

Above: Ray as Eddie Palmer and Louise Plowright as Helen in the ITV series *Palmer*, 1991. This was his first television headliner as a private detective.

Below: Ray *(left)* and Karl Draper *(right)* at Southwark Crown Court, where Ray was accused of allegedly attacking Draper.

In 1997 Ray hit the headlines for his role in British director Gary Oldman's film *Nil By Mouth*. He won the Best Performance by a British Actor in an Independent Film at the British Independent Film Awards. He is shown here on set *(above)* and with co-stars Charlie Creed-Miles and Jamie Foreman, and director Gary

Ray received further recognition for his acting abilities in 1999 when he won Actor of the Year at the RTS Television Awards for his portrayal of a bereaved father with Pauline Quirke *(inset)* in the BBC drama *Our Boy*. He is shown here with his proud daughter Jaime holding his award.

With Ray's love of football he can often be seen in his football kit for charity. Spotted here *(above)* in April 1998 for a charity football match for the British Brain and Spine Foundation at Wembley.

Below: Posing with fellow actor and close friend Glen Murphy with their shields.

With Paul Weller and Robert Carlyle at the party for *Sexy Beast* at the Hampshire Hotel, London.

Inset: At the British Independent Film Awards ceremony with fellow cast member Ben Kingsley, where Ray was nominated for Best Actor, 2001.

Ray in the theatre.

Above: From the play *To The Green Fields Beyond* with Dougray Scott, 2000.

Below: Taken from the play *The Night Heron* by Jez Butterworth, 2002.

Ray at a celebrity five-a-side football tournament held at Hackney Marsh in London, 2001.

even rubbish. Whether it was bad management or bad acting on my part, it's difficult to say. I felt I was getting worse as an actor. I was bored, stale and forgot what it was about. So I poodled around, retired for two or three years, ducked and dived. I enjoyed doing nothing, but financially it wasn't very rewarding.'

Although there were some who said he went bankrupt, according to Ray, he didn't. 'People said I went bankrupt, but I've never been bankrupt because I paid it all off eventually. Half the country was suffering. Lots of people lost houses and businesses, and I lost a few quid. You had people going bankrupt in those Thatcher years throwing themselves out of windows. You can either go that way or face up to the problem. So I went out to work and paid off my debts. We got through it. Elaine's been there all the time and it can't have been easy, but she stuck by me.'

Another one to stick by him was actor Glen Murphy, best known for his role as Blue Watch hero George Green in ITV's *London's Burning*, one of Ray's closest friends since childhood. 'Ray is the first person I call in a crisis and I think I am for him,' Murphy once told a reporter. 'We're so similar, we've got the same beliefs and principles about pretty much everything. I'm lucky to have a mate like that. If he's ever been short, I've bunged him a few quid and vice versa.'

The friendship between the two has now spanned four decades. As lads they hung around West Ham football ground dreaming of becoming soccer heroes, and Murphy can still remember the day he was heartbroken when, at 16, he was dropped from a football apprenticeship by Charlton Athletic FC. Then, as teenagers, they both showed a talent for boxing. Murphy later became a semi-professional boxer.

'Ray's mum and dad knew my mum. They'd all been mates

in Stepney, East London, so we were like brothers from the age of three,' he continues to explain. 'We boxed together as kids at Repton and West Ham Boxing Clubs. Ray was technically better than me but I was probably fitter than him and, of course, we were different weights.'

From his mid-teens, just as Ray had helped out his dad on the market stalls, Murphy worked in his father's pub, The Bridge House, in Canning Town. 'I was always helping out there and got used to that whole pub way of life. There was always someone in there drunk and aggressive; it put me off drinking. I'd go in at lunchtimes, on lovely sunny days, and it would be dark and dingy inside. Angry women would come in looking for their husbands who'd blown half their wages on booze. It made me see how alcohol can destroy lives.

'Once Ray came in to see my dad for advice, saying he really wanted to make a go of boxing professionally but he'd been offered some film part, and he didn't know what to do. My old man told him to forget the boxing and go for the role, which is what he did. The film was *Scum*.' And, although Murphy would tell you that, from there, Ray's career took off, and certainly it did for a little while, at the time, it seemed that it had come to a grinding halt.

CHAPTER 6

Marriage, Births and Death

One month after *Quadrophenia* was released in the UK in November 1979, Ray married Elaine in her hometown of Manchester and, afterwards, they carried on living in the flat they shared in Edmonton, London. The stag night, Ray recalls, 'was a real anti-climax but the wedding was a riot. The priest was drunk and got our names wrong. He called me Eamonn Rambrose Winstone. I repeated it and the place fell about. Then he called Elaine, Eileen. He came to the wedding breakfast afterwards and had a ball. We never found out what happened to him at the end of the night. We reckon he pulled a bird!' As for the wedding night itself, 'I slept in a single bed because my father-in-law drank all the champagne and fell fast asleep on our bed.'

Meeting Elaine in the first place was, according to Ray, the best thing that ever happened to him. 'I was getting up to all sorts of silly tricks before she came along. I met her at a time when all the birds were around me. I couldn't lose. But she was something really special. I thought I could conquer anything that was going at the time. But she meant the most. So I gave up my bachelor days early and I'm glad. Before Elaine I'd always run away from marriage but I reckon it's right for me.'

It was probably 'right' for him because, beneath his tough demeanour, according to those ubiquitous friends, who always seem to be on hand to comment upon showbiz affairs of the heart, Ray is something of a pussycat, and a total pushover when it comes to women. When Ray met Elaine, he was having what he called a blinding time with non-stop wild parties and, at that point, could never see himself settling down. 'But I dunno, it was like, really right from the first moment. Bosh.' Even now, today, it is much the same, even though Elaine, admits Ray, often calls the shots in their relationship.

If they have a row, he adores the making-up bit best. 'It's great, isn't it? But there's no sulking. Elaine's a fiery little thing. She can be quite evil. We are both very black and white, there is no in-between. Once I didn't talk to her for four days after a row and it killed me. I gave up in the end, I waved the white flag. I was getting deaf-and-dumb dinners. It was, crunch, "Here's your dinner,"' he admits, mimicking a plate being thrown on the table. 'Sometimes I'd look at her and imagine her wearing the plate with the dinner on. I couldn't bear it, so I went to a boxing match in Chigwell with my mates. I got suited up and called a cab. I didn't even say goodbye. It was my way of getting back.

'Anyway, about 1.30am, my mobile went and she said, "It's Elaine." I said, "I know who it is, what do you want?" She said, "Are you coming home?" I said, "Do you want me to come home?" And she said, "Yes." So I said, "OK, I'm coming home."'

Despite such fiery rows, their marriage has been a happy and enduring one in an industry not known for successful long-term unions. But, according to Ray, there is no big secret other than 'I love her. We just have a laugh. I'm romantic too, although I haven't done the flowers bit for a while. People seem embarrassed if they are happily married. It's sort of "in" to be divorced.'

The first years of his life with Elaine, though, were spent being arrested every now and then. 'But Elaine stood by me during those difficult times but that's what you do when you're a couple. If you don't, then there's no point in being together.'

The most difficult times were in the years immediately after his first big break in *Scum* as he went broke on two separate occasions and struggled to find contentment as an actor. 'I had kind of decided that acting wasn't for me because people like me didn't become actors.' His so-called bankruptcies, or, as he prefers to tag them, running out of money, one before his marriage and one after, and his inability to settle into a career inevitably took their toll on his marriage. That was when he was probably drinking heavily and getting into trouble and got himself arrested a few times for assault. 'Yeah, I got into a few fights, but not because I had problems. I was just young and foolish. I'm too old to do that any more. I probably still am an alcoholic. I do binge-drink. It's rare that I go for longer than a week without a drink and then, when I do, I really go on a binge. But I am trying to calm down.'

One of those times, when he got into trouble, according to the *News of the World*, was in March 1980, just one week before *Fox* – the new television series in which Ray had landed a role – started its run on ITV. But most of it was down to how many people saw Ray at that time – a tough guy and a hard nut. To a degree Ray himself agrees with this perception. 'After *Scum*,' he told reporter Ivan Waterman, 'I started getting funny looks. People wanted to prove I wasn't as tough as I looked. There are always occasions when you can't walk away. It's only happened to me twice – both times in pubs. Just because I might look a bit like a bloke who enjoys a brawl. I had this clown coming up and saying things like "You fancy yourself a bit, don't you?" I kept backing away but finally it was no good. He was getting braver and braver. So I let him have it and knocked him out. One of the guys who was working on *Fox* told me afterwards, "Don't ever do that again – your career will be over." He's right, I know that. So now I always go to pubs and places where I know I'm not going to get any trouble.'

He continued, 'I suppose I was too full of myself at the time. Like, after *Scum* and *Quadrophenia*, I started to get recognised when I went out. That sort of thing can go to your head. I'd be out having a drink and someone would be staring. I'd think, "What's that cunt looking at?" Then I'd realise that he probably recognised me from one of my films. You'd get the odd bit of aggravation. Blokes coming up and saying, "You're an actor, aren't you? They're all fucking poofs, aren't they?" You've just got to learn to handle that sort of thing.'

Although it is often reported that Ray claims he left an acting career behind for about two or three years because he didn't like what he was doing and considered himself really bad in what he did do, it was only one year after *Quadrophenia* that he was back in front of the television cameras for 11 out of 13 episodes of *Fox*. It was then, possibly, that he may have questioned why some actors were capable of making bad material work and he wasn't. 'I thought, "If I'm not going to do it properly, then I don't want to do it at all."' But he still carried on regardless.

Fox was a sprawling epic of family life, with a host of major characters and a large supporting cast of memorable figures. The writer, Trevor Preston, had previously worked with director Jim Goddard on ITV's 1978 *Out*, although, unlike that tightly focused revenge drama, *Fox* was expansive, and Preston weaved numerous plotlines to create a depth that is seldom seen in TV drama. Indeed, Goddard approached the series as if it were an 11-hour film, which was necessary for logistical reasons, but, even so, it took over a year to plan, shoot and complete. *Fox* was the story of the Fox family, dominated by their patriarch father Billy Fox, played by Peter Vaughan, a retired Covent Garden market porter who is regarded with awe by the residents of Clapham where most of the action takes place. He has four sons by two marriages and, although he is a family man, the sons struggle to form their own identity under his shadow. There is a particular tension between Billy and his intellectual son, Phil, played by Eamon Boland, a left-wing firebrand, which is exacerbated when he refuses to attend a vital boxing match of his youngest brother, Kenny, played by Ray, the ramifications of which rumble on throughout the series. When Billy dies, the family tries to hold itself together, but individual trials and tribulations create division, and Phil departs to America in order to work through his feelings. The resolution of the series is ambiguous and, although Phil returns, there is no real sense that the family will ever be the same again. *Fox* was quite a rarity for television, as it is unusual for a serial of the time and of such length to have one author and one director.

After *Fox*, Ray would not work in film and television for at least another year. When he was seen again on screen, it was more than 15 months later in one of his least remembered television dramas. *Death Angel* was one of six 30-minute separate plays made for children in the *Theatre Box* series that was shown every Monday from 2 November to 24 December 1981. Written by Brian Glover, it was the story of how three friends, Fergus, Toy and Bud, break into the Town Hall during a wrestling tournament, intending to mug the Master of Ceremonies, played by Bill Maynard, for the night's takings. Swapping from boxing to wrestling, Ray was cast as a wrestler named Gus and, despite not looking very convincing as a grappler of the then popular 'All-Star Wrestling', he still looked like he had just walked out of *Scum*.

Glover had been a real-life wrestler in the heyday of the popular televised sport and had become a household name along with the likes of Steve Logan, Mick McManus, Jackie Pallo and Steve Veidor, who also made a cameo in the drama. The general consensus was that Glover, who went on to make an impressive name for himself as an actor in the world of film, was well placed to write a play about the subject.

Not long after he completed filming *Death Angel*, Ray was working on yet another television series, playing a bit part in an episode of the popular detective series *Bergerac*, which ended up having a strange conclusion for Ray. While returning home from the Jersey set, he was stopped and questioned by the police. The Old Bill, Ray now laughs, 'told me it was something to do with gun-running'. Three years after that, he was held for 72 hours in a Leeds police cell on suspicion of murdering a policeman after a viewer saw a photofit picture on *Crimewatch*. In fact, when a picture that looked like him appeared on the crime series, Elaine had said, 'That's you!' Ray was later questioned by the police before being released without charge. He later joked, 'I think that was a case of the police watching too much telly. They probably think I'm a villain. They don't understand I'm actually an actor.'

The release of another film role in *Ladies and Gentlemen, The Fabulous Stains*, in 1982 coincided with the birth of the first of Ray and Elaine's three daughters who they named Lois. Ray was 24. He is a self-confessed indulgent father, saying, 'You start to look after yourself a bit more when you're a dad. When I'm out having a drink, I think, "I can do without this" because I want to be up early the next morning to play in the garden with my little girl.'

If he was worried that there would be a danger of Lois becoming 'a spoiled little brat', growing up where she did, in North London, and attending the same school that Ray did, soon took care of any concerns. If there was any concern at all, it would probably be how she became a fixture on Ray's film sets. 'When I was four, he took me with him when he was making *Robin of Sherwood*,' she says. 'There was a scene where the Sheriff of Nottingham is coming down the hill from his castle in a stagecoach, and my dad and the Merry Men were waiting to ambush them. The director called, "Action!" and I ran on to the set going, "Get 'em, Daddy!" And the director's shouting, "Cut! Sort her out, will you, Ray?" I knew even then that I wanted to act.'

A few years later, however, Lois's teenage rebellion began. She dyed her hair red and had her lip, nose and tongue pierced. 'Dad hated them, he thought they looked trashy.' So then she discovered a taste for big boots, backcombed hair and corsetry, and got into what she calls 'a whole underground London thing: going to squat parties, hanging out in Kentish Town with travellers, and MC-ing at raves'. At one point, she didn't go home for weeks. 'I was angry,' she says today. 'It was the typical teen thing. I hated school. I thought I was a big shot, going out all the time, drinking too much and not buckling down, getting sucked into a superficial world of people you think are friends.' One of the things she remembers well, though, was the time when 'Dad sold his car in 1987 so that he could take us to Disneyland and buy us presents. And we always had bread on the table,' even when money was tight.

Robin of Sherwood was an ideal opportunity for Lois to spend time with her dad, and equally for Ray to have her around while he worked. It also helped matters financially that he had a regular gig over the next three years from when the pilot for the series, *Robin Hood and The Sorcerer*, was aired in 1984 in the peak-hour Saturday tea-time slot on ITV.

Looking back, it seems remarkable that so many films have been made about Robin Hood, an historical figure who we're not even sure existed. To many, he is just a medieval nursery story that has been exaggerated over the years, but, of course, that hasn't stopped him from being a favourite for filmmakers and television producers. Five silent movies depicting his adventures had been made long before Douglas Fairbanks Snr got his hands on the role that made him a household name in 1922. Later, Errol Flynn's 1938 version did much the same for his career as it had done for Fairbanks, while in the late 50s and early 60s the British-made *Robin Hood* television series established Richard Green as probably the best and most familiar Robin Hood of all.

Perhaps the greatest and most adventurous retelling for cinema-goers, however, came in 1976 when Sean Connery and Audrey Hepburn traded in youth for maturity to play *Robin and Marion* in the later stages of their lives. But for those more familiar with the series that had started out with Michael Praed playing Robin, and Ray as Robin's rebellious half-brother Will Scarlet, *Robin of Sherwood* is probably regarded by its generation as the best version. And certainly, unlike previous adaptations of the story, it combined a gritty, authentic production design with elements of real-life history and pagan myth. Ray's characterisation of Scarlet as a much older and angrier character than the one Christian Slater later played in the 1991 film version, *Robin Hood: Prince of Thieves*, seemed perfect for him. The fact that he was playing a character troubled by his wife's rape and murder also suited him, and, in retrospect, has become his favourite kind of role.

Richard 'Kip' Carpenter, who created the series, agrees. From the start, he had always seen Ray's character as an outlaw with revenge on his mind. 'I wanted to present somebody who had actually lost his family as a result of the cruelty and oppression of the times,' he explained. 'In Northern Ireland, for instance, the reason the conflict goes on and on is because people have lost someone who's near and dear to them. It isn't an abstract, it's a personalised hatred. If you've seen your wife and children shot in front of you by either an IRA man or a loyalist, your revenge is personal. It has nothing to do with being a Catholic or a Protestant.'

Carpenter went to great pains to make sure the character he was creating for Ray would be full of hatred with an open wound, so to speak. 'He's festering, there's a psychopathic factor. That's how it started, how it grew, because I didn't want him to be a nothing character. I wanted him to be a strong character, the toughest of the outlaws. He wanted to kill and, by killing, he hopes to exorcise his wife's death, but he never can, because the only way you can is to forgive. That's something that poor Will can't do.'

Ray was certainly pleased to have landed the role because, as he explains, it got him over the stumbling block of typecasting that seems all to easy to fall into in an industry that loves stereotypes. 'It goes in stages. You don't get cast for your acting ability, as such. You get cast for what you were playing in your last job. I went through the stage of playing the hard man, the skulduggery and all that. Then I got a job in a comedy show called *The Factory* and then found myself for a few years playing comedy roles. And then, this came along, where I played the psychopathic killer who changed as the series went on and became a member of a so-called family. You actually get cast as you are. You have to play a role in a certain way to get them to see you differently. You always look for something different; otherwise, you're playing the same character all the time and you're becoming more of a personality than an actor.'

Certainly, Ray thought that Carpenter's view of Will Scarlet as a tough psycho was 'probably closer to the way things really were. In one episode, I spot this kid, and I should mug him, because, literally, that's what Robin Hood's people were – medieval muggers. You know, the word "Robin" means robber and the whole thing develops. And I always thought this whole thing about the rich giving to the poor was a bit of rubbish, let's face it, whether we're fighting for a good cause or not. So, in that episode, I sat down with Kip, because we were allowed to put a lot into the show, and I said that my character, when he goes out mugging on his own, keeps half for himself and gives half to Robin. And, in this episode, I kept the money, but Robin makes me give it back in the end because we're the good guys. Kip always tried to make my character the one who argued against what Robin was doing, as a balance to the show. They weren't all just goody-goodies, there was an element. I quite like the anti-hero.'

Carpenter also formed a close-knit unit around the cast and crew. 'What's unusual is that you normally make friends from work, say, "I'll see you again," and they're gone and you don't keep contact,' Ray later reflected. 'But I did with the guys from this show for a couple of years after the series ended, we used to meet on the first Monday of every month. I think it was because we were all different. None of us clashed.'

Even with such camaraderie, Ray doesn't hesitate in admitting that he got incredibly homesick while on set. 'I mean, there was one time we were about 200 miles from London. I would be sitting there after work, and I would get in the car, head up to London – just for the night – come back early in the morning and not tell anyone about it, because they wouldn't let you go.'

There were, of course, times on set when some of the other cast and crew might have wished him to be elsewhere as he enjoyed playing practical jokes on fellow cast and crew members. One assistant carrying supplies for a tea break was once tipped into a nearby stream. 'I couldn't resist,' confesses Ray. 'He was just walking beside the river bank, and a quick nudge from me was the ultimate temptation!'

Ray also set up a running joke when Sean Connery's son, Jason, joined the cast to replace Michael Praed as Robin at the end of the second season in April 1985. At dinner one night, Connery found an unusually tough bit of gristle in his meat. After trying valiantly to chew it, he gave up and, after removing it from his mouth, placed it on the side of his plate. But, like a beast from a horror movie, the gristle wouldn't go away. Over the next two weeks, Connery would find the somewhat deteriorating piece of grub in his soup, his beer and his water and, whenever he had disposed of it, it would return. Animating the bit of fodder was Ray, with the connivance of the rest of the cast and crew.

In some quarters, it was said that Connery deserved the creeping gristle episode. During his screen test for the role, he managed to fire an arrow into Ray's arm instead of the tree he was aiming for in front of where Ray was standing, but 'it never stuck in,' Ray jokes. 'It just bounced off, 'cause I'm a tough Essex boy!' And on another occasion he continues, 'When we were in Rickmansworth doing some publicity for the programme, they set up this camera 100 yards away, next to an archery target. I told Mark Ryan – he played the Saracen, Nasir – to aim for the camera because there was no way we were going to hit it. I shot my arrow and it went straight down the lens and caused 70 grand's worth of damage. As it hit the camera, I turned and went, "Mark! What have you done?" But it wasn't a bad shot, really! You can see it on the film, you can see the arrow spinning towards the lens. They ran it on all the news shows.'

Aside from his fooling around on set, Ray's tough-guy image gave him something of an undeserved reputation, according to Carpenter, who said, 'He's a gentleman, an absolute diamond, but he comes from a very rough background. He has a reputation that isn't warranted – that he gets into fights and things. Boxers are taught, because of their strength and skill, to keep out of trouble. Ray tends not to get involved if someone starts being silly. Ray's going to walk away from it – not because he's scared, but because he knows what he can do to the other bloke.'

It was that same background that got Ray the part in the first place. 'In a sense, Will Scarlet became Ray Winstone and Ray Winstone became Will Scarlet, and you can't see the join. He builds the character from inside. He's very clever. He thinks it through. He's a creative actor, and you can't tie them down, particularly because you write something in the quiet of your study, and they're acting it out in the pouring rain or in the howling wind. Things happen that are spontaneous and they're going to cover it with a line. If it's good, it'll stay in. If not, it winds up in the blooper reel.'

Ending up in the blooper reel were several scenes that couldn't have fit into the series by any stretch of the imagination. Instigated by Ray, the cast once burst into a stalwart, though off-key, version of 'You Are My Sunshine'. And, in another scene, Ray responded to Judi Trott's remark about a comment Robin made with a Gable-esque 'Frankly, my dear, I don't give a damn', followed by the whole cast breaking into a choral rendition of the 'Tara' theme.

All the same, Carpenter couldn't give enough praise when it came to Ray. At the time of making *Robin of Sherwood*, he thought he was an actor, who back then, was very under-rated. 'I admire him enormously, because he's an actor's actor. He'll do a job, not particularly because it's enormously well paying, but because it's an interesting part. I saw him in a club theatre playing very obscure German drama of the 1920s – an enormous part, twice as long as Hamlet. He held what was quite a small audience in the palm of his hand, and he didn't need wonderful lighting or marvellous music or big close-ups. He was just there and focused, and he was wonderful.'

There were three seasons of *Robin of Sherwood* in all, comprising a two-hour opening pilot episode and 24 hour-long episodes per series. Interestingly enough, *Robin* had been shot on film rather than on videotape, and was almost entirely filmed on location, mostly in the north and west of England. Despite rave reviews and praise for one of the most influential treatments of the Robin Hood legend, because of its realistic period setting, no more episodes were made after its final two-part episode aired in June 1986. Many believe that HTV found the series too expensive to produce and could not afford to make it themselves after Goldcrest, the production company, pulled out.

Fans of the show were further disappointed when Ray and the rest of the cast blocked the planned repeats of *Robin of Sherwood* by the BBC. 'Yeah, because they owed us a lot of money, and someone reneged on a deal towards us. So we made a decision that someone had to come to us with an offer, and it wasn't necessarily about the money, it was just that a little bit of honour was involved, y'know?'

In between shooting episodes of *Robin of Sherwood*, whenever Ray found a break in the filming schedule, he filled it with playing bit parts in other shows. One he remembers well was *Auf Wiedersehen Pet* in 1984. He played Colin Latham, a mysterious British stranger who all the regular characters, bar Oz (Jimmy Nail) and Wayne (Gary Holton), help out while out on a country fishing trip, and who turns out to be a deserter from the army serving out his national service in Germany.

What is perhaps strange is that Ray reckons he didn't meet Jimmy Nail till much later, despite sharing a couple of scenes with him. When he said they did finally meet, it was when the cast pulled a scam to get Ray out to Germany for a party.

'Yeah. I remember I was doing *Robin of Sherwood*, and the boys from *Auf Wiedersehen Pet* were having a party in Düsseldorf, and they wrote an extra scene in and it worked out with HTV to get me out to do this one scene which never existed – they flew me out there for a party! And I went out there expecting to work! But that was where I met Jimmy Nail for the first time. And Timothy Spall, who's one of my favourite actors. It was fun, being let loose in Germany, where the beer's lovely,' so one can only presume, that the party was before he was cast in 'The Fugitive' episode of the first series.

During the same year that *Robin of Sherwood* ended its run, 'I played a kidnapper in *Cat's Eyes*, and I remember doing one scene where the kidnappers are asleep and the father talks to the kid, and we actually fell asleep because we were so knackered. When it came on the telly, you can hear us snoring in the background, it's a great effect. I remember looking out me window in Maidstone, near where we were filming, and it was about two o'clock in the morning, and we'd had a drink downstairs. And I went to close the curtains, and I looked out the window and I saw this naked man in Wellingtons running across the lawn, in the snow! And I thought I was freaking out, thought I'd had too much to drink, and the next day I found out it was the night watchman – he was chasing some people and was completely naked.'

It was also during the run of *Robin of Sherwood* that Ray was shattered over the news of his mother's death. Margaret or Marge for short, as Ray called her, died from cancer in 1984 when Ray was just 27 years old. 'I'd love it if she could see my work and, more importantly, I wish she could have lived to see all her grandchildren. If I could change anything about my life, that'd be it. She'd be very proud. She was a great lady. She loved life and fought for every breath. She was only 52. It's something you never really get over.' But it was a year before he could express his grief. "I was driving from Bristol and I looked up at myself in the mirror – and I went. The tears just flowed.' To this day his biggest regret is losing her.

Ray and Elaine's second daughter Jaime was born in 1985, the year after his mother died, and was given the middle name Margaret after his mother. Jaime grew up in North London as sister Lois had done, and, like Lois, attended the same school that Ray had. She has also followed in her father's footsteps into the world of acting. Despite turning down the role of Stacey Slater in *EastEnders*, she has since become best known for her role in *Kidulthood*, and in Channel 4's soap *Goldplated*. But it was *Kidulthood* that put her career firmly on the map.

At the premiere of the film, she stepped out, aged 20, in a dress that led to comparisons with the infamous safety-pin dress that Liz Hurley wore in 1994 to the premiere of *Four Weddings and a Funeral*. According to the *Daily Mail*, if Jaime was going for the same maximum exposure, then it worked. 'She drew gasps in a daring cutaway dress, revealing more than just her stunning figure. The cleavage busting number will no doubt be leaving her father considerably distressed with the overwhelming attention it will put on his daughter. The figure-hugging black mini-dress certainly left little to the imagination, and exposed her navel as well as her svelte figure.'

Ray, however, said nothing. Well, not publicly anyway.

After Jaime's birth, at some point during the mid-1980s, Ray seems to have snapped. He can't remember where or when exactly. He just remembers that he'd had enough of bad scripts, bad choices and his own bad acting. He was ready to give it all a miss. He would be in something and watch it with his hands clamped over his face. It wasn't until Kathy Burke came to Ray's rescue, inviting him to appear in *Mr Thomas*, a play that she had written when she was just 22 years old and now four years later wanted to direct at the Old Red Lion in Islington, that Ray's fortunes seem to change, for a little while, at least. 'It was the business,' he enthuses. 'I thought, "This is what it's about." It was a huge turning-point, absolutely crucial. Doing that play, I got the buzz for acting back for the first time since *Quadrophenia*. I really wanted it again. I was right up for it. And I got some good work from that. Still, it was a slow process but I started working at the Royal Court and at the National Theatre. So it's all down to Kath that I'm still carrying on.'

The coming together of Ray with Kathy Burke was rather ironic. He was, at the time, in the bit-part wilderness, and she had been out of work for nine months. So her play was ideal timing for both of them. *Mr Thomas*, recalls Burke, 'was Ray's first gay part; he played a closet homosexual but it didn't bother him. Not in the slightest. He got off on the dialogue and said to me, "This is the first thing I've seen that reads like I talk."'

Just before *Mr Thomas*, Ray had got really bored with what he was doing because he felt he was 'becoming really crap and some of the stuff I was doing was crap. You could look at it another way, you have to do those things sometimes to learn your trade. But one day I said that if I was going to act then I should do it properly, but I wasn't really good enough so I'd leave the profession. No one noticed. Then Kathy wrote a play and phoned me up. I like her a lot. She said, "Don't be a fuckin' idiot. Go on. Do it."

'It was fabulous writing. And she was fabulous at directing it and it was a really good piece. We were promised 30 quid a week, which we ended up spending. But that gave me the buzz again, and I was back.' Up till that point, he would always remember how he would have to wait for jobs to come up because he was unemployed and he was getting offered parts that he didn't particularly care much about. And that was the trouble. 'There's no particular route to go in this business, something either happens or it doesn't. I don't think there's any set formula of working in this game. You just have to be in the right place.'

Certainly, the bit-part wilderness had driven him to the edge of madness and frustration, to the point that he admits he could 'get angry over nothing. I got to the stage where I couldn't suffer fools gladly. I was doing stuff and I became a bad actor. I thought of jacking it in but once you've stopped doing a man's job it is difficult to go back to physical graft.'

To this day he credits Kathy for the impressive stage career he had over the next 12 years including Sam Mendes's play *To The Green Fields Beyond* and Patrick Marber's *Dealer's Choice*.

One of the most successful relationships he has had within the theatre world has been with the director Ian Rickson. Strangely enough, it wasn't until the rehearsals for *Some Voices* that Rickson met Ray for the first time and some of his thoughts about the actor show why he remains at the top of his game. 'I actually didn't audition him, he did a reading of the play for the playwright – more for script than casting purposes – and made the part his. I came in and he was sitting there in a burgundy leather jacket looking like Terry Venables, and I thought, "What is this going to be like?" But, as soon as you get into a dialogue with him, you realise how charming and open he is. Normally, when you spend time with people who are famous, they're surrounded by a retinue and can't be curious and ask questions. What's lovely about Ray is that you'll see him with the taxi driver, the person doing wigs or the director, and he's as engaged and generous with his time with all of them. That's what will keep him a fresh actor.

'The kind of actor Ray is isn't coming out of drama schools. He's been a boxer, he's worked on markets, he has a background. So immediately he comes on stage he's bringing that interesting world with him. He's incredibly rich emotionally. It's the contrasts that make him so special. The contrast in him between being very manly and being tender and passionate is electric. You would have seen that in *Nil By Mouth*: this brute who's also very vulnerable.

'We go to football together. I support Charlton, he supports West Ham. The two teams are kind of friendly, and there's always a mutual cheer for the other when the results come over the Tannoy. I suppose we'd see each other more if we weren't so busy – we meet every month or two. I met him in Ireland recently only because we were both working there. He swears a lot when he's drunk, and I've had arguments with him about being so macho. I like to think I've been challenging some of his more macho traits.

'The fear when you meet a male actor who's been successful in television for a long time is that they're not going to be open to the kind of working process you need for a new play; that they're going to be a bit suspicious because they don't want to look silly, that they're going to be guarded.

'Particularly with Ray, having seen him in things like *Scum*, you also fear him being a tough guy who isn't going to enjoy the sensitivity of the theatre process. So it was a revelation to me how willing he was to play in rehearsals, what a seeking person he was. He's really interested in learning, developing, asking questions. He's a man of great curiosity, which is such an important quality in an actor.'

Rickson goes on to say, 'What I'm interested in doing is casting actors slightly off type, so that the Ray who was in *Scum*, and playing baddies in *The Bill*, I cast as someone much gentler who was a cook. That was really interesting, getting that out of him. He said to me afterwards that he based the performance on my effeminate hand movements. I'm not sure whether to take that as a compliment or not. But I was touched that he could access a part of himself that was tender.

'An exciting thing we've done at the Court is to team up a writer with an actor, the way Shakespeare did, and Chekhov too. Joe Penhall, the writer of *Some Voices*, was so entranced by Ray that he wrote his next play, *Pale Horse*, for Ray to perform.

'There are enough affinities between us to make the friendship sustaining, I think. Professionally, I see him as a real Royal Court actor, because he can be detailed, incredibly real, yet tragic, epic. That suits the kind of work we do. We're not particularly interested in plays with wigs or plays set in drawing rooms; we want to put real life on stage in all its complexity, and we look for actors who can do that.

'I'm always interested in actors who don't look like actors. He's not luvvie-like. He has that need to know, to find out. And, because he's a good listener, conversations are quite equal. He's a very powerful personality, so you have to be very persuasive and imaginative in your directing or conversation to get him to go with you. But, because he's trusting and open, that power thing is largely irrelevant; it's creative. You do sometimes feel as a director that you can't see actors socially, because there's still that power issue around. I never have to think about that with him.

'There was a big surprise birthday thing for him recently, for his 40th. All his friends were in his favourite restaurant in Enfield, and he thought he was just going there for a quiet bite to eat with his wife. He turned up looking fairly haggard, in sweatpants, and quite scruffy. Seeing him that evening, I found myself thinking, "Yes, you really can judge someone by the quality of their friends." He had people who were quite well known, and others who were not in the arts at all. It made me realise he must have a real knack of engaging with a whole range of people. He has empathy, which is what all great actors need.'

Ray was equally impressed with Rickson on meeting him for the first time, even though 'I haven't got a clue when that was. I don't even know what day it is now. He reminds me very much of Gary Oldman – although they've got very different styles, there's a feminine side to them both. When you work with male directors, they're often looking for the macho side, and they don't know the other side of a man, the weaknesses. We can all be macho, larger than life. But Ian's feminine side is quite inspirational, it makes him more of a man. Some directors don't know those other sides; that's OK, but Ian does.

'The first time I came in to rehearse, it was one of those "all sit on the floor" kind of things: "This is a map of England, and I want you to sit where you come from." Before I'd have said, "This is bollocks," but you've either got to surrender yourself to it, get on with it, and be a luvvie if you like for a minute, or don't be there, go and do something else.

'We were standing around in a circle, falling backwards –

you know that game, trusting the people on stage with you? – and I thought, "This is not what it's about." But there's something about it that works. One night on stage we had a power cut, and we just carried on as if a light-bulb had gone out as part of the play. If a daft game works for you, you do it.

'I learned with Ian, with female directors and certainly with Gary Oldman, that there is another side, that weaker side. Strength is easy to do. To show a man at his most vulnerable, that's more interesting. Ian brought that out of me when I done *Some Voices*, and we explored it more with *Pale Horse*. That was great for me, like going back to school. By the time I came to work with Ian, and Gary and Tim [Roth], you know, that's what I was looking for. They were people to learn something from.

'Ian's a Charlton man and I'm West Ham, but I have a soft spot for Charlton. There are connections between us, like Alan Curbishley, the Charlton manager, who used to be at West Ham, so I hope Charlton do well this year. We go to dos, to pubs. People you drink with, you learn something from. We're total opposites, but I think that's good. I can imagine us being friends for life, and nothing to do with this business.

'When you like people, that's when you argue. I mean, there are things about Ian which truly bug me. Like when he directs women. He's quite forceful with women where he's not with guys. He actually loves women, he's a ladies' man, but I do wind him up about not being able to direct women, and that pisses him off quite a bit.

'I like the small space of the Royal Court,' Ray has said. 'I find it like cinema acting which is so close. You can experiment – people would be all along the walls, and I'd use the phone call in the play to pick out someone in the audience, and talk to them. Ian would go, "You can't do that, you're breaking the spell of what theatre is." And I'd say, "You're bringing them into the play." When he wasn't in the auditorium, I would still do it sometimes.

'Two guys in the audience used to come in quite a bit and sit by this bed which was on-stage, and I would like lie backwards and lay my hand right in the guys' lap. You could feel the whole audience suddenly connect. And Ian used to make me promise not to do it. Maybe I would, maybe I wouldn't. But that's just experimenting, you know. I love it in the cinema when someone looks right down the camera at you.'

Working in theatre and being applauded each night by responsive audiences gave Ray not only a new buzz, but also a new outlook towards his career. He even summed up his view of acting as a profession in a different way to before. 'A job is a chore. If you love doing it, it's not a job – this is a hobby because you get paid for doing something you love doing. At the end of the night, you're physically and mentally tired, but you're buzzing, 'cos you've done a great day's work. You want to go and have a pint and talk about it a little bit before you crash and go home.' Despite his love of theatre, Ray reckons he would only be tempted to return to the stage if he could be in a play that had a six-week run. 'I worked at the national one summer, every night I'd go past people sitting in pubs. And you start thinking, "Who the fuck invented matinees? Kill em!"'

It was probably shortly after appearing in *Mr Thomas* that Ray was contacted by Laurence Marks and Maurice Gran, the creators of a new series called *Get Back*, and asked if he would be interested in playing one of the lead characters. Eventually billed as 'A Comedy For The Recession' by the

BBC, *Get Back* dealt with the adventures of a family fallen on hard times and returning to their working-class roots. Although he was told in the preliminary interview that he was 'just what they wanted' and that he had the part if he wanted it, Ray remained sceptical. 'Yeah, yeah,' he thought, 'I had been told that a million times.'

But then again, since *Mr Thomas*, his fortunes appeared to have changed for the better. He was suddenly doing television, theatre and movies that didn't always have him cast in the 'geezer' roles. In fact, a lot of the roles he did after Kathy Burke's play were what he described as romantic roles. Well, sort of. More like the boy next door. The one thing he kept in mind, though, and remembering the pitfalls of typecasting, he did all he could to avoid playing the same role over and over. He felt he had to continue to demonstrate his versatility even if it did mean that he had done small television bit parts, like playing Arthur Daly's mechanic in *Minder*, and other lesser roles in the likes of *The Bill*, *Casualty* and *Fairly Secret Army*.

He also did an episode of *Boon*. 'I was absolutely fucking terrible in that. I was playing the third henchman from the right. I looked like someone had hit me round the head with a baseball bat. And I thought, "Do I really need to be doing this?' Then I did this terrible film called *Tank Malling*. John Conteh was in it. I know that, when I did that, I should have been nicked for impersonating an actor. Without a shadow of a doubt. Fucking diabolical it was. When your own kids tell you it's a load of shit, you know how bad it's got. There's no escaping a truth like that. You can't run from yourself.'

Another of the many lowlights that sticks in his mind was *Space Precinct* in 1995, in which he had to act opposite a bizarre menagerie of aliens. 'This geezer came up, playing a monster with two eyes about that far apart,' he laughs, stretching out his arms. 'They asked me to look at him when I was speaking. I said "Which eye?" I was doing my Tommy from New York acting. It was terrible. I was pissing myself laughing. Oh, mate, I never stopped. But I was skint. And it got me five grand for Christmas, so I can't knock it. Got me out of trouble.'

In many ways, though, good or bad, it all paid off handsomely well. He was, after all, the first cast member from the *Robin of Sherwood* series to get a show of his own and, as Ray himself would put it, 'That's a result.' As he said at the time, he was very pleased with the new series he was about to embark on. It has, he said, 'real characters, people living in desperation – not all smiling with white teeth'. He also believed it would 'demonstrate the funny side of tragedy'.

In *Get Back*, Ray and Larry Lamb played brothers Martin and Albert Sweet who have used their wits to climb the ladder of success. Martin has married Loretta, played by Carol Harrison, and turned her father's outfitters into a fashionable boutique, while Albert has married Prudence, played by Jane Booker, 'an expensive thoroughbred', and runs a successful chain of jewellery shops. The brothers only return to their roots during the football season to take their conniving old father, Bernie (John Bardon), to see Arsenal play at home.

But, practically overnight, the Thatcherite dream turns into a nightmare for Martin. His business fails, the bank calls in his overdraft, his brother refuses to give him a loan and he finds himself back where he began – in his father's grotty Finsbury Park council flat. The story then focuses on how Loretta and their two teenage daughters, played by

Michelle Cattini and an unknown Kate Winslet, cope with life on the other side of the tracks. Ray remembers Kate Winslet, 'You could see then she had something. She knew where she was going'.

Get Back was aired over 11 episodes and shown in two series, five shows plus the pilot episode from October 1992 and the remaining five, oddly, from December of the following year. It seemed odd because usually a series would not be split into two series with over a year in between the two showings. All the same, and considering the first series had followed *Palmer*, Ray's first television headliner as a private detective, ten months earlier, it put him well and truly in the television spotlight.

And, according to *Inside TV* magazine, the casting agent had got it right in pairing up Ray with Larry Lamb, who interestingly enough, had gone to the same school as Ray in Enfield, looked and talked the same. 'We feel like brothers,' Lamb told reporter Fiona Knight. 'We're very different in lots of ways, but both of us can talk for hours about anything. And we even have the same-shaped forehead and nose!'

The series had been something of a reunion for Ray and Larry. They had worked together on *Fox* 12 years previously. But he was probably best-known for his role of Matt Taylor in BBC's short-lived North Sea ferry soap *Triangle*. 'For three years I took sea-sickness pills. It was the only way to survive. I haven't been near a boat since.'

Ray, on the other hand, had, according to Knight, made a small fortune, only to lose it. 'I've always lived for the moment, that's been my problem,' he confirms, 'but I don't have any regrets because I've had a great time. Thankfully, I've got more sensible as I've grown older. People assume you've got loads of cash because you're on television. They're surprised that we live in a council flat but maybe we'll move when we've got a few more quid.'

Ray's words about 'living for the moment' rang truer than he could ever have known. In 1993, one year after the second series of *Get Back* was screened, and after being reduced to another succession of bad-guy roles in television series, Ray was declared bankrupt for the second time, after failing to pay a £17,000 VAT bill. In the throes of sorting it out, he was temporarily separated from Elaine, Lois and Jaime. But Ray, to this day, insists it was for financial reasons. Although the stress of it all was reported to have almost cost Ray his marriage, his old pal Glen Murphy helped bail him out of debt.

'I lost everything overnight, including my family, because of the rows with my wife Elaine over what happened. Friends looked after me, and, yes, Glen did help me a lot. That's what us East End lads do. But our marriage has always been as sweet as a nut. There's a lot more to us splitting up than meets the eye. Being made bankrupt motivated me, more than anything.' But, of course, he's right when he says that there were a lot of people going bankrupt in those years. 'Some were even throwing themselves out of windows. You can either go that way or face up to the problem. So I went out to work and paid off my debts.' But his view of it was: 'I've been skint before. I'll be skint again. But that's life. I'm lucky. I always got by – I always do. Sometimes you haven't got the money to go out and you live on bacon and onion gravy. That's the way it goes.'

Although most agree his career up to this point had seen some decided downs as well as ups, none of it was helped by the occasional surfeit of what might be termed 'attitude'. Famously, he was auditioned for the first *Star Wars* prequel,

The Phantom Menace, at which the director George Lucas appeared so indifferent that Ray asked if he'd like to go away and have a short nap. He didn't get the part. And inevitably he ran into trouble with the law. And it wasn't only during the time he was at his lowest ebb in 1993. Two years later, when he was appearing in *Pale Horse* at the Royal Court in Sloane Square, *The Stage* reported how Ray went from the Royal Court to Southwark Crown Court, allegedly accused of attacking Karl Draper at the Green Room Club while drinking with Phil Daniels. Ray, who was then living at Weatherby Road, Enfield, Middlesex, denied causing actual bodily harm. He claimed he was defending himself after Draper called him a 'fat, bald skinhead' and tried to bite his nose. But Draper snapped, 'He had been drinking. He stood over me and then punched me. My nose was pouring with blood, I couldn't breathe and my eyes were closed.'

Another time he was cleared of a couple of other accusations of assault when people tried to get 'busy' with him or 'in a manner likely to cause offence'. It was indeed a fairly grim period. But one he was soon destined to leave behind.

CHAPTER 7

This Acting Life

It was in the summer of 1990 that Ray first heard of *Nil By Mouth*. It happened during a chance meeting with Gary Oldman at the funeral of Alan Clarke, the director they both credit with helping their careers. For Ray, of course, it was his role in *Scum*, and for Gary, in 1988, playing a football hooligan in Clarke's final film, *The Firm*, which is still regarded as one of the most notable performances in a series of powerful British films made during the 1980s.

According to Nicholas Rapold, writing for the online journal *Senses of Cinema*, Clarke was a rare director who is still regarded as one of the foremost stylists and pioneering realists of cinema. Following his untimely death from cancer at the age of 55, he received belated recognition in the form of BBC re-broadcasts and two retrospectives at the National Film Theatre and the 1998 Edinburgh International Film Festival, all of which rekindled interest in the director's work.

Later, in 2004, more sparks flew off the back of the release of an American box set of four DVDs of his films.

What is not so well known about Clarke's work is that, shortly before he fell ill and died, he had been experimenting with new minimalist style. His 1988 *Elephant* short is probably the most extreme example of how he used 16mm colour film to its best advantage. It is also a fine example of his approach to filmmaking, and is essentially a compilation of 18 murders on the streets of Belfast, without explanatory narrative or characterisation and shot in a cold, dispassionate documentary style. The film succinctly captures the horror of sectarian killing.

Sadly, critical appreciation of his work still remains somewhat muted, and there are still many critics who consider him, unjustly, to be an ultra-realist, lacking in art and artifice. Those who knew him and worked with him recognise him as an extraordinary filmmaker, who was almost wholly responsible for launching Ray's acting career.

After the funeral was over, Ray remembers, 'Gary told me that he was writing a script for a film which he'd like me to be in. A year went by and I did not hear a thing. Then, I heard on the grapevine that "Gary Oldman has written you a part in his script." I thought, "I've heard that one before." But this time I got a phone call from Gary, asking me to look at the script. It was honestly, the best thing I've ever read, even though it was not story-driven. But it was an indelible authenticity of place and character in long dialogue scenes which have the ragged, spontaneous quality of an observational documentary, about a dysfunctional working-class family living on a rough South-London estate who encounter some pretty awful domestic violence, drunkenness, drug addiction and petty crime.'

All the same, Ray continues, 'I was excited, but I had to be realistic. Great scripts often don't get made into films – or, if they do, then they are changed so much it's no longer a great script. But after I'd met properly with Gary, I realised this was going to be different. He does not compromise. If he wants something doing, then he never cuts corners. He will do it his way or not at all. I knew from that moment this was one film which would be made in the way it was written. This is a very honest film. We're not going to change the dialogue for an American market, we are not going to change it because we need a happy ending and we are not going to cut out any of the scenes of degradation. We made a film about the way people live.'

Certainly, there were many graphic scenes in the film, but one which will stick in the mind of many is the one in which Ray's character, also named Ray, beats up his on-screen wife Valerie, played by Kathy Burke, in an explosion of drunken temper after he feels that she has humiliated him by playing snooker with one of his acquaintances in the local pub. It would be the second time in his career, up to that point, that Ray had to play such an aggressor to women on film.

Ray himself affirmed that, yes, 'I beat up a woman in *Ladybird, Ladybird*, directed by Ken Loach, and there is only one way I can look at it. I think of the woman as a man. Of course, there is no physical contact at all, but it's a scene in which you need a lot of help from the other actor. I had known Kathy a long time and there was a lot of trust there, which helped me. We had met years before in the Old Red Lion, playing pool, and she beat me. I remember saying, "Are you a geezer?" She said, "Shut it, Winstone. Don't start on me." We had a drink and a laugh and have been mates ever since.'

Even so, there was a remarkable reaction among the crew after the beating-up sequence was shot. 'I would be lying to say it was all rosy,' confesses Ray. 'Kathy was fine, even though she was not very well at the time of shooting, but some of the crew were physically sick. I know I'd done it right when I saw their reaction. I even felt a bit ill myself. And Gary was very quiet.'

Ray regards Oldman as one of the best directors he has ever worked with. 'The man is a genius, which is not something I say lightly. He just gets so involved and captures the mood of the entire thing, which is just what Alan Clarke had going for him. He talks gently, but with passion, just when you most need it. He explains, communicates, directs and encourages.'

Another key scene, and vital to reveal the thoughts and actions of Ray, is the one where he has to deliver a monologue, more of a soliloquy in style, about his drunken father. He talks of how his dad is finally brought to his knees by drink problems and is lying in a hospital bed, surrounded by tubes and equipment, with a 'nil by mouth' warning to nursing staff.

'It was the tricky one of the whole film for me,' admits Ray. 'It's a man talking about himself, really. He is in denial. So he is talking about this boozer of a dad and he is trying to hide all his actions behind him. It is heartbreaking. We shot it three times. The first time was on Day One of shooting. It seemed to go pretty well and Gary said to Jamie Foreman and me, "What do you think?" We said, "Nine out of ten." He said, "Yeah, we could do better. We can do it again." So we did it again in the middle of shooting, but the film was damaged when it was sent away and they lost the whole soundtrack. So we finally did it on the last day.

We were all shattered by then, and it made the performance and the whole feel of the scene different. The movie crew went, "That's the one."'

Interestingly enough, Oldman had been talking for three years about writing what eventually ended up as *Nil By Mouth*. American producer Douglas Urbanski, his Los Angeles-based manager and partner, recalls it was always going to be a dark working-class story based in London and something that he had wanted to direct. 'I remember standing on the set of *Immortal Beloved*, with Gary dressed as Beethoven, talking between scenes about the project. He wanted it to be in a naturalistic style, which he was carrying around in his head. But having it bubbling around like that and making it take solid shape are two different things.'

Oldman finally wrote the screenplay in its entirety in five weeks during part of February and March 1995, and handed it to Urbanski at a meeting in New York that April. 'It apparently came pouring out non-stop, and that script is more or less exactly what you end up seeing. I said, "When do you want to start shooting?" And he said, "November 9th, 1995," It was as precise as that, because of Gary's other working commitments, he knew it would be impossible to start before.'

But there were immediate problems. Firstly, there was very little interest from film companies in backing Oldman as the film's director. And, secondly, he already knew that he himself was not going to appear in the film, and he was adamant that he didn't want any big-name superstars for it, who, needless to say, would have attracted the financial backing he required to get it into production. Instead, he decided that his film was going to be about the London working class with an unrelenting use of violent language.

Although Oldman has been directed by some of the very

best directors like Stephen Frears, Oliver Stone and Francis Ford Coppola (whom Oldman described as having an ego the size of San Francisco) and because he had absorbed everything from all of them, like a sponge, it didn't take a lot of working out what a good director he would actually make. But, as Urbanski argued, there had been an unfounded reputation following him around that he was a difficult actor, when, in fact, he wasn't.

One of those who didn't get on with Oldman as an actor was Winona Ryder, who had worked with him during the making of Francis Ford Coppola's 1992 *Bram Stoker's Dracula*. And it didn't help when she got vocal about it. Although their working relationship on the set had started out as a genuine bond of friendship, it quickly degenerated to such depths that, at times, Ryder could barely stand to be acting opposite him. According to Coppola, he actually instructed Winona to make believe that, instead of Oldman, she was acting opposite him or Winona's other co-star and friend Keanu Reeves. 'The issue is not that they didn't along,' Coppola elaborated later. 'They got along, and then one day they didn't, absolutely didn't get along. None of us were privy to what happened.'

According to Winona, there was no defining moment in which her rapport with Oldman collapsed. 'We hung out before the movie in rehearsals and stuff,' she explained. 'But it wasn't the same after we started shooting. I don't really know why. Maybe it's his way of working, but I felt there was a danger.'

It rankled with her, for instance, that Oldman apparently refused to depart from the character of Dracula even after the cameras had stopped rolling. For Winona, her role of Mina was something that she and her drama coach Greta Seacat had learned to squeeze her into, but for Oldman, according to Winona, Dracula was a lifestyle that he needed to live for as long as Coppola demanded it.

It did not help when Winona nicknamed him the King of Pain. 'He's a very emotional actor, very emotionally on edge,' she explained. It was that, more than anything, that Oldman told Melvyn Bragg offended him most. The slightest thing, she said, could bring that side of Oldman bubbling over. 'I'm not saying that it happened a lot, but in rehearsals it did. It wasn't like we hated each other, it's just that we both did our own thing.' And maybe she was right. All the same, if it's true that the tension between her and Oldman, in their off-set relationship, provided much of the electricity that critics noted ignited their on-screen chemistry, then it worked. Certainly, their performances imbued both their characters with an emotional strength that seems larger than life. And wasn't that the whole point?

Watch any of Oldman's film performances and you will see that most of his characters are absorbed with the same menace that he seemed to possess in playing the vampire king. In fact, his screen debut in the 1986 biopic of the late Sex Pistols guitarist Sid Vicious was so good that it won him the London *Evening Standard*'s Best Newcomer award. Since then, he has become one of Britain's leading film actors who still works regularly in big-budget movies in the United States and Europe. At the time of *Nil By Mouth*'s release, he was about to be seen in *Air Force One* as a hijacker of the Presidential jet, in which his portrayal was as disturbing as the role he had convincingly played only a few years earlier in Christian Slater's *True Romance* as the repulsive pimp Drexel, a white drug trader who sports dreadlocks and flawlessly mimics black street talk. Whether you love him or hate him, there is no denying that Gary Oldman is a breathtaking actor who, like Ray, nine times out of ten, delivers a performance so on the ball it's frightening.

The other stumbling block for getting financial backers for *Nil By Mouth* could have been down to Gary going public about his recovery from alcoholism, which somehow got translated into the fact that he was unreliable. And as Urbanski explains, if you are considered unreliable, 'then you don't have anyone interested in your movie'.

On top of that, there were even more difficulties to cope with. Oldman had decided that he wanted to film on a Super 16mm camera to work in cramped, claustrophobic conditions, and achieve a grainy look to the film. It also meant less lighting equipment and the possibility of using a bigger film magazine, so with a steady cam it would not be limited to a three-minute sequence. The one thing Oldman wanted more than anything was a realism and a voyeurism, like peeping through a keyhole at something you are not supposed to see. He had even considered, at one time, filming in black and white to recreate the feeling of how he remembers South London in his youth as bleak and colourless. In the end, though, he opted for the washed-out colour effect that Steven Spielberg used for *Saving Private Ryan* which was shooting at around the same time as *Nil by Mouth*.

'There were so many negatives, which meant we were unfinancial and unbondable,' recalls Urbanski. 'But, fortunately, our friend, the director Luc Besson said that he would be able to help finance some of the film by foreign sales, because at the time he was selling *Fifth Element*, and he had some muscle in the marketplace. He eventually pre-sold everywhere, apart from Britain.'

Even so, only $2 million of a $4-million budget was in

place. Oldman, who was under no illusions that initial interest would be muted, decided to put in the remaining $2 million himself. 'Gary did not want any financier to have artistic input into his movie,' says Urbanski. 'No one would tell him that the plot did not work; no one would tell him that an actor was not right and there would be no length restriction. Gary reasoned, "I don't collect cars or have a string of houses around the world. I have worked hard and this is my bag. This is my thing."'

Filming began on Oldman's pre-arranged date of 9 November and was completed, with a two-week break for Christmas and New Year, during the third week of January 1996.

It probably helped the overall finished look of the film that Oldman grew up in the same hard-drinking pub atmosphere which he captured on film for *Nil By Mouth*. The Five Bells Tavern, Deptford, which was used in the film, was a few hundred yards from where he was born. But Gary recalls that it was the expectation among his friends and family, rather than his own choice, which introduced him into the pub culture. 'I wasn't physically pushed into the pub, but my peers and my culture demanded it of me,' he says. 'It was a case of "You are going to learn how to drink light and keg. And you're going to stand at the bar and play darts." I hated it. I never liked beer. But I would do it and make myself incredibly ill from doing it, because it is like my graduation. It was a case of "I am a working-class boy in a working-class district and now I have reached 15 and I graduate to standing at the bar." But I am fascinated by bar-room conversation and really enjoyed coming back and being in an old neighbourhood.'

Certainly, Oldman could not have been more honest about his alcoholism than he was. Ironically, it was not the wish to be drinking huge amounts surrounded by friends in a public house which dragged him in to it. 'By nature, I'm an isolationist, so my boozing was at home thank you,' he says. 'I was not a goer-outer. I mean, I didn't drink for the taste and I did not want to be particularly social. Someone once described alcoholics as egomaniacs with low self-esteem. That is a perfect definition.'

But many stories have either been misinterpreted or reported inaccurately. 'Some newspapers said that my father used to beat up my mother, which is not at all the case. It was the result of a press conference at Cannes Film Festival and I wondered for about two months how that interpretation could have been used in what I said. I finally realised that one journalist asked which character in the film am I closest to. I said, "The little girl." They took that to mean that I watched my mother being beaten up by my father, which was never the case. What I really meant was that I was witness to a whole collage of events.'

Nil By Mouth was released in October 1997 to rave reviews, and was 'the film to see' during its premiere screenings at the Cannes Film Festival that May, where it won Kathy Burke the Best Actress award. Not that she would be shouting the news from the top of the Hollywood Hills or anywhere else for that matter.

Kathy is what you would describe as a low-key personality who prefers to let her work do the talking. She was even too anxious to attend the cast and crew screening of the film when it was shown in London. 'There is a part of me which gets very shy when all the focus is on me,' she admits. 'Even when acting – such as the miscarriage scene in this film – I find certain things very tough to do. I like scenes involving other people, rather than just me.'

Kathy, no stranger to praise, had previously worked with Gary Oldman before on his first film, *Sid and Nancy*, but had not seen him in ten years. 'He still had the instinct and the courage of his convictions that he had when I first knew him as an actor,' she recalls. 'I was offered the part without an audition and without reading for it. But I wanted to meet Gary first to talk it through and to know that we were on the same wavelength.

'I knew from the writing where Valerie came from and it was obvious that she was a victim. But I really wanted to give her a bit more strength than she should have had. Everything she did seemed to be so slow. Gary said she is supposed to be like that. She is worried and punch drunk. All the men seemed so much faster and sharper around me. But they were supposed to be on drugs, I suppose.'

She carried her concerns about her performance all the way to Cannes. 'I was gobsmacked, because I felt I was very much a supporting role to Ray, who was brilliant, so it completely blew my mind,' she says. 'When I first saw the film at a private screening in London, my main thought was one of relief because I had not shown the piece up. I was worried that I would be the one to let it down.

'I wanted this film to work more than anything I have ever done. It is very beautiful and I'm proud of it. I definitely went through feelings of hopelessness in my own life, especially as a kid – even if I don't want to delve too deeply into it – and, had I not found the theatre, I might have ended up with a guy like Ray is in the film.

'Fortunately, acting took me to different worlds in my head. The whole experience of *Nil By Mouth* made me appreciate even more what I have from my own life. It was wonderful to return to my little flat every night having spent the entire day on the Bonamy Estate [where the film was shot] and look at what I've got.'

Kathy was under no illusions as to why Gary Oldman wanted her in the film. 'Other actresses can play cockney, but I play victims,' she says. 'I knew what he was getting at. There was going to be no one around to rescue me. Fortunately, I have no difficulty in leaving the character behind at the end of each day'

Despite the subject matter and content of the film, Kathy says, 'A day did not go past when I didn't cry with laughter at some point. It was bliss, really. Usually, when a job has been blinding to do, it is a come-down to watch. Not this one. I loved it.'

So did most others. One of many was online film critic James Berardinelli. In his review, he noted that, from the beginning of the film, it's clear that three elements are going to be critical to the events that transpire: alcohol, drugs and poverty. 'Our first glimpse of the main character, played by Ray Winstone, in a stunningly forceful performance, is in a pub where he and some friends are sitting around drinking lager and trading profane stories. Oldman allows the film to develop slowly, giving us a feel for Ray and his buddies. They are all victims of society, but do the best they can to get by, and use alcohol to dull the pain of not having any real purpose in life.'

Ray is a family man. He has a wife, Valerie, and a young daughter. But all is not well under his roof. When he has had a few pints, Ray is prone to explosive displays of violence. With little or no provocation, he will lash out at anyone in range. His favourite target is his wife's drug-addicted brother, Billy, who lives with Ray's family. When Billy isn't around, there are other possibilities, including his wife. And, although

Ray never harms his daughter physically, there is little doubt that his behaviour leaves deep psychological scars.

Certainly, continued Berardinelli, 'Oldman does an excellent job of bringing the audience into a world where despair and hopelessness are the norm. *Nil by Mouth* does not sympathize with Ray, but it forces us to understand him. He is the product of a dysfunctional family and the son of a man who was incapable of expressing affection. He loves his wife and daughter, but, like too many men under the influence of alcohol, he cannot control himself, and the most base impulses of his nature emerge with devastating consequences. The film's treatment of Valerie is equally well rounded and believable. The director shows her pain, desperation and humiliation, as well as her growing determination to free herself from the cycle of violence that threatens her safety.'

By the end of his review, as in most of the other reviews for the film, Berardinelli concluded that *Nil by Mouth* 'is as powerful as it is uncomfortable, and those in search of a pleasant movie-going experience would be best served looking elsewhere. However, for anyone who isn't bothered by the thought of experiencing a shock to the system, this film is not to be missed. It approaches a serious social issue in the best, most dramatically true manner. Instead of resorting to lugubrious sermons or prettying things up Hollywood-style, it tells a simple, psychologically exact tale that illustrates the depth and breadth of pain caused by domestic abuse. *Nil by Mouth* leaves an impression that is hard to shake off, and that's the mark of a top-notch film.'

While the film was still showing at Cannes, *Variety*, the legendary entertainment trade journal, added considerable praise to what the world's leading critics were all saying about the film and, in particular, about Ray's performance.

'Winstone dominates the film with an intensely focused performance. Both Burke, as his punching-bag wife, and Laila Morse, as his tough mother-in-law, inhabit their character's skins, with Edna Dore contributing a sparky cameo as the fearless grandma. Jamie Foreman is very good as Raymond's raconteur pal, and Charlie Creed-Miles fine as the withdrawn Billy.'

However, there was one British journalist in Cannes, Ray says, 'who wrote "this does not happen." It's one thing to say you don't like the film, you'll either like it or you won't, but to say it doesn't happen is wrong. I'd like to know where he lives, because I'd love to live there.' But, all that aside, '*Nil By Mouth* was the most enjoyable job I've ever worked on, even though it was so tough, because it was so good. The writing was so good, and the actors around you were so good.

'We'd go to work even if we weren't supposed to be in that day, and sit behind the cameras and stuff. But I needed a break afterwards. You don't realise it when you're working on it but, afterwards, you take stock, you're tired and run down and you start to wonder that, if you've done these things in the film, then there must be something in you that's like that. It's really weird and, after a couple of weeks, you feel that that's all bollocks and have to stop thinking like that. But it's funny, since *Nil By Mouth*, my wife and my sister-in-law say I've really mellowed. I'm not into therapy or anything, but it was quite an education doing it, it opened your eyes and your heart a little bit to the way these people lived and the way you live yourself.'

Elsewhere, there were those journalists who wondered if he got offered parts like the one he had in *Nil By Mouth* because there was no escaping it, he was a dab hand at playing heavies. Or was it because, as he says, 'I do it properly. I've always had my feelings about violence on screen. When you watch a movie like *True Lies*, the violence is never real as it should be. Someone will pick up a chair and hit someone and they get straight back up again. What sort of message does that send to children? It's irresponsible. When you hit a man with a chair, you kill him, and you have to show that. If you're making a film like that, holding back would be like cutting the bottom off a Picasso painting. If something's violent, then you must show the real horror of it. You must portray it as truly as possible.'

Ray has said *Nil By Mouth* was the one movie that let him out of his cage, so to speak. 'It started me off and let me go. My character was just a bully who didn't know how to express himself and Kathy Burke's character loved him and thought everyone lived that way. But you can say that about a million films and, yes, *Nil by Mouth*, for example, was very realistic, but you wouldn't want to see that sort of movie every day, otherwise you'd go mad.

'People have said, "Oh, that film must have been so harrowing," but it wasn't. I've never had such a ball in my life. Don't get me wrong. That don't mean I weren't concentrating. It's just that I'd already done me homework. You imagine spending all day on set brooding about beating your wife up, you'd be in a nuthouse. I'm one of them blokes who can be laughing and joking and then it's "Action!" Bam! I'm in there. I can switch from blah-blah-blah to "You cad."'

But you have to have a laugh, he continues, 'or else you'd go off your head. Can you imagine the set of *Nil by Mouth* if we didn't have a laugh? People would have been killing each other. I hear about actors who are hostile to each other on set because their characters hate each other. That's bollocks. Life is too short.'

In *Nil By Mouth*, though, it was simply, he tells most that ask, the best script he's ever read on the subject, and the best part he's ever had, and Oldman the best director he's worked with. 'When a man actually enjoys you sitting with him behind the monitor, and takes in ideas, and makes you feel part of the filmmaking process, it's very, very exciting. If Gary hadn't given me that part, I probably wouldn't be working today. Suddenly scripts were pouring through the door. I'm glad it happened to me now, maybe I wouldn't have been able to handle it when I was younger; I might not have been disciplined enough.'

Ten months after completing *Nil By Mouth*, and just one week before Christmas 1995, Ray was filming the final sequence for *Face*, Antonia Bird's mostly underrated British villain piece, which, to this day, still ranks as one of the best crime dramas to come out of the nineties. Strangely, at the time of its release, just one month before that of *Nil By Mouth*, it was more or less overlooked, and has ended up being one of Ray's least seen films, despite it being one of the best British villain films of its time.

It did not go completely unnoticed, however. The review in Britain's *Total Film* magazine summed it up as 'a solid, slick Brit thriller, a fast-paced and noisy film which wears its heart on its blood-soaked sleeve. With a throbbing soundtrack and a razor-keen attention to character detail, this is a compelling and utterly unglamorous look at Britain's seedier side of our criminal element.'

The critic writing in *Radio Times*, however, didn't entirely agree. Even though the magazine considered the film was full of good ideas, they also thought it never quite delivered the punch it should have. 'It is a movie about betrayal, paranoia, loyalty, the morality of old-style and new-style criminals. It involves some shocking moments, both physically and emotionally. And despite fine performances from all the cast it ends up feeling like a routine crime thriller.'

Face was the story of a professional thief named Ray and his associates, whose carefully planned £2-million heist nets only a fraction of the intended sum. Friction occurs between the gang members when it becomes apparent there is a traitor in their midst. The focus of the movie becomes the need to find out which one has double-crossed the others. *Face* is not only one of Ray's least seen films, but also one of the few in which he is on the receiving end of the violence about 20 minutes before the end of the film. Sharing the thoughts of the director, Antonia Bird, many considered that is where the film should have ended, after Ray was shot and killed. Instead, it ends with the surviving Carlyle, his not-so-bright buddy Stevie and girlfriend Connie driving away from the mayhem they have just left behind.

As *Total Film* noted, 'It all sounds suspiciously like *Reservoir Dogs*, but *Face* is a thoroughly British crime flick. For one, there's no gratuitous earlobe-trimming. Two, there're no black suits and shades in sight and, three, its very British stars include *Trainspotting*'s Robert Carlyle as the eponymous *Face* (the underworld slang for thief), along with Ray Winstone, the superb Phil Davis and, amazingly, Blur frontman Damon Albarn in his acting debut. In fact, this little beauty is more reminiscent of the underworld Brit thrillers of yesteryear, classics like *The Long Good Friday* and *Get Carter*.'

To all intents and purposes, *Face* was an unashamedly genre film, exploring not just the dirty world of (dis)organised crime, but also the world of believable, ugly, flawed characters. All this is set against a backdrop of strong social, domestic and political issues, whisked into a froth with themes of love and friendship, respect and family, betrayal and deceit. And, although it's full of the usual criminal suspects, with 'shootahs, motahs, bad language, and birds', there's an awful lot more to the movie than its apparent stereotypical simplicity.

If anything, *Face* looks grimy, although it's beautifully shot. It feels gritty, mainly because it's haunted by the spectre of Thatcher's uncaring Britain, and it's streaked throughout with the sort of earthy, pithy comedy lines you might hear down any London boozer after a few jars. It just oozes realism: it's full of real people bleeding; real emotional pain; real personal histories to reflect on; real people trying to get through their lives in Britain in the nineties the only way they know how.

While the plot might be the oldest of old hats, the film still has a cracking script and stunning cast to play with. Carlyle proved once again that he is a multi-faceted actor, and is as watchable as ever. Much the same as Ray is. Phil Davis, Stephen Waddington and Lena Headey as Carlyle's girlfriend, who turns a small part into a memorable one, and 'pretty pop-boy' Damon Albarn, all provide heroic support. Even though, 'the obtrusively heavy-handed political statements might already seem dated, and the action lurches into overly frantic melodrama at the end', *Total Film* were correct when they concluded their review by saying, the film 'has more than enough to it to merit the entrance fee'.

Perhaps one of the main attractions of *Face* for the actors was the fun and excitement of the realistic use of guns. In preparing for their roles, Ray and others in the cast gathered in an Islington pub, probably the Old Red Lion, to meet some robbers who were said to have carried weapons at one time or another. One of the criminals they met was the late Bobby King, who also played a security guard in the film, and who later said that Ray had made a far more frightening blagger than he had ever been.

At this meeting, Carlyle sat quietly in a corner, letting others ask the questions, and watched in fascination as one of these veteran thugs ate a packet of crisps. The man sifted the contents carefully, demolishing each crisp with tiny, neat, methodical bites. For Carlyle, who likes to research his characters by direct observation, it was a useful insight. 'Here was a guy who was a bank robber, a very violent man, a man who would stop at nothing. I found it very interesting – the precision. That level of containment is quite frightening, and that precision runs right through their work.'

As if to prove the point, Phil Davis, who plays Julian, one of the gang who demands an extra 40 grand at gunpoint to cover his expenses, explained how exhilarating it was for him and Ray in the 'shoot 'em' up in the street scene. One can still picture the 'SAS' eyes of concentration that he and Ray had as they leaped from one explosive eruption of gunfire to another when they are all but cornered by the police. You can actually smell the cordite of fired hardware. Maybe too, it was the mixture of immense power that a gun can presumably command and, of course, the simple male-macho supremacy that goes with it. Isn't that why we play with toy guns in our childhood versions of cowboys and Indians or cops and robbers?

Another revelation that Davis spoke of was Gerry Conlon's cameo in the film. This was the same Gerry Conlon who had been wrongly convicted as a member of the Guildford Four, who police had insisted were responsible for an IRA bombing campaign in London. Davis was well informed of the misfortunes of this most remarkable and resilient individual when he read *Proved Innocent*, Conlon's autobiography, and had been completely moved by it. The book ended up as a major film, *In The Name of the Father*, starring Daniel Day-Lewis as Conlon. Ironically, Davis played a detective in the same film who brutally and violently interrogates Day-Lewis. One can only imagine how Conlon must have felt while watching Davis tugging on the ears of Day-Lewis.

A similar connection occurred while making *Face*. The scene in which Conlon, as a small-time drug dealer, is threatened by Ray with shouts and screams of 'Where's the gear, where's the *fucking* gear?' must have reawakened in Conlon the real horrors he must have been put through years before. As one would expect, Ray holds nothing back in his performance, and, although there is little compassion in either of Ray's or Carlyle's characters, pretending to be cops on a violent raid on Conlon for drugs, Ray is the more threatening and intimidating one. In fact, the scene was such a remarkable piece of acting from Conlon, when you consider what he had been through, that you have to applaud him for his integrity. If Ray felt any sympathy for Conlon during those brief minutes of utter abuse, he showed no weaknesses to his audience. But that is what Ray does best.

'He's a force of nature,' says Ronan Bennett, who wrote the screenplay. 'He didn't need anything explained to him about his character; he knew that world and the people in it, how their value systems worked, but for me in casting you can't cheat class, and when Ray plays his class – as in *Face*, as in *Nil By Mouth* – he's compelling, real and moving.'

Antonia Bird agrees. As an actor, she says, Ray 'is a rare commodity, a genuine working-class bloke from proper working-class roots. There's a received wisdom in the industry that he's a big bruiser but he's probably one of the brightest actors I've ever worked with.'

CHAPTER 8

War Zone

If *Nil By Mouth* was the best thing that ever happened for Ray's career, then his role in Tim Roth's unflinching exploration of child abuse would prove to be his toughest. '*The War Zone* hurt me,' he says matter-of-factly. '*Nil By Mouth* didn't, and so I had to take a look at myself and ask why I could give Kathy Burke a clump, and go home and not really worry about it, but I couldn't do the same after raping my [screen] child. I understand why, and I don't have a problem with that, but abuse is abuse.'

In fact, so daunting did he find the filming of the rape scene, he recalls, 'I was standing there thinking, "What the fuck am I doing this job for?" Tim was the director and I was really, really angry with him for making me do the scene, just angry with him for breathing really. I thought, "Why can't I go and get a job as a bus driver rather than do this for a living?" But Tim was absolutely right to make me do the scene and I agree it was essential to the plot because we were making a film about the subject of child abuse and we had to portray it.'

But, after filming the scene in which he raped his screen daughter, played by Lara Belmont, in a concrete bunker, while he emits terrible grunts and howls, as if he is the one being raped, he thought, 'Why did I get so angry about that kind of abuse and not get so upset about having to hit Kathy? You see? We all draw the line somewhere and you have to start to question why.' His constant refrain was that everything he does is merely acting, a job. But, inevitably, some roles affect him more than others and he is particularly forthright about what should be done to people who perpetrate the kind of abuse carried out by his character in *The War Zone*. 'I think they should be killed. It's as simple as that. And I'd have no qualms about getting a gun, sticking it in their mouths and pulling the trigger myself. After all, they kill the children inside, don't they?'

Like most other people, he has pretty strong feelings about paedophiles. He has said, 'I would put them all up against a wall and shoot them. I know it's not necessarily the right attitude but, as a father, that's the way I feel. I remember meeting Gary Glitter on a yacht in 1979 and thinking he was a nice fella. It just shows, you have no idea who these people are because they seem so normal. If I'd known then what I know now, I would have drowned him!'

If what he discovered about Gary Glitter left him cold, then playing Dad in *The War Zone* would leave him frozen. His discomfort seemed to spread as filming got under way. And he wasn't the only one to ask why, if the child abuser in one film had disturbed him, the wife-beater in the other hadn't. His explanation to most journalists that posed the question, however, was simple. In *Nil By Mouth*, his character 'just wants someone to cuddle him. He wants someone to love him. The people round him don't want to show their love. And so he explodes. His only way of doing it is in an aggressive way. And, usually, you find that those people, it's out of fear a lot of the time. I like him and I feel for him.' *The War Zone* was a different matter entirely. 'I kept thinking, "Why am I doing this? Why would I want to put myself through this and put this young girl through this?" But that's quite a healthy way of looking at it in a way, you know. She's 17, 18. But the fact of the matter is that it's still abuse, whatever way you look at it, I guess.'

But, continues Ray, 'you do feel like the abuser when you're doing it. The only character I've ever played that I didn't like was the guy in *The War Zone*, but it probably was the nearest to playing me that I've ever played. I played me as a dad. I cook my kids tomatoes on toast. I sit down and tell them stories about when I was a kid and car crashes and things like that. But there was the one moment when I actually raped my daughter which… it's not me. It's really weird that it's the only character that I detest. And I'm playing me. It's hard for me to say that. The only way I could make the film was by thinking that all the stories I told in the film were my stories, the ones I tell to my kids. It's all I could do to make it feel like this guy is someone you would have a drink with, who then goes home and goes crazy at his daughter every night. That way it made it more frightening because you saw him as a normal guy. It's a therapy,' he admits. 'I guess I cottoned on very early to that kind of technique. People like James Stewart and Gregory Peck could always be the tough guy in town, but they played it with a very human side and they weren't afraid to cry.'

Not that his daughter Jaime much liked the idea of watching it. At the time, it was said that *The War Zone* was the only one of her father's films that she hadn't then seen. And that, she said, was because, 'he's a child abuser in it, and I know what a good actor he is, so, from a daughter's point of view, I don't think I would really like to see it.'

It probably didn't help matters that the producers wanted to cast her in the role of Jessie, Ray's screen daughter, who is raped in what most reviewers described as one of the most brutal and harrowing sex scenes ever filmed. Ray, of course, refused point blank to have his own daughter in the role.

As Abbie Bernstein wrote in *iF* magazine, it's hard to imagine there would be much on screen that could intimidate Ray, but, as she noted in her December 1999 feature on the film, the rape sequence was enough to give Ray reason to pause when it came time to shoot it.

According to Tim Roth, atmosphere on the set the day the rape scene was shot was not good. But, as he explained, 'I've got to get it right, because otherwise you've got to come back. What was interesting was that we created a family that really looked after each other. I prepared the actors. The actors were fine. But, as much as you may read it on a piece of paper, nobody is prepared to actually see the reality of it. The boom guy was crying, the focus puller was crying, the operator was trying not to throw up. Tears all around me, and Lara was doing her stuff. She's a very good actor, this girl, and Ray's doing his stuff. And I'm the one sitting there going, "Head up, Lara, we can't see your face, love." Talking through the scene what is happening. "Kiss her, Ray. Tell her you love her." And then it's all done. Cut. Done.

'And, then, I'm busy setting up the next shot, and they come out of this bunker where the rape scene was shot, and everyone – there's about four or five people standing there, and they're white as sheets – they come out. There are a lot of tears going on. Lara goes straight to Ray and comforts him. Which I thought was extraordinary. And then we went to the pub and got completely drunk. But Ray, I think we could have lost him that day. It was that bad.' And, as Roth concluded, it wasn't helped by the fact that Ray's oldest daughter was the same age as Lara.

Certainly, for Ray, it was the most difficult film he'd ever done. When he came off the set, he says, 'I wanted to hit Tim. He's my friend and he's a great actor, a great director, but I just wanted to rip his throat out.' But maybe, he continues, 'I made a mistake. I kind of put certain scenes in the back of my head like they were never going to happen. And, when the day came, I wasn't fully mentally prepared to do it. It was a day I nearly just packed up and went... But, thinking back on it, it's quite healthy, in a way. There'd be something wrong with me if I didn't feel that way about the scene. You go through so much pain when you're doing a scene like that. I mean, the girl Lara Belmont who was doing it, she's the age of my eldest daughter, which kind of freaked me out. I was beginning to worry about her state of mind.'

Despite Ray's concerns, Belmont seemed to feel that everyone involved behaved with complete professionalism. As Ray says, 'She came up to me after filming the scene and thanked me, which really did disperse any ghosts. That helped me a lot. I did say, I never will make a film like that again while I was doing it, but I've changed my mind, because acting is what I do. And I'm very proud of the film. It's really responsible. It's not a Saturday-night repeater, but it's a fantastic film. The one thing I wanted to do with the part was make him initially seem to be a good guy. Because that's what child molesters come over as. That's why they very rarely get caught. It's not this guy with a moustache and a bald head and a beard and little pebble glasses that is everyone's fear of what a child molester is, a picture of this monster. It's a banker, it's a bus driver, it's a doctor, it's every man on the street. A child trusts its parent to love it and to nurture it and to protect it through its life. You know, even though I'm 42, my dad still tries to protect me now. So I understand all that. And the thing with parents who commit incest, in a way, they murder their child every day. The trust they're given and the love they're given, they abuse. They educate a child from a certain age that incest is all right, until a child gets older, and, by that time, the child is damaged.'

Even if, as Ray himself says, his experiences on *The War Zone* caused him to rethink his attitude toward his earlier work on *Nil By Mouth*, the bottom line was that in his mind, and probably most others, too, 'both films are about abuse, abuse to yourself and abuse to other people. On *Nil By Mouth*, I'd say, "Well, I don't take the work home with me. I don't come home at night as a wife-beating, alcoholic cocaine-head." I was that light about it. If I can walk away from *Nil By Mouth* going, that's another job, that was a great film, and then get myself into such a state over a film that showed abuse to a child, I had to rethink the responsibility you have when you make a film like *Nil By Mouth*. Again, I'm very proud of it; I think it's a great film, but just the way I thought about it after changed.'

Most of the reviews of *The War Zone* summed up the general critical opinion, and all agreed that Ray was at his uncompromising best as a man with a disturbing, sickening view of fatherhood. In the film, after recently moving from

London to Devon, Ray and his seemingly functional middle-class family try their best to readjust. There follows a series of refreshingly plotless scenes that do nothing to further the story, but that provide priceless insight into the leading characters. We are introduced to Ray's tough but loving wife, played by Tilda Swinton, while newcomers Lara Belmont and Freddie Cunliffe play their children Jessie and Tom.

When you watch the film, it is hard to believe that Belmont and Cunliffe had never thought about acting before. And even harder to fathom how Tim Roth plucked Lara off the street. 'She was shopping. She thought we were going to steal her purse. We would go up to these people and say, "Do you want to read for a film?" And most people would say, "Fuck off." But some would say, "Yeah. Why not?" And she said, "Yeah!" We gave her the script to read. She said, "I think I can do this." And I believed her.' She was just one of 2,500 hopefuls that were auditioned.

They certainly had the critics on their side too. One can imagine how difficult it was for them both to play their parts. Cunliffe as Tom, 15, and Belmont, as his 17-year-old sister, are very close in the film, but fight as passionately as most typical teenagers of that age do. Their characters both seem bored by the enforced solitude of the breathtaking Devon countryside and long for the frenetic energy and anonymity of London life. The problem is, they're stuck with their demanding dad and are faced with all the responsibilities that go with having a new baby sister in the house. The controversial element at the heart of the storyline is that, as the film progresses, Tom discovers that his father is having an incestuous relationship with sister Jessie. And, already feeling alienated by the move out of the city, Tom feels even more isolated as he carries the burden of his terrible discovery.

As one reviewer noted, 'The only negative aspect of *The War Zone* is that the whole thing is extremely hard to stomach. Some might find it too much of an ordeal. If you do give it a go, just remember there is a meaning behind the madness. This one gets under the skin and stays there.'

But, as Ray suggests, if the film made kids aware that being abused is not right, then the film did its job.

Whether it did or not, one thing was for sure, Channel 4's film arm, Film Four, who bankrolled the project, were very reluctant to cut any scenes from the final print of the movie. So determined were they for the public to see it as it was intended that they said they would rather not release it than see it released cut and tampered with.

Michael Bor, the then principal examiner at the British Board of Film Censors, agreed. In the end, he chose not to censor the film in any way, judging it to be a very important movie. 'There is no taboo subject that should never be tackled in a film. It all depends on how it is handled. It is incredibly valuable showing how sex abuse can tear apart a family. Certainly, films that were highly controversial have proved to be immensely important not just as entertainment but to society as a whole.'

Looking back at some of the films that had caused controversy, *Natural Born Killers* (1994), the tale of a young couple on a random murder trail, was accused of glamorising killers and being excessively violent. In France, Florence Rey was convicted of four murders after becoming obsessed with the movie. Another, *Lolita* (1962), an account of a middle-aged man's obsession with a prepubescent girl, was criticised for encouraging paedophilia, and the BBC film *Cathy Come Home*, Ken Loach's gritty tale of homelessness in the late 1960s, was attacked for its bad language, but is now acclaimed for raising the issue on a wide scale for the first time.

However, 30 years later, some critics fear filmmakers are breaking new taboos just to create shockwaves. And, as audiences become increasingly familiar with sex and violence, movies have to push the boundaries further with explicit material to have impact. But not *The War Zone*. As Tim Roth rightly says, the reality, however grisly it is, has to be fully portrayed. 'I think you have to show what these people do to their children, what they go through, how awful it is. You either deal with the subject or you don't. I wouldn't have shown it if I had to cut my film. Very straightforward. I told them, "You cut one frame, I take my name off it." And they didn't. But they wouldn't anyway. They're very cool people.'

Soon after *The War Zone* was released in September 1999, the British film industry was beginning to change the way they thought about Ray as an actor. Much of that was down to his role in *Nil By Mouth*. 'All of a sudden good scripts were coming through,' he remembers. The BAFTA nomination for his performance in the film, the European Actor of the Year nomination for *The War Zone* and a British Independent Film Award for his portrayal of a bereaved father in *Our Boy* also helped. 'I never thought that awards really worried me before, but, yeah, it is important, because, all of a sudden, your status goes up, the scripts you're getting are of a different quality, you're more in demand, so then you're getting the top jobs and your money goes right through the ceiling. I wouldn't want the quality of the work to suffer for the money to go through the ceiling because, in the long run, how much money do you actually need? But it's nice when people in your industry nominate you. You've been accepted. And it's lovely when someone in the audience gives you a slap on the back and says, "Well done."'

It wasn't surprising that he won the Best Actor nomination for his role in *Our Boy*, a compelling BBC1 drama written by his old friend Tony Grounds (who went on to write *All In The Game* specifically for Ray, as well as the acclaimed *Births, Marriages and Deaths*).

Births, Marriages and Deaths was a drama about three East End men who have been friends since school, and whose lives begin to unravel when past deeds return to haunt them following a drunken stag night.

Ray played Alan, but he didn't see him as the bad person audiences did. 'I mean, I don't like his brashness an' all that. But he's a good-hearted man. Before these events take place, he's fine. But, to him, anyone who fucks with your family and friends... he's gonna top them. It may not be the law of the land, but it's the law of the jungle, in a way. I may not be as extreme as Alan, but, if someone fucked with my family, there's no reprieve in the world that would stop me going to find that person. Mind you, if Alan really was such a big potato, he'd own up to the things he's done. But he doesn't. He bottles it.'

Any misgivings about the series would, a *Time Out* journalist said, be the throwaway ending, but Grounds believed in this piece of television, just as he believes in any TV written by the likes of Ken Loach, Alan Bleasdale, Alan Clarke, Alan Bennett and John Sullivan. He has high hopes that *Births, Marriages and Deaths* will enter the pantheon. 'That may sound like conceit. But I think people who get into it will really love it, and I do think it captures the mood of the times. It's so easy to patronise the medium of TV,' continues Grounds forcefully. 'It's reaching the point where everyone is sitting and watching stuff and then thinking, "I could do better than that." That's not the way to come to art, thinking you could do better than something that's shit. Lots of people can write, but not too many people actually have something to say.'

Ray and Grounds's friendship is revealed in the banter they took part in for the benefit of the *Time Out* journalist. Asked to describe each other in a nutshell, Grounds says, 'He's fat, I'm thin.'

Ray: 'I'm handsome – he's ugly. And short-sighted. But he's a staunch friend.'

Grounds: 'And, like all mates, I know, if I'm in trouble, I can phone Ray first.'

Ray: 'And I'll tell the missus to say I'm busy. How much does he want this time?'

Grounds: 'Well you get paid more than me.'

Ray: 'I'm fuckin' entitled to.'

It was this kind of humour that lay at the heart of *Births, Marriages and Deaths* as it pinpoints the place where the playground banter stops being fun – or even a hidden emotion – and becomes a refusal to grow up, where abuse is tolerated, betrayal is commonplace and love is more easily expressed through the violent big gesture than simple respect. Certainly, Grounds and Ray have located that place and exposed it to the light, the end result being that women may never look at their fella and his mates in the same way again. Not that it is to everyone's taste.

And, if *Births, Marriages and Deaths* wasn't everyone's cup of tea, then nor was *Our Boy*. That was a different kind of story completely – of how a working-class couple from the East End of London cope with the death of their only child,

Lee, killed in a hit-and-run road accident. Woody, played by Ray, is sent almost mad with grief, sleeping in his son's bed and then eventually in the old garage where his son's body was found. His wife Sonia (Pauline Quirke) reacts in a more natural way, grieving, but then, after many months, trying to resume their lives and carry on. As Woody refuses to allow his grief and reactions to abate and turns in on himself and what happened, it splits him and Sonia. He also suspects that the man who has been arrested for the killing was not actually driving the car. DS Spence, who has looked down on Woody and his family and dismissed them as scum, is shocked when a young boy confesses that he was in the car that killed Lee, and that it was driven by Ricky, Spence's son. When Woody finds this out, he goes after Ricky.

'Woody's the nearest to me that I've ever played,' Ray confessed. 'I was brought up in Plaistow, where *Our Boy* is set, so making this was like going home. Woody ducks and dives, does a bit of building – the sort of thing I'd be doing now if I hadn't got into this game. He loves his family, has a lark about with his mates, he goes to see West Ham. But then his world falls apart.'

He also admitted that Woody's initial reaction to Lee's death couldn't be divorced from what he imagines his own would be in the same situation. 'My first instinct is "an eye for an eye"; I would want to kill whoever was responsible, end of story. But that don't bring your kid back, does it? Please God, that none of us are ever in the situation.'

At the time, Ray said that *Our Boy* would touch anyone who has children of their own. 'I'm very proud of it, maybe more so than anything I've ever done,' he declared at his agent's office in London's West End. 'It's very honest, very truthful, and I like that. Tony Grounds is a top writer – he really knows his stuff.

Although Ray is always willing to give credit to others, it is his portrayal of one man's mental torment and anguish that anchors *Our Boy*. So, how did he summon up the intensity of Woody's grief? 'I suppose the closest I've ever come to feeling as empty as Woody was when my mum died, although that was almost a relief in some ways because she'd been suffering for a couple of years. But I didn't draw on that for this. You have to make it up because unless you've been through it you can't relate to how it must feel to lose a child. And I wouldn't want to go and talk to someone who had. Why should I intrude on someone else's grief to help me play a part?

'Actors work in all sorts of ways but I find all that sort of unnecessary. I just imagined what my own grief might be like, how I might react, because the minute you start thinking about what other people would do, you're making barriers for yourself.'

After all, he continues, 'It could come to an abrupt end tomorrow but I'm having a ball at the moment. I'm getting good work, and if you can get good work the rest is up to you. Any job you enjoy doing is easy in a way because it's not a chore. I'm not saying what I do is easy, but I like doing it and I want to do it as well as I can.'

Another bonus of making the film was having many of his family and friends around on the set, who had all landed parts as extras, probably with Ray's help, much like Elvis normally got parts for his buddies in most of his movies, usually as extras in the fight scenes. But perhaps the biggest bonus of all for Ray was having his sister Laura playing a small part.

Two months after *The War Zone* was playing out on

screens across the country, Ray was next seen in *Fanny and Elvis*, a major departure from the kind of roles audiences were used to seeing him play.

At the time, Ray said, 'I wasn't looking for a romantic comedy, because I didn't think anyone would want to cast me in a romantic comedy. But director Kay Mellor wanted to make a romantic comedy about a man and a woman, not the male model and the female model. I went to see it with an audience, and they're crying, they're laughing and they're enjoying it. There's me kissing someone instead of punching them, and it's kind of cool. I'd much rather kiss someone than punch them, especially when they're really attractive. But no, I didn't consciously pick that. You don't do a gangster film and think, "Right, next I want to do a musical." I think some actors plan that way, and it's to their cost, because then they go and do a piece of shit. But this turned out all right.'

The film, which premiered at the London Film Festival in November 1999, was summed up perfectly in the Festival brochure by Sandra Hebron as 'a warm and witty romantic comedy set in the North of England at the end of the millennium'.

The story centred on a writer named Kate who has finally completed her debut novel, but her exhilaration dips when a trip to the doctor reveals that she is running out of time to get pregnant.

Realising she will have to rethink her priorities, her situation worsens when her husband Rob leaves her for a younger woman and she is faced not only with heartache but also with a biological clock ticking even louder. She and her gay lodger-cum-best-friend hatch plans and scheme, but neither matchmaking nor medical intervention provides a solution, until chance and coincidence throw Kate into close proximity with Dave, the ex of Rob's new girlfriend. But, feminist though she is, Kate still has romantic dreams, and the flashy, macho car dealer seems unlikely to fulfil them – though his happy band of kids from earlier relationships proves that at least his sperm count is up to the job.

'This directorial debut from writer Kay Mellor, best known for her TV dramas *Band of Gold* and *Playing the Field*,' concluded Hebron, 'sees Kerry Fox and Ray Winstone playing delightfully opposite each other, with the latter confirming his status as one of our most versatile screen actors. A definite crowd-pleaser, *Fanny and Elvis* will have you humming along with Dusty and Elvis on the soundtrack and leaving the cinema with a huge smile on your face.'

The review by Neil Norman in the London *Evening Standard* shouted much the same message. 'For anyone who thinks that Winstone is restricted to playing gangsters or abusive husbands and fathers, his performance in this romantic comedy will be a revelation. Kay Mellor's script may trawl every cliché in the book of Northern Mills & Boonishness but it's the performances that make the film wonderfully watchable. A cuddly teddy bear of a movie and a definite crowd-pleaser.'

Film critic Alexander Walker agreed. 'Winstone adds another feather to his acting cap. Soon he'll be able to fly just by nodding his head up and down.'

And another review in Blockbuster's *The Scene* magazine echoed what most other critics were applauding. 'Fresh from deserved acclaim for starring roles in harrowing films like *Nil By Mouth* and *The War Zone*, tough-guy actor Ray Winstone makes a welcome departure with *Fanny and Elvis*. He stamps his authority on his leading role though, giving a typically believable performance and swapping jibes with Kerry Fox with as much relish as he swapped punches in *Scum*. Together he and Fox work up their romantic friction into a veritable froth before the film reaches a heart-warming and moving climax.'

Perhaps much of the acclaim was helped by Ray and other cast members appearing at the Gala screening of the film at the Festival to answer questions from the audience. One of the audience members was Alison Carter, who now runs the *About Ray Winstone* fansite on the internet. She remembers that 'Ray was wearing a long grey coat, no beard, hair quite dark. He said hi to his wife and kids who were there and who he hadn't seen for a while – presumably because he's been filming *There's Only One Jimmy Grimble* – and answered a couple of questions. One was about West Ham football club and how badly they are doing at the moment, and one was about whether he enjoyed playing a romantic hero after his hard-man roles.' Ten days later, the film was released into cinemas throughout the UK, further establishing Ray among the upper echelon of British actors.

CHAPTER 9

Paradise –
Spanish Style

In the summer of 1999, soon after completing *There's Only One Jimmy Grimble* alongside his *Face* buddy Robert Carlyle, Ray was high on a hill above the village of Agua Amarga, close to Almeria in southern Spain, laid out across the patio of a designer villa in a pair of yellow speedos under a blistering hot sun. He was shooting the opening sequence for director Jonathan Glazer's debut feature film, *Sexy Beast*.

In the film, Ray is Gary 'Gal' Dove, a retired London con contentedly enjoying a new life sunning himself in the delicious heat of Spain. Alongside his adoring sexy wife, and ex-porn star, Deedee, played by Amanda Redman, his loyal pool-boy Enrique (Álvaro Monje) and his long-time friends Aitch (Cavan Kendall) and Jackie (Julianne White), he's living out his days in lovely suntanned, calorific glee. It's a blissful, simple existence that he and Deedee have worked and properly suffered for. That's why Aitch's news of the arrival of Don 'Malky' Logan (Ben Kingsley), a man clearly from their long-buried pasts, is met with sheer dread. He wants something from Gal, but no one is sure what. But it soon becomes clear. He wants Gal to return to London for one last job, an elaborate bank robbery which involves breaking into a safety deposit vault through the swimming pool of the neighbouring Turkish steam rooms.

The idea to turn *Sexy Beast* into a movie was the brainchild of Glazer after he met writers Louis Mellis and David Scinto on a project which subsequently fell through. So instead, says Glazer, 'We decided to continue to collaborate as we had similar sensibilities about films and what we felt was missing in the business today. They gave me projects which they had originally written as stage plays.' And it was in this haphazard fashion that he discovered *Sexy Beast*. The whole thing blew him away. 'It appealed to me because it has a very simple plot dynamic, but is very powerful and visceral, almost operatic in style. I could share their love of these characters. They also take a lot of risks in their work, because they are not slaves to structure, and I think great stuff can come from that.'

One of the attractions of the film to Glazer, though, whose then recent experience in commercials and pop-music promos had honed his visual skills, was to work on a piece driven by character. 'I was more interested in working in an area which I was weak in, and to collaborate with the writers. Their stage directions are so specific, and illustrate the particular way they see the world they are writing about, so that I could use them as maps.'

Even though Glazer admits that *Sexy Beast* is hard to categorise, he describes it as a very simple story about the redemptive power of love. It is set in the world of London gangsters. 'The gangster genre creates its own autonomous society, operating on loyalties and extremes. Shakespearean in a way.'

Another figure who helped bring *Sexy Beast* to the screen was producer Jeremy Thomas. By then, he had already made his mark in finding some of the most exciting directors of international cinema including Bernardo Bertolucci, Nicolas Roeg and David Cronenberg. When *Sexy Beast* came up, he was again on the look-out for new directorial talent. 'I had been aware of Jonathan Glazer's work as a director for some time and was pleased to be approached when he was ready to make his first feature film,' says Thomas. 'This is the first time in many years that I have been so excited by a script and a first-time director.' On top of that he had seen Glazer's previous work that had included groundbreaking videos for Jamiroquai and Radiohead, and had been impressed by what he saw. He was convinced that Glazer would become a major figure in world cinema in years to come: 'I recognised that Jonathan has an original voice and a strong visual sense which will translate to feature film.' He, therefore, had no qualms about the director being able to sustain his story-telling with original visual flair.

Thomas also applauded the script by Mellis and Scinto, as a fresh and original work. 'It's in the gangster-movie genre but with an original twist. Here in Britain we have a tradition of gangster movies, with such beacons as *Get Carter* and *Performance*, both of which gave the audience something they hadn't seen before, as this does. It's overwhelmingly a love story, set in the gangster world, but with a different vernacular and different approach. Mellis and Scinto are talented writers, whose plot and dialogue are totally innovative.'

Glazer agrees. 'Jeremy has an extraordinary pedigree, and has eclectic tastes, so he was happy that we wanted to create a film which, although British, has a European flavour and wide appeal.'

Even so, for the Spanish line and co-producer Denise O'Dell, the script threw up one major location problem, and that was finding a villa on a hillside for the opening scene of the film, where a boulder would be likely to roll down the hill and damage a swimming pool. It probably didn't help that the script was set on the Costa del Sol, the traditional early-retirement home of choice for those Britons who may have made their cash in less conventional ways. The production team searched the coast at Marbella, Malaga and as far north as Cadiz. They initially found nothing because, as O'Dell points out, most people wouldn't build a villa in such a dangerous position, so she began looking around Almeria.

She knew the area well, and having had over 30 years' experience of living and shooting in Spain, and knowing that David Lean had been the first filmmaker to use the area in *Lawrence of Arabia*, it seemed a perfect location to scout. Even if Lean's epic hadn't made it famous, then Clint Eastwood's trilogy of spaghetti 'Dollar' westerns probably did. Not only that, but O'Dell herself was involved in filming sequences for *Indiana Jones and the Last Crusade* on the rugged landscape. 'It's the wildest in Spain, and lends itself to being shot as a desert location, some of which we have used for Gal's dreamscapes.'

The production team eventually found Gal's villa, an architect's home, perched high above the perfect beach cove in the tiny village of Agua Amarga, some 30 miles east of Almeria. 'Perhaps only an architect would build on the site of an old coal mine,' O'Dell jokes. 'On the side of a hill where there is a very real possibility of rocks tumbling down a hillside on to his property.'

Accommodating the cast and crew was not such a nightmare as it had been to find the location. Most stayed in the village which, out of the summer season, has a population of only 300 people. As Thomas confirmed, 'When you are working on location, you are at the mercy of certain outside forces, like the weather, and filming becomes a very intense experience. Also, by giving up some degree of control, you are leaving a door open and very often something unexpected enters the equation, enhancing the final film.'

Certainly, Glazer wanted the locations for the Dove's surroundings to be as anonymous and simple as possible. 'For the first two-thirds of the film, we don't show the landscape for the sake of it. It's all about how the characters react to each other. It's also a bleached place that Don Logan [Ben Kingsley's character] would hate and want to smash to bits.'

The title of the film has raised some questions. Whenever Glazer is asked about who the *Sexy Beast* is, he explains that the answer is really in the characters. 'All of their mistakes are sexually driven. It's a cradle for the whole film, it's also impressionistic and a bit brazen.'

Making *Sexy Beast*, Glazer admits, was a major step, and to a degree he had thrown himself in at the deep end. After years of making commercials and music promos, jumping straight to feature films was indeed a brave jump. 'In a pop promo, for instance, you already have the cast, the band and the script, the song, and the director's job is to illustrate this as best he can. The sheer momentum of making a film, the marathon involved, is a lesson. There's value in each discipline. My aim is to make a film that people want to see, not just something to show in an art house to seven of my friends. In Britain we are so reserved in our tastes. We can only approach passion in films from a distance. I want to get back to a cinema that I admire. The cinema of the great passionate filmmakers who give you a whole new dreamscape.'

He also wanted to find the perfect cast and, when the casting process began, he already knew that he wanted Ray to play the lead role of Gal, the criminal who has found his own paradise in Spain. 'Even though Ray's character is a criminal, I wanted him to play against that type, to strip away his macho side and show the vulnerability of Gal.'

Fortunately for Glazer, Ray had no qualms about accepting the role. 'It's one of the few scripts I've read where you shouldn't change a single word. Usually, I'm known as Ray "Paraphrase" Winstone, but with this dialogue the language is so particular, that, like Shakespeare, if you alter it, the whole scene can play differently, going off in the wrong direction. The writers have caught the poetry of a certain kind of London language.'

Ray, however, describes his character as a good guy, but with weaknesses. It is after all, one of the few films in which Ray was playing the antagonised rather than the antagonist. 'In playing a role, I like to find the good in the bad guy and the weakness in the good guy. That's what is interesting for an audience, and for me. There are moments in the story when Gal should be sorting things out but he goes the wrong way about it.' Having grown up in London's East End, it probably won't be much of a surprise that Ray has actually met people like those portrayed in the script. 'Gal loves his wife, and won't risk getting caught again because they would be separated. I've known guys who have given up dodgy work because they realise they don't want to spend years inside, away from the family.'

Working with Glazer, for Ray, was simply an added bonus to what he considered a wonderful script. He had nothing but praise for the director's talent. 'He knows how he wants to shoot the scene, but will let you rehearse it the way you want to do it, then somehow manoeuvres the actors to work with the camera where he wants it to be. He has the gift of being able to communicate his vision to the actors, which not all directors can manage.'

To Ray, *Sexy Beast* is a film with three distinctive moods. 'Part one, where Gal is at home in Spain, is bright and happy, like an Elvis movie on the surface, but with skeletons in the cupboard, lurking in Gal's subconscious. Part two, after Don appears, is almost a horror movie, then part three moves into the territory of a sixties London gangster movie, where a dark job is taking place. The film has a pace and a widescreen Hollywood look to it, like the movies you saw when you were young.' Playing the romantic hero was an unaccustomed pleasure for him. A different kind of role. 'Usually, I get to punch the geezer, not kiss the girl.'

Thomas also agreed with Glazer, 'Ray's great talent is to take a character from the same geographical background as himself, and delineate between Ray the man and Gal the character. That's why an audience finds him so convincing and compelling, because he alone knows where that line is drawn.'

To cast the role of Don Logan, Gal's nemesis, Glazer's final choice from the cream of British actors was Ben Kingsley. 'I knew we needed a great actor, to pitch against Ray as Gal. Kingsley is acclaimed internationally for his work, but has never been associated with any "Brit-pop cinema gang", and, as soon as I met him, I knew he was the perfect choice. Working with Ben is like driving a Rolls-Royce. He doesn't shrink from his responsibilities but he realises that you have to throw most of it away, and resist the temptation to try to make the scenes dramatic. The combination of Ray's more method approach and Ben's classical training works on screen.'

Kingsley agrees, but he also compares his work as an actor to that of a portrait painter. 'I approach my work in a clear and practical way, and accept a role if I am curious about the man, and want to know more and want to tell his story. Don Logan intrigued me. I liked his purity, his singularity in being welded to his mission to put together a team for a big heist.' But, above all, Kingsley saw Logan as a man on a professional assignment who could equally and easily be working for the police or the SAS, pointing out that successful police officers and successful criminals have one thing in common. Both have very good imaginations. As an actor, says Kingsley, 'It is important to stick to one agenda, presenting your character without judging or moralising. That's something the audience must be allowed to do. And the task of the director is to assemble these pure colours into a picture on screen that makes the eyes dance.'

Like Ray, Kingsley also praised Glazer for his talent. 'Jonathan has the strength and clarity of overall vision to keep the characters on their own narrow tightrope. He has a boundless curiosity to explore the human condition.' And again, like Ray, he was attracted to the writing of the script: 'It is unique in structure, relying, like Beckett and Pinter, on the rhythm of words, with each main character having a totally different rhythm. The level of mythology is so dense and explosive that it sets the script apart.'

The casting of heist boss Teddy Bass came easily. Almost

from the first draft, Glazer had envisaged Ian McShane in the role. 'The spine of the film is the trinity of Gal and Don, in opposite corners, with Teddy Bass in the middle.' Teddy Bass is the dark charismatic centre of the film, the immaculate leader from whom all power emanates. Watching *Lovejoy*, McShane's hugely successful television series in which he plays the title role, a loveable-rogue antique dealer, Glazer's enjoyment came from McShane's performance. 'Ian was so obviously playing against the story, which gave the show an edge.' He also felt that British cinema has overlooked McShane in recent years, because of his television success. The actor points out that, in his first film role, *The Wild and the Willing*, he was directed by Ralph Thomas, father of producer Jeremy Thomas, and that he made two British gangster movies in the 70s, namely *Sitting Target* with Oliver Reed and *Villain* with Richard Burton.

Another to rave about the script was Amanda Redman. 'Simply one of the best pieces of writing I have read in years. It's poetic writing, with a plot that is exciting, so it's not an art movie.' To Redman, the script is a beautiful love story that happens to be set in the world of gangsters. For her, everything that happens is as a result of Gal and Deedee, and their friends Jackie and Aitch, trying to protect their love. 'It's a fairy story – good versus evil. This couple, who each have a past that the other knows all about, have set each other free. Their love is unconditional, and they don't have children, so everything is channelled into the relationship. Then Don, the outsider, the psychopath, arrives and everything changes; but they are prepared to kill for each other.' Redman relishes the chance to play a strong woman, particularly in such a male-dominated genre, and a woman who is the equal of her man.

Having Redman play his wife was another added bonus for Ray. She is his favourite actress that he has ever starred alongside. If you had to cast someone to be a real-life wife to Ray in a movie, it would have to be her. 'She's one of the finest actors we've got. Probably in the world. I can't believe she isn't doing more films. I mean, *Sexy Beast* was acclaimed. I don't know why things didn't take off for her.' But, then again, it is widely considered that it is much harder for women to get roles in their forties than it is for men. Not that Ray would entirely agree. If anything, the suggestion baffles him. 'Oh, I thought there were a lot of good women in their twenties and a lot of good older ones, so in the middle group you'd have thought that would be good for her. She's got the most amazing eyes you've ever seen, Amanda has. I suppose there's not that much being written for them.'

Not only that, but Redman is also a family friend. When Ray's eldest daughter Lois had started her teenage rebellion and dropped out of an art course at Southgate College, because she was, as she says 'all over the shop', she was taken under the wing of Redman, who gave her a place at her Artists Theatre School in Ealing, West London. 'It helped me through a tough time,' she says, 'but I wasn't quite ready for it. I was so undisciplined.'

Ray's memory of the shoot in Spain, he says, is that it was good fun. 'We were in a national park, on the coast in a beautiful village.' The preparation wasn't bad either. 'My rehearsing was lying on a beach for two weeks, eating and drinking because I had to put on two stone. Fantastic.' But then Ray isn't the kind of actor who likes to have things too worked out before he turns up on the set. 'I might get it all wrong, and then I'd have wasted all that energy. I've heard of people going to work in factories for nine months to get into a part. If I'd wanted to work in a factory, I'd have done it as a job.'

Good acting is, he says, all about truth, and that comes from digging deep into yourself. 'We've all got that nasty little fucker in us somewhere.' And what is acting, but making the unbelievable believable. 'We've all got this dark side,' he says, 'but we all choose how far to take it, you know? In *Sexy Beast*, Ben Kingsley had to play a really nasty gangster and I was thinking, "This can't be right – he's Gandhi." But he was great and he said to me, "This is me, this is a part of me." So I suppose we all dig deep.'

Not quite so unbelievable was what Elaine thought when she first saw Ray as he appeared in the opening scenes of the film. 'Everyone out there wears these surfing trunks and I was in those Speedos with my dong hanging out and she kept saying, "You can't wear those!"'

When *Empire* magazine caught up with him, there were just ten days of shooting left in Spain and there appeared to be a lot of pressure placed on everyone's shoulders. Not least of all on Ray himself, when, on one of those ten days, he had five pages of dialogue to commit to film, and was rehearsing his lines into Glazer's ear in a sinister whisper. It was, apparently, an unsettling sight.

Off set, though, Kingsley kept himself pretty much to himself, whereas Ray, whose life motto is 'when in doubt, give it a clout', had been partying long into the night after shooting wrapped and still, quite impressively, made it into work the next day on time.

But, three weeks later, in a notably chillier trailer parked up outside the diver-training water tank just off the M25 in Waltham Cross, Ray was filming the underwater climax of the film, in which his character drills away in the tunnel of a Turkish bath that has a subterranean access to the bank vault that he and his fellow characters are about to break into. The tank may have been familiar to filmgoers as it had been used in any number of cinema's other sub-aquatic scenes, including the one in *Trainspotting* where Ewan McGregor disappears down the most disgusting lavatory in Scotland. But, by the time *Empire* journalist Jasper Rees arrived on the set, Ray had just hoicked himself up the ladder, out of the pool and into a deep-pile dressing gown, lit up a B&H and lovingly reflected on how great the Spanish leg of the shoot was.

All the same, it was pretty clear to Rees, and other journalists that Ray spoke to at the time, that he had revelled in portraying the vulnerability of Gary Dove as the character is reluctantly dragged back into his criminal past and wrenched away from his beloved Deedee.

'That was the thing that appealed to me,' he states. 'Normally Ben Kingsley would've played Gal and I would have played Don. I'd have been the psychopath, the loonpot. I love the weaknesses and the strengths of Gal. It's totally different to the way I'd play it. If someone came and threatened my family, it'd be a different kettle of fish. But then you start getting into it and understanding the power of what Don is – he's the fucking devil.'

In its final cut, *Sexy Beast* is a hyper-stylish proposition offering the visual pyrotechnics to be expected from someone with Glazer's background and simply sterling performances from Ray as Gal and Kingsley as the demonic, insanely intense Logan. Better still, it manages to plant a distinct flag in increasingly overpopulated terrain. Glazer admits that he grew twitchier with every month the film spent in post-production as yet another Brit gangster film was released.

'Oh yes, of course,' he confessed, 18 months on from the Spanish shoot, ''Cause you can do nothing about the timing of things. The film took so long in post-production and you saw the British public growing progressively more and more bored of British gangster films. But we were always at least confident in that the film was a psychodrama which really could take place in the court of King Arthur if it had to. It's more of a character duel, really. It's a film for me that happens within the genre, rather than about the genre. That's the key.'

The film also led to Ray reflecting on some of his favourite places he had visited, whether with a film crew or as a tourist. 'I remember when I was a kid, I saw pictures of the Maldives, you know, palm trees on a beach, and I said, "I'm gonna go there. I don't care how I get there, but I'm gonna go there." And then I got a cheque from a job I did and I said, "Right, we're going." It lived up to every expectation. It was just amazing. The sea is like turquoise glass. It is the eighth wonder of the world. It's the Hanging Gardens of Babylon. It's everything. And it's one of those places I know I'll go back to again and again and again.

'The islanders are fantastic. They get a pittance and you're told not to tip 'em by the tour company. Don't spoil 'em. We went with Gary Oldman's sister, Mo, and her husband, Jim, and this little guy who was looking after us, we each gave him £100. And I suppose it's like a year's wages, but he can send his kid off to school now, and that's not us being good or anything, it's just a thing you do. I mean this guy really looked after us. We used to go out on boat trips in this *dhoni* – that's what they call it – and there are loads of islands that are deserted, and he'd take the family out for the day to this deserted island. And he'd catch fish and cook them for us – there on the beach.

'You could walk out for miles, it seemed, up to your waist. I remember standing there and I could hear this noise behind me. Whoosh. I turned round and this thing, this marlin or swordfish, whatever it was, dived out of the water behind me and straight over the reef. Now it's one thing seeing that on telly, but seeing it for real... And I turned round and realised that nobody else had seen it and I was gutted, because you want to share it. It was fantastic... unbelievable.

'Another time, I was snorkelling with the kids and this shark came in. A little shark, about as tall as my youngest, swimming about. And I went over to the kids and – it's amazing how calm you become – I put them behind me. Someone else might have put them in front, I suppose. But we just watched this shark circle around us, about a hundred yards away. Then away it went. It was an experience I will remember and treasure for the rest of my life. It was as it should be. I shall go back there. I want to do a shoot there. I keep coming up with these story ideas and they're all set in the Maldives, but so far I haven't been able to get anyone interested.

'But one of my favourite holidays was in Newquay. There's a hotel called the Atlantic. I went with my family and my mate Karl Howman – you know *Brush Strokes*, *Babes in the Wood* and all that. And he'd taken his family and we were in a 100mph gale. This hotel was run by, well, they were fabulous people, but it was a bit like a cross between Fawlty Towers and the Addams Family. You went in the bathroom and it was so big and draughty you could fly a kite. There was always some event going on in the evening, like a fashion show – you can imagine what a fashion show in Newquay was like – and old-time singers. It was the funniest holiday I've ever had. I never stopped laughing from the minute we got there.

'I love Scotland as well. A couple of years ago, at New Year, a few of us rented the west wing of this big old house in Tarbert, on the west coast. On New Year's Eve, just before midnight, the door opened and four people walked in. It turned out to be Lord Irvine's son and all that mob. They were really good people, a bit "chappy" – not like the Labour party you'd expect, but then that was before the Labour party got in.

'We sold the cars once, to go to Florida. We were all skint. But it was more important to get away than to have a car. You can always buy another car when you come home. We had four weeks over Christmas and New Year. It was just something I wanted to do… the idea of having Christmas dinner and a Christmas tree round the pool. Florida was one of the best places for fishing. I'm not a fisherman really, but we chartered a boat and we caught 120 fish. There were these two puffer fish we called the Dangerous Brothers.

'They used to come up to the top of the water and we'd catch one, and the other one would keep following us. So we'd put the first one back and then we'd catch the other one. And it went on like this. We kept putting them back, but every time we caught one of them you could see his mate getting the hump. It was almost like they should have had dark glasses and porkpie hats. I always think it's better to rent a villa or a house. In a hotel, you've got to worry about what everyone else thinks or whether you're being too loud in the bar and upsetting someone. I like to be a little bit loud when I go away. As you can imagine.

'I love architecture and Barcelona's one of my favourite cities. That is one great city. I love New York, too. I like to go round places like Harlem and the Bronx. I just put an old coat on and have a walk about. I want to see the real places. I don't just want to see where the holidaymakers go. In LA, I walked around Watts. Probably quite dangerous. I had a walk down the Falls Road, in Belfast, about eight years ago. I must have been completely insane. But I want to see a city for what it is.

'There are places I would never have gone to if I hadn't been an actor, like Agua Amarga, where we filmed *Sexy Beast*. There were times when I really got the hump with Spain. I was going to Puerto Banus quite a bit and it's like Bethnal Green in the sun. But Agua Amarga is in a national park, a little village set right by the sea. It was absolutely stunning. There's all these places and they're just there for everyone to see. I've even taken my kids out of school to go on holiday, because I think it's that important. They can speak French and some German, and I'm really pleased about that. I only speak English... and I even have a bit of trouble with that.'

Even so, and despite the location being like a travelogue of sea, sun and exotic scenery to die for, there were some who thought that *Sexy Beast* – on its release in January 2001 – was nothing more than an excuse for Ray to play a gangster in yet another of his gangster movies. But that wasn't strictly true. As Ray points out, 'There's this concept that I play gangsters all the time, but I don't. I've only played one once, in *Love, Honour and Obey* [in 2000]. In *Face*, I was a thief, and that's a different breed of person altogether. One's an extortionist and one's a thief, and I know there don't sound a lot of difference, but there is. A thief ain't necessarily a violent man. And I'm not a gangster in this – I'm a thief. The gangster is Ben.'

CHAPTER 10

Heroes and Villains

Ray's idea of playing a gangster in *Love, Honour and Obey* wasn't quite what one would have expected. And that was largely down to the script. As each of the main characters' first names match their real-life names (this did not apply to minor characters), and as the directing team of Dominic Anciano and Ray Burdis also wrote and produced it with small cameos for themselves, the movie was much more of a film to be enjoyed than critiqued. Certainly, no one was trying to create grand cinema. And in many ways the film was more like a home video that some kids cooked up in their backyard, with a fly-by-the-seat-of-your-pants hand-held camera.

While video seeks to chronicle a family's life, it is also used to reflect and even laugh at the past. There are several sections of the film that laugh at the standard mob movie. Ray's character, Ray, the boss of the South-London mob, doesn't want to fight with his North-London counterparts; he wants to be friends and doesn't feel the urge to take over the whole shebang, which is almost unique for the gangster-movie genre. There's even a scene in which his group is having a shootout with the other side from behind parked cars, a situation abated when Ray breaks into uncontrollable laughter.

As one online reviewer commented, 'It is almost as if the film sets out to rub out the layers of what it's like to be part of a "family" imposed by its predecessors. Each member of the group is almost normal, with wife and kids and homes in suburbia. The film also makes use of simple humorous details. Before one heist, each member of Ray's group passes around Viagra to try out its effects. One of them brags about pleasing his woman for four hours, so they all jump on the bandwagon. Normally, this would lead to a certain amount of cheesiness, but not here. It gets a laugh instead. While they are pulling off their stunt, each has a boner, and their victim ends up more scared of being raped than losing his precious diamonds.'

In fact, it was while shooting that particular scene that Ray's own real sex life got a boost after he swallowed the pill rather than holding it in his mouth until the directors could shout 'cut'. He laughs at the memory. Yeah, 'I actually swallowed my tablet by mistake; I think I'm the first guy to take Viagra on screen. It gave me a funny feeling, but I was all right for days after.' And Elaine certainly wasn't complaining about Ray's new potency. 'She loved it. She had a smile on her face for weeks.'

Despite the notoriety of the cast and crew, who, interestingly enough, had all worked together on another of Ray's films, *Final Cut*, the film was barely marketed and there are still many to this day that have never heard of it. It seemed as though the production team was more interested in playing with their equipment rather than building acclaim. The fact that *Love, Honour and Obey* is not trying to be anything stunning, but instead comes across as two hours of simple fun and entertainment, is in itself a salute to being creative.

Everyone who worked on the film adored the freedom of the production. Working to a basic script, Anciano and Burdis allowed the cast free rein to act out scenes within the allotted framework in terms of dialogue. This is a method much enjoyed by Jude Law. 'Fifty per cent of it is us,' he says, 'fifty per cent is character. What's amazing is that we've out-Mike Leighed Mike Leigh. People think Mike Leigh is improvised, but it's very stylised.'

The movie was narrated by Angelina Jolie's first husband, Jonny Lee Miller, whose character works in a dead-end job as a courier but dreams of a more glamorous lifestyle – one that could be made possible by convincing his old school friend Jude Law to let him join the notorious North-London mob, run by Jude's uncle Ray, the biggest gangster in London. Ray, whose obsession with karaoke is legendary, is not initially convinced but eventually relents. The character is not your run-of-the-mill tough guy, and it was this untypical take that attracted Ray to the role.

'I'm not playing the clichéd film gangster with the overcoat around his shoulders, puffing cigars, winding the car window down slowly – none of that. I'm not saying all films should be made like this, but it'd be great to do one of these a year. Ray and Dom can have me back any time.'

The credit-card scam that is Jonny's introduction to the North-London mob works a treat, and he is initially happy with his newfound life in the 'fast lane'. The 'family' settles back into its usual daily routine of low-level, non-violent crime and Ray and his soap-star girlfriend, played by Sadie Frost, set about planning their wedding. Meanwhile, Anciano and Burdis, who are the gang's bouncers, try to sort out matters rather closer to the heart, which is Burdis's problem with impotency.

His wife Kathy (Burke) is feeling redundant as a woman; she is in her mid-thirties and still childless – a problem not helped by Burdis's impotence. Anciano and Maureen, played by Denise Van Outen, suggest sex toys could be the key to the problem and, in a hilarious X-rated scene, Maureen suggests ways in which Kathy could solve Ray's problem by demonstrating – much to Kathy's disgust – her expert 'oral' technique on an oversized cucumber.

Jonny, frustrated by the North-London gang's lack of interest in 'real' crime, sparks a gang war with the South-London mob by stealing their secret stash of coke. The South Londoners are headed by Sean, played by Sean Pertwee, for whom this was his first experience of working with Anciano and Burdis. And, although he was initially dubious about the process, he now has all the zeal of a convert. 'It's incredible,' he says. 'They latch on to traits that you as a person maybe aren't too aware of, then pull them out of you. It's made me fall in love with this job again because, for the first time in ages, I really feel like I'm flying by the seat of my pants. You show up on set not quite knowing what's going to happen, and that's extraordinarily liberating.'

In the film, peace is eventually reinstated between the rival gangs – a process shown through a series of very funny sketches. The 'Jonny' problem is resolved and equilibrium restored, resulting in the inevitable return to harmony, as Ray invites both sets of hoodlums to get back to what they really enjoy in life – and that is karaoke.

The movie is peppered with vignettes of the various characters performing their favourite songs, and we are treated to the delights of British actors exposing a side of themselves hitherto unknown. 'We discovered that all the cast have great voices,' says Burdis, who dresses up as an Elvis clone for his duet with Kathy. 'We all sing the title song, which is the greatest song ever written,' says Anciano. 'It's called "Avenues and Alleyways". We do a line each, like that "Perfect Day" video that the BBC did.'

For Anciano and Burdis, however, the best comedy is found in the most unlikely places. 'We're not interested in people in funny situations, but how people are genuinely funny in the most terrible situations. That's more realistic,' notes Anciano. 'Real life is much funnier than comedy.'

The karaoke singing that Ray is seen performing along with the other cast members over the opening credits of the film must have been a dream come true. Especially for Ray. 'I'd love to be a singer more than anything else in the world but my balls dropped and that was it!' If you asked Ray whether he had ever considered a singing career, he would say 'no': 'Have you heard me? You tell me. I don't think so. I do lots of karaoke when I'm out. I like to sing a bit of Frank Sinatra. My two favourite renditions are "Summer Wind" and "I've Got You Under My Skin". Then I go into a bit of Dean Martin and Harry Connick Jr. My family have usually left the room by then! Once I've got the microphone I don't want to give it up. But I think everyone's like that.'

Not that Ray would be doing any singing in his next role, as Vince Dodds, in Fred Schepisi's *Last Orders*, a movie based on Graham Swift's prize-winning novel. The story begins shortly after Jack Dodds (Michael Caine) has died, and his friends Ray (Bob Hoskins), Lenny (David Hemmings) and Vic (Tom Courtenay) are fulfilling his wishes by taking his ashes from South London to Margate, to scatter them off the pier of his favourite seaside resort. They enlist Jack's car-dealer son, Vince, played by Ray, to make the drive in a spacious Mercedes, wherein they swap the memories that become the spine of the film.

As Matthew Bond noted in his review in the *Mail on Sunday*, it was not what you would call a commercial film, 'but in its own strangely old-fashioned way, it is an interesting and thought-provoking-picture about love in all its many forms and the inevitable passing of not just time, but lifetimes. It feels like a throwback to the Sixties. It may be set in the late Eighties but it's a world where men still wear porkpie hats; fireplaces have brown tile surrounds, and Helen Mirren sits reflectively by the Thames with no makeup on and, apparently, a tea-cosy on her head.'

She is Amy, Jack's wife, who has decided not to join in the pilgrimage to Margate, instead she's set out on a very significant journey of her own, a visit to their mentally handicapped daughter June.

The road trip begins from the Coach and Horses pub, where Ray, Vic and Lenny have gathered to raise a glass to Jack for the last time and brace themselves for the journey that lies ahead. In a series of flashbacks, the emotional mystery unfolds as they try to come to terms with Jack's death by reliving their life with him – the war, the children, the affairs, the good times and the bad. Stopping along the way to pay tribute to Jack in the way he'd most appreciate it – in a pub – tension eventually builds to boiling point between Lenny and Vince when it's revealed that Vince made Lenny's daughter, Sally, pregnant and then ran off to the army.

Vince's anger is exacerbated by the painful recollection of Jack revealing he wasn't his real father and learning that Amy rescued him from a burning house when his own parents were killed during a bombing raid. Vince takes a detour, to Wick's Farm, where he and Lenny fight it out in the middle of the field, where ironically Jack and Amy first met before the war.

With a requisite stop at Canterbury Cathedral, Ray's mind is elsewhere. He's always secretly loved Amy ever since Jack first showed him a black-and-white photo of her in his wallet during their army days in Egypt. For six weeks, Ray and Amy had an affair. Ray understood her and sympathised with her about June, where Jack failed to, all of which comes spilling out on the road to Margate.

Filming of *Last Orders* began on 18 October 2000 and was shot over nine weeks in what was an unpredictable winter in Britain. Because the story spanned from the World War II right up to the 1980s, the structure of the film required numerous flashbacks, in order to reveal a little more about details in the lives of each of the principal characters. Scenes were shot with actors playing young versions of Jack, Ray, Amy, Vic, Lenny and Vince so a pre-shoot period was worked into the filming schedule in order to capture a summer Kent for hop-picking scenes.

On location, Peckham and Bermondsey in the heart of Southeast London were commandeered for scenes in the Coach and Horses pub, Dodds Butchers and Vic's funeral parlour. In the East End, Smithfield Market was also used, which was by now becoming a very familiar filming location for Ray. Other locations included Canterbury Cathedral, the historical Chatham War Memorial, Eastbourne, the pier in Margate and hop fields in Kent. A disused warehouse in Peckham was transformed into a temporary studio where sets were built for the interior of Jack and Amy's home and Ray's flat.

It was very much a London film, and something close to the hearts of the cast. 'It's wonderful. Working in London is terrific,' recalled Bob Hoskins. 'I get to go home every night! I've been working in Sarawak, Poland, Sarajevo and the Philippines, so working in London's a treat. It's a holiday. I loved every minute of working on this film, and working with such amazing actors; you're not just a prop like in some of these big action movies, it's a chance to really get your teeth into something.'

Michael Caine agreed, especially about the shooting of the film in Peckham. Four hundred yards down the road from where he was filming was Wilson's Grammar School, the school which he attended as a boy. 'I've gone full circle. From Hollywood, the bright lights and the Academy Awards, I'm back in Peckham after 40 years in the movies. It's funny.'

But, for Ray, crossing into South-London territory, from his East End roots was something of an alien experience. 'Ray might say you need a visa to cross in to South London,' laughed co-star David Hemmings.

But, according to Ray, although 'I'm an East End boy, I think it could be based anywhere in the world, families and friends are the same everywhere.'

Helen Mirren continues: 'It would be difficult to do this on the backlot at Warner Bros in Los Angeles, that's for sure. It's much better to be here in Peckham. You know, the whole process is to do with imaginatively putting yourself somewhere, so it's very important that the environment is authentic. It's nice doing a film in London about London. I haven't done that too often. The people who come from this part of the world know that really well; they recognise those sorts of places as being very special. I've always felt that British filmmaking is better when it does something truthful and authentic to itself. *The Full Monty* is a perfect example and many other films back through history of British filmmaking. Ironically, that's when they find an audience abroad.

'We've all been in the industry for a long time, and we've all had a level of success as actors and we're all still here. There's a real level of comfort with who people are. There are either no egos or a lot of egos to balance each other out, I'm not quite sure which it is. I mean, I was hugged by Ray which was fabulous, I got hugged by Michael and then I get hugged by Bob.'

Ray was equally complimentary about his fellow stars. 'Helen plays my mum, so I'm quite a lucky boy. I've always been brought up with lots of uncles but you should see the uncles I've got here – Bob Hoskins, David Hemmings, Tom Courtenay. I remember as a kid watching Tom, David, then later Bob, in some of my favourite films. Michael Caine, of course, says Ray, 'opened the door for us, when you think of *Alfie*. Yet in *Zulu* he was the posh one. But there he is, this bloke from South London who worked in the meat market. Even if you were a kid from Liverpool, that made a difference. It was like me watching Albert Finney in *Saturday Night and Sunday Morning* or Richard Harris in *This Sporting Life*; they were geezers like us suddenly making films. And, where I came from, if you thought of becoming an actor, if you had any heroes, they were it. So to be playing opposite them is quite daunting at times. These were people

I watched as a kid. The people who made me want to become an actor. I thought, "Fuckin' hell, this is fantastic."'

But, of course, it could have gone the other way. What if, when Ray got on to the set for the first time, he found that they were all, as he puts it, 'wankers', and hadn't lived up to his expectations. 'They're all my heroes and it would have been so awful if I'd have been disappointed by any of them. But they were all smashing. I loved them all to bits. I wasn't intimidated because it's not their style to make anyone feel like that. I had all these little drinks, little talks, with Michael Caine. Blinding. And David Hemmings. Great man. Don't take no shit. I love him.'

Though a 'man's' film, with a largely male cast, *Last Orders* is far removed from British films such as *Lock, Stock and Two Smoking Barrels*, which was criticised by some as an inaccurate representation of East End gangster life.

Ray agrees. 'The thing you can say about director Guy Ritchie is that he knows how to sell his films. Vinnie Jones was blinding in it and the posh kids were great, but, no, it wasn't realistic. But you can say that about a million films and, yes, *Nil by Mouth*, for example, was very realistic, but you wouldn't want to see that sort of movie every day, otherwise you'd go mad. *Lock, Stock* was entertaining, and there's nothing wrong with that.'

Last Orders remains one of Ray's favourite films, and perhaps it's not surprising when he got to act with some real 'proper geezers', as he puts it. In fact, he was in acting heaven. 'We did the journey, from Bermondsey in South London to Margate, and we just told stories, and some of these guys' stories were fantastic. Loved that film, but it just wasn't sold properly in Britain and that really upset me.'

Overall, though, 'it was nice to watch myself in a film

where I wasn't shooting, stabbing or hitting someone. I do have a little scuffle with David's character in one scene, but it's a pathetic, sad little fight really.' What he was probably pleased about, though, more than anything, was that he proved once and for all that he could act with more than his fists.

Aside from working with some of his favourite actors, the film also offered him the chance to work alongside his eldest daughter, Lois, who played his on-screen daughter in what was her first feature-film debut. But, according to Ray, it was a nightmare. She was only in one scene, but she still made an impact on her entrance that no one would forget in a hurry. Tottering around in a 'slapper's outfit' including a mini micro-dress and leopard-skin belt, Lois remembers her dad couldn't stop 'gawping' at her. Probably from shock. 'He forgot his lines and couldn't concentrate. But I felt really confident for the first time. I mean,' she concludes, 'I came across as a sexual person, which is what I am.'

In the scene, Ray had to throw the keys to her, 'and when I did it she said, "Dad, you don't throw keys like that." She was right. I was looking after her so much I couldn't think about what I was supposed to be doing. When she first came on set I thought I wouldn't tell anyone that she was my daughter, then you'd see all the crew leering, and I'd say, "That's my daughter!" They'd say, "Ray, we didn't know!" "Well, you know now." Complete nightmare! But she was blinding, that was the first thing she'd ever done.'

Even though the filming itself got a little tense at times, due to the tight schedule that had to be kept to, making the film, Ray says, was one of the best experiences he's ever had on a movie. One of the fun times, as he calls them, was when they were filming in Margate. 'Some youngsters were coming up and asking me for my autograph. There I was with all this mob and they were asking me for my autograph, and Tom [Courtenay], who was always winding me up, had this mac on and a cap and he slid up behind these kids, who were waiting for me and said, "I played Lear, you know!"'

Even though the film was in development for three years, Ray, like most of the critics, found the film 'very funny and very sad, and I like that. It's good if you can laugh and cry at the same time.' But much of that was down to American producer Elisabeth Robinson. She was working with director Fred Schepisi prepping a feature film based on the story of *Don Quixote* in 1997, when she brought Graham Swift's *Last Orders* to his attention.

Robinson said of her choice of Schepisi for the role, 'Primarily, I thought he'd be right for it, based on his previous work, particularly *Six Degrees of Separation*. Like that film, *Last Orders* is about a very particular place, but a universal experience and needed to be told with subtlety and elegance, which I believe Fred does better than anyone.'

So, in the autumn of 1997, Schepisi and Robinson persuaded Graham Swift to allow them to acquire the rights to adapt his Booker prize-winning novel for the screen. Swift was apparently impressed by three short-term options created by Robinson. It was music to his ears, as countless adaptations of various other best-selling works have been left in limbo for years, much to the frustration of the authors. One such adaptation was Susanna Kaysen's *Girl, Interrupted* which took nine years to get into production after it had been optioned by Columbia Pictures.

Once Schepisi confirmed he would write and direct the film of *Last Orders*, a three-year option was secured from Swift on the understanding that each of the options could be renewed unless several major elements were in place. This galvanised everyone into progress and the initial option was taken out for six months.

By September 1997, Schepisi set about the daunting task of adapting a book that covered 40 years of four men's lives. With a first draft written by the following February, Schepisi had meetings with potential cast members that culminated in commitments from Caine, Courtenay, Hoskins and Ray, enabling the next one-year option to come into play.

By early 1999, it was time to raise the finance in order to fulfil the final option. Although Robinson was an accomplished film executive in the States, she needed a British collaborator to assist her with financing if the film was to be shot in the UK. As Helen Mirren said, it was not the sort of film that could be made on a Hollywood studio backlot. Familiar with his history and reputation, Robinson recruited Nik Powell and his independent production company, Scala, who, in turn, brought in additional European financing from a German-based production company.

Once Robinson and Schepisi went public with their plans to make the film, 'It was such a terrific story, there were a lot on actors knocking on our door,' says Schepisi. 'All the cast jumped at it as soon as they'd read the script. It's a story they could relate to and it touched them all in a very personal way. Ironically, Michael Caine said he'd always known he'd play his father one day. A group resonance existed throughout the shoot, which brought an amazing spirit to the whole thing.'

Certainly, when Robinson first read the novel, she immediately felt a film version would offer wonderful roles for the cream of the British acting fraternity, and 'to have them all together in one film is rare, but it's exactly what happened'.

Caine agreed. 'It's a little gem. I remember the first read-through, everything felt right and everybody was so good.'

Helen Mirren shared Caine's opinion. 'I don't normally like read-throughs, I get bored, but this was wonderful. It was very funny to see all of those actors sitting together. It was kind of moving and quite powerful.'

Interestingly enough, Ray had read the script two years before shooting commenced and was immediately hooked. 'I just really badly wanted to do it.' But at the time he became attached to the movie he had no idea who was going to be in it. 'If I remember rightly there was talk of Michael Caine, but I had no idea about anyone else who was going to be in it. That was a bonus, when I found out that Tom Courtenay, David Hemmings and Bob Hoskins were doing it too.'

But, according to Hoskins, 'It was a con. Fred Schepisi told me that Michael, David, Tom, Helen and Ray were already doing it and he said, "You'll do it, won't you?" So I said, "Yes." On the set we realised he'd told each of us that everybody else was in it when he didn't have any of us. I think he'd tried to find a skinny Bob Hoskins, but couldn't.'

In the production notes circulated to the press prior to the film being released, Ray explained the attraction of playing Vince Dodds, the second-hand-car dealer and son of Jack, who is affectionately known as 'Big Boy' to all of his father's friends. 'Even at the age of 45, if you've got a powerful figure in your family, there's that thing of them making you stiffen when you're around them. You love them to bits and they love you, but it's about being controlled and never being allowed to grow up. Vince's decision not to follow in Jack's footsteps causes friction between a father and son, as "Big Boy" was expected to inherit the family butcher's business, just as Jack did from his father. Starting the car dealership is Vince's way of rebelling. The journey is not just about taking Jack's ashes to Margate, but about four men who've been controlled by one man all their lives in one way or another. As the journey unfolds, they settle their differences and all grow up. The one thing I didn't want to do with Vince was make him a clichéd, flash car-dealer type. He's a man in turmoil.'

The hardest casting decision though was selecting the younger actors. As Schepisi noted, 'It's all very well to talk about Michael Caine, Helen Mirren, Bob Hoskins, Ray Winstone, Tom Courtenay and David Hemmings, but who plays them when they're 19 and 21 years of age? They had to have the same star quality and charisma, it was quite difficult.'

The search for the young stars was entrusted to veteran casting director Patsy Pollock and her team, who scoured the country, every drama and theatre school and even the East End gym where Ray used to box in his youth. The painstaking search finally paid off and JJ Feild came on board as the young Caine, Kelly Reilly as the young Mirren, Anatol Yusef as the young Hoskins, Cameron Fitch as the young Courtenay and Hemmings's son Nolan as the young version of his father's character. Playing the young Ray was Stephen McCole, who Ray thought was brilliant. 'He is more me than me, and he's Scottish! That's a performance. He's playing a Londoner too. We sat down beforehand and established some mannerisms for the character. They were all fantastic, the kids in the flashbacks. Everyone talks about us older ones, but the kids are actually the ones who are doing the acting because they're playing us.'

As Ray repeats, 'I had such a good time making that film. The frightening thing is you get really excited about working with such great actors and then you think, "What about if I turn up and they're all horrible?" But they weren't, they were all really nice and it was a happy film for me. We're all still mates and I'd love to work with any of them again.' Little did he know then that he would team up again with Hemmings two years later when they were offered a script for a television sequel to one of Ray's previous dramas that proved irresistible to both of them.

CHAPTER 11

Still The Daddy

Four months before *Last Orders* had its world premiere during the 26th Toronto International Film Festival in September 2001, and received rapturous notices, Ray and Elaine had some exciting news of their own. They announced the birth of their youngest daughter, Ellie Rae, who it seemed they may have named after themselves by shortening and altering their own names.

Some men may have found the idea of becoming a father again at the age of 45 daunting, but Ray simply loved it. Those who know him can see that being a dad again clearly suited him. He himself has said, 'I'm a lot more relaxed this time, because the first time you become a parent, you're a nutter, a raving lunatic.' He was even talking about how he would like to have some more in the future. He reckoned having a family of eight children would be a perfect number, 'but that's probably pushing it. Anyway, it might be hypothetical. I could be firing blanks from now on.'

Ray has explained that one of the reasons he and Elaine had Ellie later on in their lives was because 'we had just moved to this big house in Essex with a huge garden and there were no kids running around. It just didn't seem right. We missed having babies and we were lucky enough to get one pretty quickly. I was 24 when I had my first child and 45 when Ellie was born. You start to look after yourself a bit more when you're an older dad. It's great to be a daddy again. It just makes everything complete.'

And, of course, he continued, 'It's so much calmer now I'm older. Now I can sit Ellie on my knee and I'm in no rush to go anywhere. When the baby wakes up in the night, I don't think, "Oh no!" It's like, "Good, let's get her into bed with us" and she is asleep again. It's so much easier. And, with our older two all grown up, we missed having babies. We were lucky enough at our age to have Ellie Rae. I can't imagine being without her now. Everything in your life changes when you have children. When you're young, you think you're going to live forever and have no fears. Then, all of a sudden, you start to have fears for your kids. In a way, having Ellie Rae has made me take more care of myself. I have a panic attack every now and then and try to slow down. I want to see her grow up and blossom. But there's no rules to the game, is there, with kids? You can treat two of them the same and they both turn out different. You've just got to trust your kids, and be there for them when they need you.'

Lois and Jaime were just as thrilled as Ray and Elaine at the arrival of Ellie Rae. 'The girls love her to bits,' Ray smiles. 'It's like she's got three mums. And Elaine looks so well it's unbelievable, it has taken 10 years off her. She's always been active, but it must be a nature thing because everything starts blossoming again. We have a little wood at the back of our house, which is in the countryside on the borders of Essex and Hertfordshire. I take great delight in going out and planting wild flowers there. I love going up to the wood and playing little games with Ellie. I fucking love it. I'm a city boy who's always wanted to be a country boy.'

In fact Ray is so besotted with his entire family, he makes sure Elaine, Lois, Jaime and Ellie Rae accompany him to far-flung film sets whenever possible. There's no point in being married or having a family otherwise, he insists. 'My kids and my wife come first. There ain't nothing else. Being anywhere without them kills me. I miss them so much I just want to jump on a plane and fly home.'

Just one month after Ellie Rae arrived into the world, Ray had just finished filming director Liliana Cavani's *Ripley's Game*, the sequel to Anthony Minghella's *The Talented Mr Ripley*, released in 1999, starring Matt Damon, Gwyneth Paltrow and Jude Law, and which centred on a character first created in a series of works by novelist Patricia Highsmith. In the book and the movie, Tom Ripley is sent to Italy to coax the son of a wealthy executive back home, but ends up committing murder.

The seeds of the Ripley character were first planted when Highsmith saw a man walking on a beach in Positano, Italy. 'I wondered why he was there at 6.00am,' she explained. 'Later I thought about a man sent to Positano on a mission, and maybe he failed.' Over the course of five novels, readers saw Ripley go from a man of barely modest means to a prosperous gentleman who also happens to be a murderer. 'I rather like criminals and find them extremely interesting,' Highsmith once said. 'I find the public passion for justice quite boring and artificial, for neither life nor nature cares if justice is ever done or not.'

Minghella's film was based on Highsmith's first novel published in 1955 and, like the book, the central plot of the movie centred on what happens after Tom Ripley kills his friend, Dickie Greenleaf, and takes over his identity.

Despite the fact that most critics considered *Ripley's Game* superior to *The Talented Mr Ripley*, Ray hated the film. 'It was shit. I knew it when we were doing it. I haven't got a clue what they were doing. I kept getting the giggles. It's hard to say that about a film when there are so many people involved in making it, but some things don't turn out the way you'd hoped and you have to stand up and be counted for that.'

Many other films based on Highsmith's novels have been made over the years. *Ripley's Game* was based on the third novel about Tom Ripley, written in 1974. One film critic, Roger Ebert, said it was, without question, the best of all the films, and that John Malkovich, who played the role of Ripley, was precisely the Tom Ripley that Ebert had imagined when he read the novels. *Variety*'s critic David Rooney agreed. 'If anyone was born to play Tom Ripley, it's John Malkovich; the aloofness, erudite manner, cool charisma and chilly superciliousness of his screen persona make the actor a perfect fit for the cultured killer. Malkovich's elegantly malicious performance gives the film a magnetic centre, complemented by Cavani's efficient direction and an enjoyable retro feel that recalls the British Cold War thrillers of the 1960s. Despite some pedestrian plotting and a final act that could be tighter, this is suspenseful adult entertainment that should find a receptive audience.'

Cavani, an Italian, born in 1933, was a good choice to direct a Ripley film, because she was comfortable with depravity as a subject. Her best-known film is *The Night Porter* (1974), starring Charlotte Rampling as a survivor of the Nazi death camps, who finds one of her former guards, played by Dirk Bogarde, in what has been described as the best performance of his film career, working in a hotel, and so she begins a sadomasochistic relationship with him. Even though there were some critics who didn't like the film, it shows Cavani using some of the same objectivity about perverted values that she used in *Ripley's Game*.

If there were any noticeable departures from the book, they were the relocation of the principal setting from Fountainbleu, France, to Italy's Veneto region and a time shift from the 1950s to the present. The action starts, however, in Berlin, where Ripley walks away from a business deal gone sour, taking $3 million worth of Renaissance forgeries while parting ways with his thuggish British partner, Reeves, played by Ray.

Three years later, he is living in luxury in a sumptuously restored Palladian villa in northeast Italy with his beautiful harpsichordist wife, Luisa (Chiara Caselli). At a village party given by British picture framer Jonathan Trevanny (Dougray Scott), Ripley overhears the host make a disparaging remark about his ostentatious taste. Since no simple form of revenge will do, Ripley seizes an opportunity presented by Reeves, who resurfaces needing an unknown face to erase a Russian mobster encroaching on his Berlin nightclub turf. Knowing Trevanny is terminally ill with leukaemia and financially vulnerable, Ripley suggests Reeves approach him.

Playing on Trevanny's need to provide financial security for his wife, played by Lena Headey (who had played girlfriend Connie to Ray's partner-in-crime, Robert Carlyle, in *Face*), and son (Sam Blitz), and, dangling consultation with a Berlin specialist as further bait, Reeves corners the reluctant man into the job. When Reeves then pressures Trevanny into a second hit, Ripley's annoyance that the pact is extended prompts him to board the Berlin–Dusseldorf Express, where the murder is to take place, and assume control of the situation. One of the most vivid sequences from Highsmith's novel, this is sharply done in the film, and provides a suspenseful centrepiece laced with black humour.

Things go wrong when one of the victims doesn't die and Reeves's attempt to make the killings look like a gang war between Russians and Ukrainians fails to convince either side. They come after Reeves, who turns to unsympathetic Ripley for help. This leads the Mafiosi back to Italy, where Ripley and Trevanny hunker down in the villa to wait for the assailants, an unexpected bond slowly crystallising between them.

As one critic pointed out, 'While Malkovich could be accused of being far too Malkovich, the actor dominates every scene with his deliciously sinister portrayal of a man of mordant wit and supreme manipulative power, able to remain cool in even the most extreme circumstances. Scott is simply no match for the more seasoned thesp, not helped by the script's sketchy psychological grounding for Trevanny's transition. The sense of Trevanny as a plaything for Ripley's diabolical amusement could have been more strongly developed, and Scott conveys the confused emotions, moral ambiguity and sense of entrapment of an innocent family man steered down a criminal path in fairly obvious terms. All the same, Caselli provides sexy, feline grace as Ripley's complicit wife, while Headey, shapes a warm, intuitive character out of Trevanny's increasingly alarmed spouse.'

The same critic, however, wasn't quite so convinced about Ray's part in the film. 'He was so good in films like *Sexy Beast* and *Last Orders*, he is underused in a role without much definition.' But, he continues, 'Director Cavani's depiction of the dark relationship between the Bogarde and Rampling characters in *The Night Porter* has vague echoes in the tormentor-victim setup here, underscored as in Highsmith's novel with the faintest trace of homoerotic tension. Absent since 1993's undistinguished drama about a deaf-mute couple, *Where Are You? I'm Here*, Cavani handles the action, atmosphere and tension with assurance, faltering only in a closing act that seems to fumble for a suitable ending.'

Even if Ray didn't like the film – and one of the things he said he particularly didn't like about it was how Cavani messed about with the character's motivations by making the Trevannys middle class – he didn't have long to mourn. Something that would be more to his liking was waiting just around the corner.

The role of DC Lenny Milton that he had first created for *Tough Love*, the critically acclaimed police drama that was first shown on ITV in October 2000, was one he was very keen on. In 2002, he was invited to reprise the role for a sequel written by one of his favourite scriptwriters Stephen Butchard. The fact that he also got to work alongside David Hemmings again was simply the icing on the cake.

As the *Observer* critic Euan Ferguson noted, Ray had perhaps never found a better vehicle than Lenny Milton. 'His capacity to be heartbreakingly vulnerable and then suddenly turn and fill the screen with life-wrecking violence has never been better.'

Ray would probably agree. But, as he himself explains, *Lenny Blue* followed on from where *Tough Love* left off. 'In the first show, it was about Lenny and his mate, and Lenny not sticking up for his mate, and doing what he thought was morally right. It was a story about two blokes who happened to be policemen and their relationship. This one is about Lenny, and his life and how he's supposed to be the bad guy, but really he's just a bit of a mess. It was great to do. It's a great format and if there are any more, then, lovely.'

In the second show it was about how Milton was trying to come to terms with the murder of his best mate and colleague Mike Love. Since the tragedy he has moved to another police station but all of his new colleagues know about Milton informing on his corrupt mate, as a result he is treated like dirt. He is at the bottom of the heap. Although he has moved on, Milton still has to deal with the same old problems such as drug dealers and gangsters.

Tough Love was more about two men. It was about the moral dilemmas of their friendship. But, as Ray adds, '*Lenny Blue* is more about the police force.' He admits he has tried cannabis but he is concerned about the effect drugs are having on today's society. 'Personally I can't smoke cannabis. I tried it and fell over. It's not for me but then I drink vodka and scotch. It's the biggest problem in the world today. Countries are paying off national debts through the drugs trade. I guess people could stop it tomorrow if they wanted. They keep trying to deal with the problem here but they could stop it where it originally comes from. I don't know whether legalising some drugs is right or wrong. I had a mate who was very, very ill and the only way he could stop the pain was to have a joint. So perhaps cannabis should be made legal. But it is a very difficult subject to comment on. There is an argument that drug users progress from cannabis to heroin but I'm not a great supporter of that theory. I think it's usually more to do with the circles you knock about in.'

Not so topical was the scene which had Ray returning home to catch his on-screen daughter having sex with an older man on the sofa. In the film he went berserk but what would he have done if it happened in real life? Well, he wouldn't be very happy about it, that's for sure. In fact, 'I'd probably grab the geezer by the scruff of the neck and throw him through a window.' But would he really? Well, 'I'd be most angry at how stupid they'd been. Why not use an upstairs room? Why show disrespect towards me and Elaine by doing it where they could easily get caught? As for being with an older man, I wouldn't be that keen. But, if my daughter really loved him and he looked after her, their relationship wouldn't cause me a problem.'

Writing in the *Radio Times* in July 2002 during the week the two-part drama was screened, critic Alison Graham offered one of the most concise summaries of the programme. 'Though the plot gets a bit impenetrable, *Lenny Blue* has some stylish, classy moments, and a fabulous soundtrack. It all feels realistic enough, and for a change, a tough, no-nonsense copper who is happily married, though his teenage children are giving him much cause for concern. But it really is stupendously tough and gritty, a bit like a 21st-century *Sweeney*. Just about every police character smokes, to the point that, when they meet for briefings, it looks as if someone's started a bonfire. And the testosterone washes everywhere, which – along with all that smoking – possibly accounts for the policemen all having very gravelly voices, particularly Winstone, though this, of course, only adds to his sex appeal. Ladies, he may not be everyone's idea of handsome, but he has the kind of charisma you can cut into slices and eat on toast.'

Strangely enough, or at least to some, it was playing scary, violent types, and in particularly his role as Lenny Milton, that appeared to turn Ray into an unlikely sex symbol. When he heard that, his response was disbelieving. 'If people think I'm sexy, then the world has gone mad. I'm 46 years old with a fat stomach and cropped hair. Maybe it's because people mix me up with the parts I play. Dangerous men with a weak side. But I love that. I don't mind showing a weak side. We all know geezers can be macho, but the weaknesses are the strengths.'

If the critics and television-viewing public alike thought that his character of Lenny Milton was like a modern-day Jack Regan from *The Sweeney*, then they wouldn't be far wrong. Five years after *Lenny Blue* was first aired, Ray was linked to a new £5-million big-screen remake of the classic television cop show that had run over four years from the mid-1970s, and in which, interestingly enough, Ray had his first-ever acting job, appearing as a 'second youth' in about three scenes in an episode in 1975, the year before he was cast in the television version of *Scum*. According to an exclusive story that appeared in the *Sunday Express*, journalists Henry Fitzherbert and York Membery reckoned that Ray was being hotly tipped for the role of the hard-drinking, hard-talking Regan, immortalised by John Thaw. And Ray's soon-to-be screen son in *All In The Game*, Danny Dyer, was also being named as the favourite to play the Dennis Waterman role of Regan's sidekick, DS George Carter.

The idea of making a new movie version had been partly inspired by the success of *Life on Mars*, the BBC show in which John Simm's modern-day policeman wakes up in the 1970s and is paired with an unreconstructed, sexist policeman played by Philip Glenister. Producer Allan Niblo confirmed that *Life on Mars* 'helped rekindle interest in that era but what we really want to do is to make a fast-paced, almost Bond-style version of the original set in contemporary London. They'll obviously be living in the modern world and have more modern attitudes but it will still be a very hard-hitting film.' Certainly, Niblo continued, '*The Sweeney* was one of the most iconic of the past 40 years and has a ready-made market. It comes with a huge recognition factor.' And, like *Lenny*, it seems to be the perfect role for Ray.

Basking in the warm glow of his most successful television drama yet, Ray went from one great role to another. Two weeks after *Lenny Blue* was shown on two consecutive evenings on ITV in July 2002, Ray joined Nicole Kidman and his *Love, Honour and Obey* ally Jude Law, and headed out to Romania to film *Cold Mountain*, Anthony Minghella's epic of Charles Frazier's acclaimed bestseller about the American Civil War.

Set in the 19th century, it is the story of a Confederate infantryman named W.P. Inman, played by Law, who, after recovering from a devastating injury on the front lines in 1864, decides to desert and make his way back to his home town of Cold Mountain in North Carolina. He wants to get back to Ada Monroe, the preacher's daughter, played by Kidman who he hopes is waiting for him. He doesn't know whether she will be waiting because it has been three years since they last saw each other, and they hardly know each other. Their interaction before he went to war was brief, but has left a lasting impression. However, the trek back to Cold Mountain proves to be an arduous one. Along the way, he meets a number of odd people, some of whom are interested in helping and others who see him only as a way to make a profit. There is a good price on the head of a deserter.

As in most stories of the heart, Ada has indeed been waiting for him to return, and once he does, towards the end of the movie, a beautifully intimate love scene follows. Kidman and Law both appear naked, with Kidman revealing more than most A-list actresses would at the prime of their careers. She left many people applauding her bravery to expose what has been described as one of the most beautiful and desirable bodies in Hollywood. But it wasn't the first time she had taken her clothes off for the voyeuristic benefit of the cameras and its audience.

She had bared all, four years earlier, when she filmed Stanley Kubricks's *Eyes Wide Shut*. But there was a difference. For Kubrick's movie, the explicit scene at the beginning of the film, which started off with a gratuitous glimpse of Nicole naked, bar a pair of high heels, was, as far as she was concerned, important to the film. It had to be harsh and gritty looking, almost pornographic. 'That film deals with sex and sexual obsession and the scenes could not have been of me in my bra and panties pretending to have sex with somebody. It also had to have a graphic quality to it.' And although the scenes she filmed for Minghella could hardly be called 'harsh, gritty or pornographic', they were still explicit.

Once again, she bared pretty much all, and, where perhaps no-one was surprised to see close-ups of her behind, breasts and nipples, she took it a step further in the five second sequence where she opens her legs to allow Law's hand to slip up in between them revealing glimpses of her pubic hair. Some thought the scene was not really necessary, others considered it very explicit for a mainstream film. Either way, it worked, despite the criticism from some quarters that it was not needed. In reality though, said one reviewer, wouldn't Inman and Ada have consummated their love with a blown-out candle, a closed door, and a few wispy clouds suggestively passing across the moon instead of the few minutes of peekaboo montage and heavy breathing.

But not everyone agreed. And it is undeniable that the scene was beautifully photographed. As Ray points out, 'it was stunning watching her. She really knows her business. Over fourteen takes, she would play the scene differently each time, to really give the editor something to work with.' Since working with Kidman in *Cold Mountain*, Ray freely admits that she has become one of his favourite actresses: 'She's one of the gang, a real geezer bird. And she's got a good soul.'

The idea of the sex scene was, as Minghella said at the time he went public with his plans to make the film, 'to do justice to the vast emotional and visual landscapes of the story and I am delighted to be helped once again in those efforts by my film family of Ann, Walter, Gabriel and John as well as Script Supervisor, Dianne Dreyer, First Assistant Director, Steve Andrews and casting directors David Rubin and Ronna Kress, and the legendary production designer Dante Ferretti, who is a tremendous new addition to the team.' And he was right. In a story in which nature and the weather played an integral part, most critics agreed that the filmmakers had rightly chosen to combine locations in the United States with the remote mountains and valleys of Transylvania, Romania, to recreate a primitive and unforgiving landscape that, without question, will transport audiences back to the time when the story was taking place.

Long before the much debated sex scene, the story unfolded a series of setbacks for Ada, the first being the death of her father, played by Donald Sutherland. This causes Ada to let the farm fall into disarray, until the arrival of Ruby Thewes (Renee Zellweger), a plain-speaking free spirit who offers to help her rebuild the farm in exchange for meals and lodging. A bargain is struck and the two begin a mutually beneficial partnership that develops into a friendship. But troubles lurk. In one of the 11 scenes cut from the final movie, for instance, the horror of the times was fully awakened when the script called for Natalie Portman's character Sara's fate to be much worse than was seen in the released version in which she and her baby are terrorised by three Yankee soldiers until Inman saves them both. In the final film, you see the naked baby saved from freezing to death in the outside winter, and Sara from being gang raped by the soldiers. But, in the scene that was deleted, Portman sings to her baby until it dies, and then commits suicide by shooting herself.

Other scenes, especially the ones in which Ray appeared as Teague, the head of the local home guard, were equally powerful. He had been empowered to kill deserters, and the one deserter he has sworn to hunt down is Inman. He is also after Ada's body and her land. Most critics described Ray's portrayal of Teague in *Cold Mountain* as one of the most menacing performances of his career. Audiences breathed a sigh of relief when Jude Law finally shoots Ray's character dead, with his own gun towards the end of the movie.

Although Minghella had considered other American actors for the role of Teague, he later said that his final decision to cast Ray proved to be the correct one. 'When I was looking for an actor to play Teague, I kept thinking of the way that Ray had created a man whose behaviour was always unconscionable but whose humanity was impossible to deny. Teague needed that ambiguity.' He continues, 'I longed to find someone who had the qualities that Ray has. In *Nil By Mouth*, Ray gave one of the most extraordinary, complex and unsettling performances that I can remember.'

Pictured on the set of the 2003 £6 million television biography of *Henry VIII*, in which Ray took on the role of the oft-married monarch and fellow Brit. Actress Helena Bonham Carter played Anne Boleyn, one of his six wives.

Above: A still from *Sexy Beast*, 2000. Ray plays an ex-con and expert safecracker whose world is turned upside down by the arrival of an old criminal associate, played by Ben Kingsley.

Below: Director of *Cold Mountain* Anthony Minghella (*left*) and Ray meeting Prince Charles at the film premiere, December 2003. *Inset*: With fellow cast members Nicole Kidman (*centre*) and Jude Law (*right*).

Ray takes the family to the London premiere of *The Chronicles of Narnia: The Lion, The Witch and The Wardrobe. (Left to right)* Daughter Jaime, his wife Elaine, youngest daughter Ellie and eldest daughter Lois.

Above: On the set of the award-winning TV detective drama series *Vincent*.

Below: With fellow cast member Suranne Jones.

Above: Ray visits the England football team in Germany during training for the World Cup 2006 in his capacity as an ambassador for England's football fans. Pictured here with *(left to right)* Gary Neville, Steven Gerrard and David Beckham.

Below: With a supporter before England's match with Sweden.

Above: Ray, Vicki Michelle *(centre)* and Danny Dyer *(right)* attend Channel 4's *All In The Game* launch party at Soho Hotel on April 27, 2006 in London, England.

Below: One of the first publicity photos to be released from the set of Ray's biggest film yet, *Indiana Jones and the Kingdom of the Crystal Skull*. Ray is shown here with director Steven Spielberg and co-stars Shia LeBeouf, Karen Allen and Harrison Ford.

Above: Ray with Cirsty White and Joshua Mills, showing his support for National Game Playing Week by playing board games with children at Haven House children's hospice. Ray, a committed patron of Haven House, visited the hospice in 2006 in order to launch National Game Playing Week in partnership with the Association of Children's Hospices.

Below: Ray appears on the famous *Parkinson* show, October 2006.

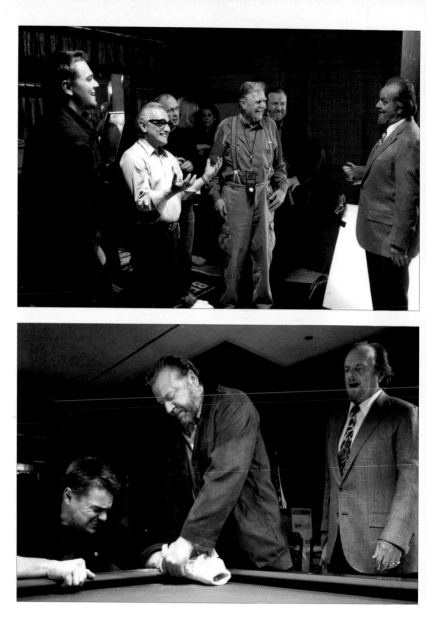

Above: On the set of *The Departed*. *Left to right:* Leonardo DiCaprio, director Martin Scorsese, cinematographer Michael Ballhaus, Ray Winstone, and Jack Nicholson.

Below: Ray plays Mr French, the powerful mob boss' brutal henchman. This film shows him ripping Leonardo DiCaprio's plaster cast and pinning his broken arm down for Nicholson to beat with a shoe.

What is perhaps most interesting of all about the way Ray played his character is how unrecognisable he was when he was on screen. 'It's my first American character. Someone had the foresight to think I could do it. I'll always go where the script is good as I want to do good stuff.' It was his first Hollywood epic and, since then, he says, 'I've been offered three films in Hollywood, being the guy in the right-hand side talking bollocks, and I didn't want to do that. So I could have gone and, if I'm lucky enough to be offered a good script, I will go.'

The only problem, adds Ray, is that 'I have three daughters and if I went to America I would never see them. I had the chance to be in the TV series *The Wire*. It had a fantastic script with good people, but I didn't go. It would have meant seven months in Baltimore for five years. I would have been able to have Ellie Rae with me but I would just not have seen my two elder daughters. So at the end of the day there was no competition. I'm very happy working in this country.'

Even so, there were several aspects of his *Cold Mountain* character that he had to acquaint himself with before he could shoot any of his scenes. One was to learn to ride a horse and the other was to do a convincing southern accent. The last thing he wanted was to be criticised for saying 'toe-*mah*-toe' when he ought to say 'toe-*may*-toe', even though it would be like damning Rembrandt because he painted one nostril larger than another. 'I've got a horse called George and I'm being taught by the top horse rider and stuntman in the country, so I'm very happy. I want to learn to do it properly, so I can ride in my spare time.' One year later, he had. 'I'm pretty capable on a horse now. I love it, I wish I'd learned 20 years ago.'

Cold Mountain was released for Christmas 2003 in Britain

and America, a lavish production which didn't really fill the criteria for a seasonal movie like, say, *Little Women* would have, but did, all the same, rapidly became both a critical and box-office smash. Perhaps, the only drawback to the film is how depressing some thought it was. Overall though, the general consensus was that it was an outstanding film with great performances from the entire cast. Even more pleasing to Minghella was how it was also applauded for its realistic portrayal of the Civil War and for elaborating on some of the darkest civilian aspects in the history of war.

As Mick LaSalle said in the *San Francisco Chronicle*, 'At 154 minutes, *Cold Mountain* is long and seems long, at times inspired, at times merely dutiful. But in most of the important ways, it succeeds. It's impossible to watch the film without hating the home raiders, for example, or caring whether Inman makes it home. More enduringly, *Cold Mountain* changes our image of the collapsing Confederacy in the same way that *Saving Private Ryan* changed our collective notion of D-Day. You just know it had to be this bad and that, if anything, it was worse.'

Ray's memory of the shoot, however, is one of distaste. This was mainly down to the fact that he simply hated being in Romania. And, as far as he was concerned, there was nothing worse than the six-month shooting schedule that Minghella instituted. 'It was also a big movie with more cameras and more time to get it done. I enjoyed making it but it was the first time I realised there were two different ways of working in film. Being on a film for six months was also a shock. In the UK we normally have six or eight weeks to make a film, which I prefer, to be honest. On a six-month film, you get tired trying to keep your concentration going. It was tough sitting on the top of a mountain in Transylvania for six months, with just brown bears and a bottle of vodka for company. I had to put garlic on the windowsill, or the vampires would have got me!'

Transylvania was, of course, the place that had given rise to much of the Dracula legend, created in Bram Stoker's original tale. According to history, Vlad the Impaler, a principal figure in Stoker's novel, was the medieval Romanian King whose lust for human blood was spilled in the decidedly unsupernatural field of battle. This age-old tale has invoked a whole spate of movies: Ted Browning's 1931 *Dracula*, which established Bela Lugosi as King of the Counts; Herzog's 1979 *Nosferatu* remake; the host of the British-made 'Hammer Horror' Dracula movies that had made household names out of Christopher Lee and Peter Cushing; and, of course, more recently, Francis Ford Coppola's 1992 re-telling starring Ray's *Nil By Mouth* ally, Gary Oldman, as well as Anthony Hopkins, Winona Ryder, Keanu Reeves, and, another of Ray's former co-stars from *Love, Honour and Obey*, Sadie Frost, who most reviewers believed constantly stole all of Ryder's scenes.

Over the years Dracula has been anthologised, humourised and deified. His image has been immortalised to sell everything from bad pornography to kids' cereal *Count Chocula*. He has been turned into a rabbit by authors Deborah and James Howe in *Bunnicula*. He has even been set to music by the English rock band Bauhaus, whose first single was an eleven-minute opus called 'Bela Lugosi's Dead'. He has appeared in theatres and church halls the world over. And he has been killed so many times that even immortality no longer provided an adequate explanation for his constant comebacks.

On top of finding the shoot arduous, Ray also missed his family. 'I didn't see them for six weeks, which was the longest I've been separated from them. It was really difficult. I was terribly homesick.' One of the reasons Elaine, Lois, Jaime and Ellie didn't visit him on set was because, as Ray explains, 'there was a dangerous road from the airport to the film site. It was like dicing with death every time you went over it and I wouldn't let them come out to see me.' But that didn't stop him from going to see them. He flew home in the middle of filming when he wasn't needed, even though they still wanted him on set, and in the same country where the set was.

As Ray points out, being away for so long just means 'when you come home no one knows you. So I made the decision that, for long jobs, they come with me if they can. I mean, if you let me loose on location, I'm staying in a hotel and I'll be in the bar most nights. You get really lonely. So I went home; I just got on a plane. They phoned and said, "You're supposed to be here," and I said, "Well, call when you want me for the next scene." I wanted to be home. I had a little baby and she changes so much every day. It's a selfish thing. I don't want to be away from them. I get very homesick. I'm not manic depressive, nothing like that, but I just get a bit miserable, a bit down.'

Not that he would be at all 'miserable' or 'down' when he attended the Royal Premiere in London in December 2003 in the presence of Prince Charles, whom he told reporters was very nice. 'He actually said to me, "And who do you play?" When I told him I played a character called Teague from North Carolina, he asked, "How did you find the accent?" I said I found it OK, and on the way out, he found me and said, "You were very good."'

According to the *Mirror*, it was Ray, and not the star of the film, Jude Law, who was surrounded by scantily dressed groupies, held court and even gave his opinion on Prince Charles. He recalls asking Nicole Kidman how she felt about meeting the Prince, and she told him that she was shitting herself because she was so nervous. He laughs at the memory, because he remembers telling her that he had just been seen playing a king on the small screen and Charles was still waiting to be one. And that was his greatest secret wish, to see Charles on the throne with Camilla at his side. 'She's his dollybird. She has put a twinkle in his eye, and she looks like a right goer, too.'

It was at the same time that he was spouting off about Charles and Camilla, at the after-premiere party for *Cold Mountain*, that Ray spoke out about being offered a role in *EastEnders*, 'But I didn't fancy it,' he says. 'I think the actors in it are fantastic. Perry Fenwick and Elaine Lordan are good friends of mine, but I'm not a lover of the programme itself. I think *EastEnders* is very depressing, you never see a geezer pull up in a great big car with a nice suit on or people having fun. And fun is vital, it's what happens, life isn't all death, doom and destruction. The East End has been built on many things from Jack the Ripper to getting bombed in World War II, and there was always humour there that I don't see in that programme. Also I couldn't be stuck in a soap opera, it is too much like a nine-to-five job. I'm not knocking it at all, but it's not for me.'

With a $14,574,213 gross in its opening weekend across 163 screens, *Cold Mountain* enjoyed one of the most successful openings of a non-typical Christmas movie, and would go on to overwhelm the following year's award ceremonies with nine nominations at the Golden Globes and seven nominations at the Academy Awards. Renee Zellweger walked away with Best Supporting Actress at both, and put the film firmly on the map. Whether you loved it or hated it, there was no denying that *Cold Mountain* was a breathtaking achievement, so it was understandable that Ray wasn't interested in a role on a soap opera on BBC Television. No one could blame him for turning it down. He had bigger fish to fry, so to speak.

CHAPTER 11

The Kings And I

To some, the idea that Ray would take on the role of Henry VIII almost beggared belief. It was as if Quentin Tarantino had announced an adaptation of a Danielle Steele novel. The shock was perhaps understandable too, for nowhere in Ray's career to date had he suggested he had ever dreamed of doing a costume piece, let alone playing one of England's most beguiling monarchs in history, who, to this day, continues to fascinate Britain, centuries after his death.

To this day, people remain fascinated by the destruction Henry often left in his wake during his extraordinary reign. From the moment Henry Tudor cast aside his first wife, the faithful Katherine of Aragon, for the bewildering and determined Anne Boleyn, he sets himself on course for a series of disastrous marriages and violent conflict, both within the population and the church, which left England reeling while its complex and charismatic King turned from handsome playboy to a bitter invalid desperate for a son and heir to the throne.

Certainly, the casting process was the first thing that got *Henry VIII* off the ground, says producer Francis Hopkinson. 'We had been working with Ray on *Lenny Blue*, when someone said, "Imagine Ray as Henry VIII," and it just fit. And so we started looking for a script. If you ask people who they would like to see as Henry VIII, they don't know. But straight away most people can see why he was a brilliant choice. He seemed to capture all those facets of Henry. And, because he's a big star, you could see he was going to bring a different perspective, and, even though it's true that there were some people who didn't like the idea of him in the role, I think their objection was purely down to the fact that he wasn't posh.'

Some people, he continues, 'expect their kings to speak like the Royal Shakespeare Company, but I find it a bit depressing that some people still have that view. The RSC went through a seismic change in the 60s. People with northern accents were appearing on stage and people objected to it, but they came around. I'm a bit startled about that sort of snobbery still existing, but it's only among very few people. And, besides, they can't quite argue with the fact that nobody knows exactly how anyone talked back then, anyhow. Henry VIII is the greatest story in English history: it's a love story, a story of an extraordinary character and a story that changed English and European history, and, arguably, the history of the world. There are so many conflicting stories about Henry, although, in the end, all you can really say for certain is that he had a psychotic temperament and had a lot of people killed, including two of his wives.'

Despite the criticism, both Hopkinson and screenwriter

Peter Morgan were determined that Ray, without doubt, should play the part, and Helena Bonham Carter should be Anne Boleyn. What happened, Morgan remembers, was that 'I had already written a rough script but I went and spoke to Helena, and the fact that she didn't tell me to sod off meant that I started to write the subsequent drafts more with her in mind. Ray was absolutely who we were going to go with straight away. In my mind, there is no one else who could play Henry VIII today. He was essential to the whole project. With Helena, I really don't feel that there is another actress of the right age who is powerful enough to hold the screen with Ray. His extraordinary screen presence and charisma would have blown any other actress off the screen. Despite being so petite, Helena certainly punches as much screen clout as Ray.'

There were the other critical objections, such as why on earth would anyone want to retell the story of Henry VIII again, when it had been done so adequately, so many times before. But, as Morgan defends, 'There's really no bad time to tell the story of Henry VIII, although I was initially resistant to the idea. But then I thought that nobody had ever really done 'the Henry story'. I mean, very few people know that Henry was the second son, that his older brother should have become king but he died of tuberculosis. Henry was the forgotten son really, a bit neglected, which is probably why he was such a larger-than-life character. All historical books and television documentaries seem to focus on his many wives, which is, no doubt, an amazing story, but I really wanted to tell the story of Henry and use the wives as a linking device.'

Strangely enough, though, when the project was first announced in March 2001, two years before it went into production, the *Guardian*'s media correspondent Matt Wells reported that Granada Television had commissioned Alan Bleasdale, to pen the drama, and, although Ray was at that point already attached, it seemed Bonham Carter wasn't. The only actresses mentioned as possible candidates to play two of Henry's wives were Anna Friel and interestingly enough Ray's *Nil by Mouth* co-star Kathy Burke. But, then again, actors and actresses often get linked to projects that either don't come to anything, or the stars in question don't end up doing, for any number of unexplained reasons. There was, however, an explanation as to why Bleasdale later left the project. It was apparently because his idea to begin the series with Henry arriving in Hell was rejected.

With or without Bleasdale writing the script, Ray was still enthusiastic. 'It's a fantastic part for an actor to get his teeth into. I'll have to sit down to talk with the production people on how I'm going to play him.'

But, as one journalist noted, 'Little did he or his drama teacher at Corona realise that several decades after he had been kicked out of the school for his reckless behaviour he would end up receiving lavish plaudits for his portrayal on television of Henry VIII as a paranoid East End gangster.'

Ray continues, it was very brave of Granada to cast me as the King. 'I mean, it's not the norm, is it? He's been played before by very talented people and always done very well. I'm just trying to look for different angles, to play him as a man and let everyone else worry about him being the King. It's a tough job, it's physical, mental, everything, and there's pressure. I'm not finding it easy, but sometimes you have to put your head on the line.'

What was also exciting about the latest incarnation of Henry was that it promised to be quite different from the atmospheric and rather restrained period films that had gone before: Alexander Korda's 1963 *The Private Life of Henry VIII* with Charles Laughton was the first talking version and was followed by *A Man for All Seasons*, the multiple-Oscar-winner of 1966, with Robert Shaw; Richard Burton's 1969 *Anne of the Thousand Days*, another 10-Oscar-nominated picture, and the highly acclaimed 1970 BBC production, *The Six Wives of Henry VIII* starring Keith Michell, that had also made it to the big screen two years later.

For the Winstone retelling, though, there would be guts and gore aplenty, warned director Pete Travis. 'This is *The Godfather* in tights. In Ray we have a man who has a wonderful animal power, very like that which Henry would have had. It's violent and sexy and that is what the world was like then. People have not seen history done like this before. Being the king is about being wonderfully charismatic. I think Ray is probably the only British actor who can do that ruthless power but also be incredibly vulnerable. He can switch from being a little boy to an ogre in the blink of an eye. If you weren't casting Ray, the only other actors you'd be looking at are Robert De Niro, Al Pacino and Russell Crowe.'

High praise indeed for Ray, who agreed with the Travis summation. 'You get the feel of a *Godfather* thing, in that they are conspiring all the time and there is loads of paranoia. It has a Mafia feel, everyone is jostling for position; everyone could be your enemy.'

To prepare Ray for his transformation, it took at least an hour each day in make-up and costume, with body suits, prosthetics and even padding in his mouth to make him look and sound convincing as the portly monarch. 'The costumes have been good, they are comfortable but pretty heavy. By the end of the week I'm dead on my legs. I get to wear all the heavy chains and other jewellery. Some days I've felt like MC Hammer. But I usually wear a pin-striped suit, so it's been a bit of a giggle.'

He even lost two stone for the role, working out at a gym and cutting back on his diet so that he was in good shape for the jousting, horse-riding and fight scenes. His only regret is that he wasn't allowed to do more of his own stunts, for insurance purposes as much as anything else. 'I start it and someone else finishes it!' he grins. 'But, really, it isn't easy. The stunt boys make us look good. There should be an academy award for stuntmen, though they'd probably just say, "Put our money up."'

The only downside, perhaps, was when ITV were accused of sensationalism for depicting Henry as a rapist, as Ray is seen assaulting Anne Boleyn after they argue about her failure to produce a son. Even if cast and crew didn't share that opinion, the scene, argued the critics, had no apparent basis in fact, and television watchdogs and historians joined in the controversy by adding that it looked like it may have been included to boost ratings.

John Beyer, director of Mediawatch UK, said, 'I think there is far too much emphasis on rape, violence and sexual assault on television today and to put this rape in some kind of clever historical setting is very far from what viewers would expect. Television makers do this sort of thing all the time. They write in particular scenes, sex it all up, and it adds to the idea that this is an acceptable activity, which it isn't. I am sure they include things like this to attract more viewers and improve the ratings, and including the rape scene in *Henry VIII* is just another example of this.'

Derek Wilson, a historian who specialises in the reign of

Henry VIII (1509–1547), joined in with the criticism. 'This rape doesn't seem as if it ever took place. It goes against everything we know about their relationship. Although he was known for being a bully as he got older, in his younger years the King was extremely courteous and witty and he abided by the conventions of his time. Including this scene is just unnecessary, as the original story of Henry VIII and his wives is a sensational one anyway.'

Surely, he continued, 'This is a move by the producers to get more viewers and sex it up, but why didn't they just realise a true story like this doesn't need that sort of treatment?'

Christopher Haigh, a lecturer in history at Christ Church College, Oxford, said much the same: 'This rape incident is not something I am aware of at all. I have never heard of it before. I think the action would be quite out of character for Henry.'

Although the scene was a difficult one to film for Bonham Carter, who was at the time pregnant with director Tim Burton's first child, she was sort of expecting it to shock viewers. 'That was a pretty unpleasant scene, but it brought home just what a monster Henry could be.'

Peter Morgan, of course, defended his decision to include the scene in his script. 'Plenty of historians will find what we have done scandalous. But I'm aiming to stimulate greater interest in history, rather than to score points with a particular version of events. The idea of the "gangster king" very much informs the piece.'

Adding fuel to an already blazing critical fire was Granada Television's controller, Andy Harries. He confirmed that *Henry VIII* was partly inspired by Channel 4's Mafia series *The Sopranos*. At around the same time another ITV historical dramatisation, *Boudica*, was also criticised for a scene where the queen's daughters were raped in front of her.

Henry VIII was screened on British television in two episodes over two weekends in October 2003. It had been compressed into 200 minutes of primetime television from the 20 hours of film that had been shot in April that same year during a £6-million, 12-week shoot on location at Arundel and Leeds castles, and at Pinewood studios in Buckinghamshire. It was filmed on 'M' Stage, just past the shed where they make *The Weakest Link* and the Albert R Broccoli 007 Stage. While they were shooting, Ben Kingsley was frequently spotted walking around dressed like a Thunderbird puppet for the upcoming live-action version of the television classic.

Despite the criticisms, on the whole, the two-part dramatisation of *Henry VIII* was well received. The *Daily Mail* called it 'a handsome, lavish and lively production, with plenty of action, bloodshed and romance'. The same message was echoed in the *Sunday Express* who said, 'A triumph... It was gritty, film-like and realistic.' In their applause for Ray, the *Evening Standard* said he was 'stunning as the ruthless, egocentric monarch'.

In retrospect, Ray's fascination with Henry should not have been all that surprising. It had many of the characteristics of his favourite kind of role. 'My idea of Henry is quite mixed,' Ray notes. 'I think he was a very troubled man – paranoid and psychotic at times, charming and funny at others. The last words his father left him with were "you must have a son", which preyed on his mind for the rest of his life. When Katherine of Aragon couldn't give him a son, Henry had to start making decisions, and that's when it all started to go wrong for him.

'This is a man who allowed two of his wives – women he

loved passionately – to be murdered. At the same time, he wrote beautiful love letters, understood science and, to a certain extent, was a great ambassador. He was an intelligent, gentle romantic man who lost his way when it came to love. He sells his soul for his country and for the duty he inherited, and from then on it became easier and easier for him to discard the women he loved. Jane Seymour finally gave him the son he wanted, but he lost her and that must have destroyed him. Back then, there was a strong belief in God, death, heaven and hell, and I guess he punished himself for her death for the rest of his life.

'Powerful men usually have a weakness and that always seems to be sex. Also, if you look at other powerful men throughout history, they had to be leaders and have that evil streak in them to survive. Everyone is fighting for his or her position, and people like Henry didn't know who their friends were. There must've been a lot of paranoia and Henry had to keep his wits about him. In my mind, only winners make the history books, though you have to read a little between the lines. For example, I've tried looking at things from Anne Boleyn's and the Boleyn family's point of view, trying to understand why they wanted to become so involved with the King when it would have been safer to stay away. It's good to look at that kind of stuff and get a greater understanding.

'Pete Morgan has done his homework. All I had to do is just come in, dress up as the King and bring all the emotion, pain and joy that goes with it. Henry's passion for being an Englishman, his passion for being in love – I can relate to that. The passion for wanting to be violent at times – I can also relate to that. But to actually hurt someone you love, I can't understand that. I think you would have had to be [violent] to survive in those times. There's certainly no room for nice guys. It was dog eat dog. So no, I'll leave the Tudor Court to the 16th century. Definitely not for me!

'But I've really enjoyed wearing the costumes, as I'm usually in a pinstriped suit! You see pictures of people throughout history and you think they are these stiff characters who are nothing like us. But they are. They walk, talk and have the same haircuts as us and that's how I've approached this costume – it's just like putting on a suit. The dialogue has been tricky, and it's hard to make tricky dialogue your own and make it conversational and demanding and powerful. So that's been the trick, trying to melt that altogether.

'Every day has also been very diverse. For instance, there was one day when I had sex with Anne Boleyn, she gave birth, we got married and I raped her – all in the same day! Also I'm playing a 30-year-old Henry right through to 50-year-old Henry. So you've really got to try to remember what's happening, and what stage you're at because it's not all done in chronological order. Sometimes you forget which scene you're in and where you are, but that's half the enjoyment and the challenge.'

Equally challenging, although for different reasons, was his role in Jerry Bruckheimer's *King Arthur*. In the film Ray plays a character named Bors, a pugilistic and fearsome fighter who is also the veteran of the pack in Arthur's knights. 'His speciality is hand-to-hand combat. He is down and dirty and all that fancy swordplay is really not his thing. He fights with an axe and his fists. He likes getting in there but he is getting a bit old. He is slowing up a bit, a lot like me, and he hurts a lot more. Bors has five children and three wives, and could be kind of a big shot in his own town.'

He's also on a final tour of duty with Arthur and his knights before he can return to his far-off homeland. He emerges as a killer with a certain humanity and humour. Ray says, 'He's macho but, underneath it all, he has feelings, and he's a family man. This is an action movie, but I believe you've also got to make the character interesting, you've got to bring in some humanity. I made him a bit melancholy because he missed home.'

Interestingly enough, he almost turned down the role. 'We didn't have a script to read when they first offered me the part. All I had was a story to go by. The only reason I did the film was because of the director Antoine Fuqua, and not for anyone else. I took a risk with him and he didn't let me down. He came up with the goods as far as I'm concerned.' Another bonus of eventually accepting the part was having the opportunity to work with Clive Owen. 'That swung it for me, too. He's a really talented boy, and, along with the fact that I'm 47 and have never done an action film before, I thought this might be my last chance.'

The story that appealed so much to Ray had been written by David Franzoni, who had worked out a new approach to the King Arthur legend that offered a more historically accurate story. 'There's a moment in history that we can actually pin down,' he recalls. 'There is a name and there is a battle. The name was Lucius Artorius Castus and the battle was the Battle of Badon Hill. This battle changed the face of Britain and created a legend which has survived for generations and has been reinvented many times. I thought it was a great opportunity to go back and try to find out what these people were like and to tell their story realistically.'

It was one of the reasons why producer Bruckheimer wanted to make the film in the first place. To be able to go to the movies and watch a big epic film, and the fact that he loved making films that change people's perception 'through telling a story in a much more realistic way. That is what *King Arthur* does; it tells you the true story about what was going on during that period.'

Certainly, Franzoni's script would do exactly that. 'This is *King Arthur* as *The Wild Bunch*,' he raved. 'The Sarmatian cavalry or knights were the last Roman Special Forces unit with Artorius Castus as their commander; they are assigned one last mission in enemy territory. All around them, the Roman Empire is pulling out and collapsing. These men have ruthlessly and brutally suppressed everyone around them for the sake of Rome. There's blood all over them and their bond is that blood. It's a bond of what they have done and what they have known.'

To capture the unromantic, harsh essence of King Arthur, Bruckheimer sought Antoine Fuqua, director of *Training Day*, a starkly realistic police drama set on the streets of Los Angeles. 'I had been a fan of Antoine's for many years through his videos and commercials. He did a video for us for *Dangerous Minds* and, so, I had always wanted to do a movie with him.'

Fuqua, a native of Pittsburgh, was raised surrounded by the myths and movies of King Arthur and the Knights of the Round Table. 'I grew up watching stories like *King Arthur*, the big epic historical movies,' Fuqua remembers. 'Through the years, I have studied mythology and related matters and specifically the legend of King Arthur. As a kid, I used to play knights with my friends and then, as an artist, I wanted to make a film like this. When the opportunity came through with Jerry Bruckheimer to do this film, I didn't hesitate to make it. I think Jerry thought I was the right guy for this film because I believe this movie is gritty – you can actually taste and smell the violence and death. You can feel the cold and the despair. It's very apocalyptic. In the world at that time, there wasn't a lot of hope – hope is what Arthur represents.'

This is what both producer and director wanted the basis of the new King Arthur film to be – an action drama that charted the 'bloody' adventures of King Arthur and his band of knights. But, continues Fuqua, it had to be much more reality based as opposed to the fantasy. 'It excited me because it's King Arthur as you've never seen him before. What appealed to me was that it was based on a sense of a reality. There was historical research done and there were some facts we found that we didn't know before. It's thrilling to discover that there is this hero that you grew up with who actually really existed. That's exciting.'

Despite his life-long interest in Arthur and the knights, Fuqua had never heard of Castus until he read Franzoni's script. 'I didn't know anything about Artorius or the Sarmatian knights, but, after reading the script, Jerry and I got together and we did quite a bit of research. We flew to England, visited Hadrian's Wall and spoke with some Arthurian experts, including John Matthews. I also visited the museums to see what the knights wore. As I researched, I found out that people of any nation who had been conquered by the Romans could have become knights. And I also found out that chivalry didn't exist then; these guys were very much about blood, guts and no glory. These guys were fighting every day in the mud and the cold weather. They must have been the toughest guys alive. I believe that *King Arthur* will give people a sense of the reality of the man; the person behind the legend. Arthur wasn't just a legend, he was a real man: someone who sacrificed himself to become a leader and earned the right to be called King.

'The reality of it is that it only takes one person to stand up and fight against evil. *King Arthur* is essentially about good against evil; it's basic mythology. You have to face the demons; you have to slay the dragons. You cannot run away. To me it's important that we stand up as individuals, as human beings. We have to face evil. You can't run away from who you are. It only takes one person to step up and be ready to do battle and you'll be surprised at how many people will follow you. That's why I respond to this kind of material. Take *Training Day* and Ethan Hawke's character: someone had to stand up to Alonzo at some point. Otherwise you get beaten down and we get dictators. As an actor, Clive Owen gets to the heart of what Arthur is about.'

After reading Franzoni's script, it was easy for Owen to see what Franzoni was getting at. It was then he saw Arthur as 'the one who feels a sense of unfairness, a sense of responsibility to intervene and make the world a fair place. The knights, as loyal as they are to him, are much more like military machines – they want to do their thing and move on. But that's why Arthur is the leader – they all recognise that there's something different about him and they can't help themselves from following him. Arthur has a line in the film: "You have your deeds, but deeds are meaningless unless they serve some higher purpose." That's really what shapes Arthur, everything he does has to be for the greater good.'

According to Bruckheimer, *King Arthur* is the definitive story of the leader and warrior who emerged to lead the Britons against the Saxons. 'It is the story of the man who became King Arthur. And that's what excited me about this film. It's a new look at a tale that we thought we were familiar with. The truth is that King Arthur lived in a much earlier time period than you see in most of the movie versions, in the Dark Ages.'

After six months filming in Ireland, Ray almost felt like he was in the Dark Ages himself, but he also confessed that it had given him the taste for action movies. It was also very different to the kind of films he had been making. 'Films I've made before were a much quicker process. With a smaller budget you don't have time to mess around. But on *King Arthur* you could find yourself doing a scene for three or four days. It's a different way of working, but, if you're surrounded by the people you want to be surrounded by, it's fine, you get through it.

'It's not like you're just doing physical stuff for an hour; you're doing it all day, every day. It was tough, but you haven't got a choice. You just get up and do it. Yeah, it was knackering but it's part and parcel of the job. I think, once the adrenaline's going, it gets you through it. But, with a film like that, you have this comedown at the end of it, and that's when you feel tired.'

Everyone, that is, except Keira Knightley who Bruckheimer had recruited from his *Pirates of the Caribbean* set to play the role of Guinevere opposite Clive Owen's Arthur. 'She was probably the toughest of us all,' Ray recalls. 'Instead of going on holiday on her three weeks off like the rest of us would have, she trained every day and she's just this little baby. She gets better every time I see her. And of course some of the Irish actors on the set were amazing as well. This country is so talented, there should be a lot more done here, especially big movies like this. It's important that the Irish film industry supports its own. I say let's stop making big American movies and make great ones at home like this.'

All the same, Ray admits, the spectacular battle scenes were down to director Antoine, especially the much-talked-about battle on thin ice sequence, which the *Hollywood Reporter* described as 'one of the great cinematic fight scenes of all time'.

Ray agreed: 'It was clear that we were working with a very, very talented director, not just technically but also the way he rallied his troops. It's quite wonderful what he's done with it, especially the immensity of it all, and you don't get the full picture until you actually see it on screen.'

The first time Ray realised he was working on a big film was when he came over the hill at Ballymore Eustace, the film location in County Kildare, and saw the reconstruction of Hadrian's Wall, which was a kilometre long and cost £6 million to make. So impressed was he that he said he wished he could shoot every film in Dublin.

'I think the best part about filming in Ireland is that you are so close to home, you're only across the pond. It was great because my family could be on a plane and be here in an hour, but also we're very similar people, we're city people and when you come to Dublin we understand one another. I was brought up in London around Irish people all my life so when I come here I don't feel like I'm in another country. I feel that I'm just part of what I've always known. It's true that coming to Dublin put 20 years on my life; I often didn't see my bed until four in the morning after a really heavy day of shooting. But, at the end of the day, if you're going to shoot anywhere in the world and you're going to be away for six months, then it has to be Ireland. Why would you want to go anywhere else?'

King Arthur opened in Britain on 30 July 2004 and in the United States three weeks earlier. Within two weeks, it had taken $30 million at the US box office; ultimately, its gross topped $51 million and its makeup team won an IFTA at the Irish Film and Television Awards. Later, it was reissued on DVD as an Extended Director's Cut, in a version that was longer and more explicit than that released into cinemas.

With two more well-received performances behind him, and his production company, Size Nine – set up with producer Joshua St John and his agent Michael Wiggs to develop projects for himself – up and running, plus a significant role as the voice of Mr Beaver in *The Chronicles of Narnia* for the Christmas movie of the following year, things couldn't have looked better.

In fact, it was at the premiere of *Narnia* that young Ellie Rae stepped into her own spotlight when she told journalists who her dad was. Ray laughs at the memory, 'We were walking down the blue carpet with all the flashbulbs going off. I looked down and she's talking into the microphone, giving interviews, going, "My dad's Mr Beaver." And I thought, "What have I created?" She's very, very funny.' And playing a beaver, added Ray, was a first. 'I don't think I've been a beaver yet in a movie so that'll be interesting and I've never been married to Dawn French (Mrs Beaver) either, so I suppose it's all quite an experience for me.'

For director Andrew Adamson, it was like a childhood dream come true. '*Narnia* was such a vivid and real world to me as a child, as it is to millions of other fans. *The Chronicles* were an important part of my childhood and I hope to bring to the screen a movie that is as real to the audience as it was to me.' And, according to the critics, he did that as well.

Adapted from one of C. S. Lewis' seven-volume series of children stories, Narnia is one of the most beloved fantasy adventures ever written and is regarded as a timeless tale of sheer imagination. Even if the film was literally years in the making, it was all worth it. As the book itself still remains the most popular tome for children after J. K. Rowling's *Harry Potter*, it was no surprise that it ended up as the seasonal box-office smash that it did.

It is perhaps interesting to note that, although Ray says providing the voice to the film was a first, it was also in the same year that he contributed his voice to the big screen version of the second most popular teatime television favourite *The Magic Roundabout*.

CHAPTER 12

Act Accordingly

Angelina Jolie was apparently so furious on her first day of shooting *Beowulf*, in which she stars alongside Ray, that she told the producers she refused to work with him unless he apologised. She shut down the production and walked off the set. She was fuming because, according to the *Hollywood Reporter*, Ray had apparently told reporters that she was getting married to Brad Pitt. And, as far as Angelina was concerned, that was a no-no. She and Brad weren't quite ready to go public with their plans. In fact, they had hired Tom Cruise's former public relations guru Pat Kingsley to improve their love-rat reputations before any wedding plans could be announced. And so the film was on hold, which apparently left director Robert Zemeckis and his film in turmoil. But did it really?

According to some sources from the set, it did, because 'most of Angelina and Ray's scenes also feature Anthony

Hopkins, John Malkovich and Crispin Glover, so Robert risks losing these big names unless he reconciles the feuding pair,' which as some online discussion groups have said is all very convincing, except that Anthony Hopkins and John Malkovich had already wrapped their stuff and gone home a couple of weeks previously, while Ray and Angelina's scenes only have the two of them in, which means that 'the source hasn't read the script, knows nothing of the shooting schedule, and isn't involved with the film in any way, not even distantly'. The general theory on the set was that one of the gossip magazines had planted the story online so they could then deniably 'report it', which is as credible as any other.

But Ray, it seems, did let it slip to Britain's *Mail on Sunday* journalist Chrissy Iley that Angie, as he refers to Jolie, was indeed already engaged. 'She's getting married, isn't she? Yes she is.' As Iley pointed out in her October 2005 feature and interview with Ray, she was somewhat 'startled that he's given me this scoop'.

According to Ray, 'It was funny because before she'd even arrived on set they reported here in the papers that we'd had a terrible bust-up on the set and I don't know how that was possible because she hadn't even arrived. It's a shame what they do to this girl, she's a really good kid. And a fabulous actress. In fact, I spent a whole day kissing her and, you know, it was tough, it was hard work. And I went home that evening and my wife and little girl was there and I was very quiet, as you would be. And my wife says, "What's the matter with you?" And I said, "I've just been kissing Angelina Jolie all day." And she goes, "Well, somebody's got to, babe."'

At the time of writing, *Beowulf*, in which Ray plays the

title role, is in production and many of the details of the film remain under wraps. Jolie is thought to play a queen of darkness who tempts the Viking Beowulf, Ray, during his quest to become king.

Written between the 7th and the 10th centuries, *Beowulf* is an action-packed epic poem about a Scandinavian hero named Beowulf, who fights fierce battles to defeat a man-eating monster called Grendel (played in the film by Crispin Glover). Regarded as one of the most famous poems in Anglo-Saxon and Old English literature, *Beowulf* was written in England, but the events it relates to are set in Baltic Europe. After Beowulf defeats Grendel and his evil mother, he returns home and rules as king for 50 years until a dragon begins to terrorise the countryside. He eventually dies in a dramatic confrontation with the beast. This new Zemeckis version is set to give Old English poetry a buzz to surpass even the excitement caused by the Nobel Prize winner Seamus Heaney's translation of the work in 1999.

In the film – due to be released in November 2007 – the actors will be seen as animated versions of themselves, by using the performance-capture technology that Zemeckis previously used in *The Polar Express*. The director made this choice because '*Beowulf* is a timeless, epic tale of heroism and triumph. Digital rendering will allow us to depict this incredible story in ways we would never have dared imagine.'

Interestingly enough, the script was originally written with Roger Avary by the British sci-fi writer Neil Gaiman seven years before the film went into production. If you asked Gaiman today to describe *Beowulf,* he would tell you it is 'a sort of Dark Ages *Trainspotting*, filled with mead and blood and madness'. It was originally offered to Steven Spielberg's DreamWorks, but they didn't like it. Eventually, Zemeckis,

Gaiman and Avary found the backing of Shangri-La, an entertainment company headed by Steve Bing, the millionaire who had once dated Elizabeth Hurley.

Even in pre-production, it sounds great fun, raved Dr Paul Cavill, an Anglo-Saxon specialist at Nottingham University. 'Some scholars are a bit sniffy about Seamus Heaney or about *The 13th Warrior* [another film inspired by *Beowulf*], but I think they add enormously to people's enjoyment of Anglo-Saxon literature. Anglo-Saxon is, in many ways, inaccessible because you have to get someone's version of it or you learn the language. One is longer than the other. So I always welcome these things. They have to be done very badly not to contribute something to the accessibility of the literature.'

In an interview on the internet film site IGN, in December 2006, another member of the cast, John Malkovich, pointed out that none of the cast was providing *just* voices for the film. 'No, it's not that. You do everything but then it's given a form of computer animation afterwards. But, no, we were all on set. We were all acting. It's not film. There's no film, there's no lights. There are video references that the specialists and technicians utilise, but it's actually all recorded on computer and all the data is fed to the technicians and then they will animate it.'

But, as Malkovich continued to explain, 'I will, to some extent, look and sound like myself, but Ray, who plays Beowulf, will be seven feet tall and will look sort of like an amalgam of portraits of Jesus and Ray. It was really an amazing experience. I know they are still hard at work on it. We shot it last year, and there's probably still a year to go.'

Malkovich also disclosed that he occasionally hears rumours that he might or might not shoot some supplemental material. 'It was a very interesting experience, great, because you'd just wear these suits with lights on them and you'd get there and you act all day. You sort of run and cut and then run back to place to start again. But it's really like doing a play. You just never stop working.'

Anthony Hopkins, however, who also stars, felt that, as an actor, working in this way he was missing some of his tools. 'You miss everything. You don't have anything. Say you have a cup or a mug or some sort of medieval thing, a drinking goblet, it's made of steel and it's all hollow. If there was a bottle, there'd just be a piece of steel construction with nothing in it and you'd have to do this. I don't know. It's weird. It's a modernised version of it but it's set in its period.

'What seems to me so strange is that they designed costumes for it. I remember going in and they put a beard on you and everything, huge cloaks and all that stuff. It's out of the period, medieval period or Dark Ages, really, 10th century, whatever it was. Then they photograph you and put you through a computer and then you never see it again. That's it. But then they dress all that in later. So it seems to me, I don't get the purpose of it.'

Whether Ray got the purpose of it or not, one thing was for sure. Determined not to move to live in Los Angeles permanently, Ray had rented a house in Malibu for the nine weeks he was needed to complete the filming of *Beowulf*. Even if he had been making his living in Hollywood alone, he says he would have no desire to live his life there as well. 'No, this is not my home. I'm an Englishman. Even nine weeks is too long to be away from my family. I couldn't be apart from them for any longer than that. I'm a husband and father first. Acting comes after that.' He had little choice about being in Hollywood this time, though, as, apart from

Beowulf, he had also been working on another film – the biggest of his career – *The Departed*, directed by Martin Scorsese and starring Jack Nicholson, Leonardo DiCaprio and Matt Damon.

In his recollection of how he got the part, Ray says he went to see Scorsese at the Dorchester Hotel in London one Sunday morning. 'I think he was seeing other English actors anyway, but the producer of the film who is an English guy, Graham King, was a fan of mine and I've met him a couple of times, so I was a bit lucky. And I went to see him and funnily enough I have the "Cavalry Charge" on me phone, and one of me mates rang up, so, as I walked in the door, it went off.

'And it was my friend Yatesie and I said, "Hold it, Tone, I'm just going in to see Martin Scorsese." And he went, "Yeah right." And I ended up sitting there for about an hour and a half just talking to him. He liked my coat, which, funnily enough, he got me wearing in one of the scenes. I think I got the part because of my jacket but what I loved about him, you go and see these people and they always have a way of ending the meeting, the secretary comes in and says, "Don't forget you've got a phone call." And it never happened and, in the end, I had to call an end to the meeting because I had my Sunday dinner, and I won't miss my Sunday dinner for anyone, not even the Queen. So I said, "I've got to get home from the Dorchester. Come with me if you like. We've got plenty." And he passed on that. And that was it really.'

Clearly, he loves Ray's work, but to most journalists that met him in his trailer, they say he tried to downplay the fact that he was on the set of a Scorsese gangster movie.

Scorsese seems to have been equally enamoured with Ray.

'I had always wanted an excuse to work with him because he's a fine actor, and it was a miracle that he was free to do it. He is such a powerful presence in the movie.'

It wasn't the first time that the director had tried to get hold of him for one of his movies. Scorsese apparently had a role for him in *Gangs of New York*, but Ray turned it down. At the time, Ray says, he preferred to wait for a film that was more in keeping with the director's earlier classics. 'I don't know who the hell I thought I was thinking that way,' he laughs, 'but this one [*The Departed*] was more the kind of genre film that I'd watched of his, like *Mean Streets* or *GoodFellas*.' And to all intents and purposes that was the kind of Scorsese film he wanted to be involved with.

Based on the 2002 Hong Kong crime thriller *Internal Affairs*, the film is set in South Boston, and tells the story of how the Massachusetts State Police Department is waging an all-out war to take down the city's top organised-crime ring. The key is to end the reign of powerful mob boss Frank Costello, played by Jack Nicholson, from the inside. A young rookie named Billy Costigan (Leonardo DiCaprio), who grew up in South Boston, is assigned to infiltrate the mob run by Costello. While Billy is working to gain Costello's trust, another young cop who came up from the streets of 'Southie', Colin Sullivan (Matt Damon), is quickly rising through the ranks of the state police. Earning a spot in the Special Investigations Unit, Colin is among a handful of elite officers whose mission is to bring Costello down. But what his superiors don't know is that Colin is working for Costello, keeping the crime boss one step ahead of the police.

Each man becomes deeply consumed by his double life, gathering information about the plans and counter-plans of the operation he has penetrated. But, when it becomes clear to both the gangsters and the police that they have a mole in their midst, Billy and Colin find themselves in constant danger of being caught and exposed to the enemy, and each must race to uncover the identity of the other man in time to save himself.

Cast opposite Jack Nicholson, Ray played Mr French, Nicholson's brutal henchman, who Ray describes as the dustman of the film. 'I clean things up. French is without emotion, nothing rattles him, nothing frightens him. To him, everyone is a rat. If you get in his way, he'll kill you without a second thought. He's one of those guys you get nothing from. He doesn't trust anyone, doesn't like anyone, and probably doesn't like himself.' That was most evident, Ray says, from the scene where he is seen ripping Leonardo DiCaprio's plaster cast and pinning his broken arm down for Nicholson's mob boss to beat with a shoe. 'It takes a special sort of man to do that to someone, almost like an undertaker. But, as an actor, I'm always trying to find the emotion in a character, the weaknesses as well as the strengths.'

The film, and the experience of making it, could have turned out so differently. Especially if Scorsese hadn't quite lived up to Ray's expectations of him. But, Ray confirms, he wasn't let down. 'He's beautiful, a really nice man. He is everything you want him to be, you know? He's just a really blinding guy... I did say to him that there was one scene sort of short of a part I wouldn't mind doing, and he wrote it in. It's the scene where I'm talking about my wife and certain things happening and that. And it making a friendship rather than being a guy in the background that's just the heavy. We see enough films like that, where they have an extra there because they don't want to pay him any more. And I think if this is going to be someone this guy trusts they've got to have some kind of relationship. Maybe that was me being clever but it made it a better character.'

But, as Ray continues to explain, 'There's plenty of directors out there who are great technically and plenty who are great with actors but to get a director who is great with both is brilliant. He's one of those directors who makes you think it was your idea. To give you an example, I was standing behind him and he's got all the screens there and he's kind of editing it as he goes along. And there's a scene where one of the main actors comes through and he looked at the wrong time and if you're watching it you can see that but, if you're acting, it doesn't necessarily always register. But instead of going out to the actor and saying, "You should look then," he went up to him and talked to him and the actor said, "Maybe I should look then." And he said, "Great idea."

'And what that does for you as an actor, that gives you great confidence that you're bringing something to the table, you're contributing to the making of the film. And even though my bit, I've got a cameo kind of role in the film, but I never felt once that I couldn't bring an idea, that I wasn't part of making the movie and that's the sign of a great director.'

But, then again, Ray has never been one to be assailed by self-doubt. Ray's daughters, Lois and Jaime, agree. They always think that it's good for the Hollywood fraternity to meet their father. As Lois points out, 'He's so comfortable with himself and so natural. All the fawning around stars is bad for everyone. I mean it's taken my dad years to get where he is, but he's never arse-licked anyone. That's a really important thing he's taught me.'

Jaime shared much the same opinion. 'I've sat next to

Martin Scorsese while he's doing his thing, directing Jack Nicholson and Leonardo DiCaprio in scenes with my dad,' she says. 'Once you get over the shock of that's Jack Nicholson, and that's Leonardo DiCaprio, with my dad, you realise the process is the same. They work exactly like they would over here on an independent film that costs a grand to make. And you learn the lingo. It makes the whole thing less scary.'

For Jaime, though, it's probably a lot easier than it is for others. After all, how many other young actresses could spend their spare time on a Scorsese movie set in New York and talk about consorting with the likes of Leonardo DiCaprio, Jack Nicholson and Matt Damon? 'It wasn't that exciting, actually,' Jaime sighs. 'There's a complete zone around the big stars in American films, which takes the fun out of it. In London the vibe is that everyone talks to each other, but, with Hollywood, people have their assistants pass messages to other people's people or whatever. It was amazing to see these huge actors at work, and I got a really nice feel for what goes on behind the screen. But it is a huge bubble of fakeness where you can lose touch with the real world.'

Filming, however, was not without its problems. Like Ray and Damon, it was the first time DiCaprio had worked with Nicholson, and today he admits that he found the Oscar-winning actor both frightening and uplifting to work with. 'He's a force of nature and you have to be prepared to roll with the punches,' he says. 'There were moments during filming when I didn't know what was going to happen next. If you hire Jack Nicholson to play an Irish Mob kingpin in a Martin Scorsese film of this genre, he's going to make the role his own and that involves going on to the set every day expecting the unexpected. He is going to throw curveballs at you and you have to be completely prepared for anything. There was tons of improvisation with him. I was never sure which side of his character he was going to be playing on any particular day. It makes you terrified as an actor, and it ups the stakes.'

One particularly outrageous stunt that Nicholson pulled was during the bar scene in which DiCaprio had to try to convince Nicholson that he was not the mole in the mob. They filmed the scene once and Nicholson said to Scorsese, 'I don't think he's scared enough of me; I have to be scarier.' So, when DiCaprio came in the next day, 'Jack's hair was all over the place. He was muttering to himself and the prop guy tipped me off that he had a fire extinguisher, a bottle of whisky, some matches and a handgun somewhere. So I sat down at the table not knowing what to expect, and he set the table on fire after pouring whisky all over the place and stuck a gun in my face. It changed the whole dynamic of the scene, and that's what he does. He makes you so much better and he makes you react as an actor, and you take more chances because your character is reacting to this homicidal maniac.'

The Departed was released in October 2006 to rave reviews. And in almost all of them, despite having a smaller part than the rest of the cast, Ray was praised for his portrayal of Jack Nicholson's henchman, Mr French. One of a dozen online reviews suggested that audiences should compare Nicholson's acting in the film to the superb work of Ray as his psychopathic henchman. 'Nicholson is always *on* – a movie star performing for the camera, while Winstone simply *is* his character.' It couldn't have been better if Ray had written it himself. Most other reviews followed suit. The great reviews may have helped when it came to the recognition the film received at the following year's Academy Awards ceremony. It was nominated in five categories: Best Achievement in Directing, Best Achievement in Editing, Best Motion Picture of the Year, Best Writing, Adapted Screenplay, and Best Performance by an Actor in a Supporting Role (for Mark Wahlberg). It walked away with four of them.

As *The Departed* was playing out on screens across the country, Ray returned to the small screen for the second series of *Vincent*. The new batch of four films followed much the same format as the first run of shows and was again shot in Manchester, doubling up for London. In many ways, it was better shooting the dramas in the northern city than it would have been down south. Well, it was according to Ray. 'You can imagine how big a city London is. You can take two or three hours to travel to another location. It's absolutely impossible. But, in Manchester, everything is within arm's reach. You can be anywhere within half an hour. On a bad day, it can be 45 minutes. It's easier to film. It's harder for me because, obviously, you can be away from your family for a while. But they come up and you can go home at weekends, so it's OK.'

Not so good, however, was the first story in which Vincent attempts to uncover the truth about the murder of hotel chambermaid Eva Krackowic. That was probably the hardest day in front of the cameras for Ray. The storyline included a harrowing scene where Vincent gets drugged and wakes up in bed covered in blood next to the dead body of Eva's best friend, played by Ray's daughter Jamie. 'It was a very difficult one to do because I never knew she was up for the job, believe it or not. And she got the part. I'm not saying dads don't help their daughters, because you do. But that was something she had done on her own.'

In fact, continues Ray, 'The first scene I had to do with her was waking up in bed with her throat cut. It's not a nice view to see. I worried about it more before than when I was doing it. But she's a working actress. She told me she was getting paid and that was fine. It's that kind of world. There's the undercurrent in every city, in Manchester, in London. I'm afraid these things go on.'

But for Jaime, it was quite a surreal undertaking. 'I didn't really think about it myself but, watching my dad, it must have been much harder for him to be staring at his daughter dead on a bed. It was scary but amazing to work with him. I learn from him every time I'm with him.'

Not that there was any question of Ray trying to persuade her not to become an actress. 'If you want to do something, you do it. And if you're lucky enough to be working, it's a great job. If that's what my kids want to do, I can't think of a better way to live, if you're working. You travel all over the world, you meet people from all walks of life and it's a kind of education on its own, without the actual filming.'

With or without his daughter in the first episode, Ray reckoned the second series had gone up a notch in his estimation. 'It's darker and I think it had to become darker. I think the first four were great, really excellent, but you're talking about a man who watches other people's lives, you know, he's a voyeur and he's a hero. They want a hero, there's a format in TV where I think TV is very scared of showing the other side of something. They like what they show already but I keep trying to take it a little bit further on, I don't think there's anything better than an audience growing to like someone and then someone who they like turns out to be someone they're not. Not that we've done that in this series but maybe we will get to that.'

Writing in the *Sunday Herald*, reviewer Damien Love agreed. 'The new series of *Vincent* is equally as strong as the first. Ray Winstone plays the eponymous private eye, drifting around London like a grumbling storm cloud. He's backed by a dizzyingly strong team – Suranne Jones, Ian Puleston-Davies, a deeply strange Joe Absolom. But it's Winstone's show. He lends it an unreconstructed strength. *Vincent* taps the stuff that made *The Sweeney* an institution, and has enough humour and nous that it doesn't need to caricature it. It's superb. I was almost punching the air by the end of the first episode; the only drawback is there are only three more this series. Here's to another 15 years of it.'

But perhaps the most concise of critical summaries was when *The Times* critic Carol Midgley wrote, 'Ray Winstone is the dog's bollocks of British acting, and he is always worth a look given that he can lift even the dodgiest script to semi-Bafta level. In fact a TV critic could almost get away with not watching anything he is in, merely writing "Ray Winstone was brilliant in … (fill in title of programme)" and going back to sleep.'

Vincent was no different, so perhaps it wasn't surprising when it won the Best Actor nomination for Ray in the 2006 International Emmy Awards. As Jaime said when she collected the award on behalf of her father, 'He's like highly inspirational, an amazing dad. I love him.'

Even though Ray was unable to attend, he was just as proud and thrilled as Jaime was. 'It's a real honour to be recognised internationally. But it's the show that has won because Stephen Butchard and the production team have created such a great role for me.' And, of course, he was right.

Even though he hadn't warmed to the character during the making of the first series, Ray had been attracted to take on the role in the first place because 'I knew it was being made by Andy Harries's department. I was really keen, because I worked with him on *Henry VIII* and I really like him. Granada's a blinding company to work for because they treat you really well. Also, I know the writer Stephen Butchard because he wrote the scripts for *Tough Love* and *Lenny Blue*, which I starred in, so I knew the scripts were going to be good. Stephen's brought a really human element to *Vincent* and delves into so many different issues, but what's really great about this script is, as Vincent's unravelling other people's problems, he's also unravelling his own. Also Stephen hasn't used any corny jargon like, "Roger, Roger, over and out."'

All the same, Ray continues, 'I really enjoyed playing him, and you don't always have to like your character as a person to enjoy playing the role. Vincent's working in a profession where he's uncovering people's deepest, darkest secrets, and could potentially destroy their lives and others around them. I kind of like that darker side a little bit more. This is a guy who's sneaking around people's windows and dustbins and takes pictures of them making love to someone else's wife, so the first thought that comes into my mind is scumbag, he's a dog. At the end of the day he's being paid by someone, to investigate the cases, be it a murder, adultery, fraud or whatever, but all he's trying to do is earn a living so you can't knock him for that. I feel sorry for him because he's a softie at heart and still clearly loves his ex, Cathy. I like the element that the audience can start to like him, but still be a bit uncomfortable about what he and the rest of the team do, but maybe he's quite a good man, and maybe private investigators are good people, who are trying to change the world for the right reasons.'

As far as executive producer Sita Williams was concerned, it was a role Ray was always going to play. It was not so easy, however, to cast the role of Beth, Vincent's sidekick. She had to be young and attractive, but also big and strong, says Williams. 'Beth is Vincent's moral conscience; she's always telling him off, so we needed an actress who wouldn't be dwarfed. Ray's a very big presence and she has to be his equal.'

At the time of the audition, Suranne Jones was just about to leave *Coronation Street* in which she had played the emotionally unstable Karen McDonald for four years. 'She was the first one we saw, but it's like buying a flat – you never feel you ought to take the first one you see.'

Everyone was impressed by Jones's reading, but reluctant to employ an ex-soap star – mindful perhaps of much-heralded post-soap careers that have sunk without trace, Jones went to Australia 'to shed my last few Karen McDonald demons' while Williams continued her search to find an actress.

'Eventually, we decided our only choice was to screen test a handful of actresses with Ray,' Williams recalls. 'We gave them a very difficult scene to play, in which Beth has to attack Vincent after he's done something stupid. We knew that, if the actress could do that to Ray on a first meeting, she could do the job. Jones went into the screen test reeling from jetlag and was greeted by Ray in feisty form.

'He said, "Ello, Suranne, last time I saw you, you was legless at the Baftas." It's true,' says Jones. 'I'd gone up to him backstage because I admired him so much and started introducing myself. He said, "Oh, I know who you are, darlin', my missus has *Corrie* on all the time." We spent the rest of the evening drinking together and that was that. He couldn't wait to remind me of that evening. I was thinking, "Yeah, thanks a lot, Ray. It's all right for you; you've already got the job. I haven't."'

Jones's party reputation, however, evidently didn't do her any harm, for, by the time she'd flown back to Sydney, the producers had made their decision. 'I was walking over Sydney Harbour Bridge when my phone rang,' she says. 'I did an interview six years ago in which they asked me, "Who would you most like to work with?" and I replied, "I'd like to be Ray Winstone's arsekick and sidekick in something." I left *Corrie* and got it straight away!'

So, when *Radio Times* critic Rupert Smith caught up with her for an October 2005 interview, she asked him if he could print that she now wanted to work with Julie Walters.

Maybe, though, casting Jones wasn't that surprising to Ray. He was said to have had his eye on her for a while. 'I watched her in *Corrie* and thought, "That girl's a cinema actress." Soap acting is very hard; you have to walk on, hit your mark, you've got four cameras on you, and you have to produce the goods, day in, day out. The good ones can leave a soap and do just about anything. Suranne's completely different in *Vincent* from what she was in *Corrie*. She's not pushing it out like you do in a soap; she's acting for the screen with her eyes and her face. She's a proper actress.'

There were the usual amount of behind-the-scene high jinks during the making of *Vincent*. One that Jones remembers particularly well is how Ray got very frustrated during the filming of the first series. 'He wanted to come out partying with us, but he couldn't. He had to stay in and learn his lines because he's in practically every scene. So, after we'd finished the first two episodes, he threw a big party for everyone, in the Rovers Return replica bar at

Granada Studios, which was quite strange for me. He hired karaoke equipment and, of course, it ended up with me doing a song, then Ray doing a song, basically fighting over the mic. Ray does all the Frank Sinatra stuff, usually with a cigar on the go. And I do 'Baby Love' with a glass of wine in each hand.'

Clearly, karaoke is one of the best ways to forge a great screen partnership, says Ray. Not that one can imagine Katharine Hepburn and Spencer Tracy ever indulging in such antics, or even *The Avengers*' John Steed and Emma Peel. But, for Vincent and Beth, 'there's definitely chemistry there. You get the feeling that these two characters could be together, except for the age thing, she's 26 to his 48. And working together did seem to forge a certain kind of screen magic for them, but to be honest,' Ray continues, 'Suranne reminds me of one of my daughters. She's mouthy enough. She tells me off like they do, on screen and off, and I should really smack her arse. I wanted that relationship to come across a bit awkward, somewhere between boyfriend and girlfriend and father and daughter. She's probably the person he should be with, but they've gone beyond that.'

Jones agrees, but still puts the success of the partnership down to Ray. 'There are some actors you have to work very hard with. Not Ray. It just flies out of him. When we do the shouting scenes, it's real for him, and so you just come straight back with your best. He's got a hard reputation, but I know he's a softie underneath.'

It was during the same period that *The Departed* and *Vincent* were wowing viewers and audiences everywhere that Ray's second big-screen feature to be released in 2006 received its European premiere at the *Times* BFI 50th London Film Festival during the Blackberry Gala. Jude Law and

Robin Wright Penn joined director Anthony Minghella to introduce the Gala screening of *Breaking and Entering*, in which Ray appeared in a minor role.

Filmed in the summer of the same year that Ray had worked on *The Departed*, the film is a modern drama which revolves around a series of criminal and emotional thefts and set against a backdrop of London's changing geographical and cultural landscape.

Will, played by Jude Law, is a partner in a thriving landscape architecture firm which he runs with his friend, Sandy (Martin Freeman). Professionally, things could not be better but Will spends less and less time at home with his beautiful, melancholy partner, Liv (Robin Wright Penn), and her troubled 12 year-old daughter, Bea. Will's office has recently relocated to King's Cross, the centre of Europe's most ambitious urban-regeneration site and their state-of-the-art studio repeatedly attracts the attention of a local gang of thieves. After one of the break-ins, Will follows teenaged freerunner Miro (Rafi Gavron) back to the apartment he shares with his mother, Amira (Juliette Binoche), a Bosnian refugee. With his relationship already in crisis, Will embarks on a passionate journey into both the wilder side of himself and the city in which he lives.

Ray was cast as police detective Bruno Fella, for which he was ideal. Ideal, that is, when you consider his own upbringing in the East End. Who better than someone who had experienced first hand the experience of the displacement of low-income families through 'regeneration' and the resentment often engendered by the seeming progress. As Ray explains, 'You're left with pockets of people that have always lived there and they get the hump because they're building these beautiful things but it's not for them. They get shipped off somewhere and people who can afford to live there move in. I believe that the planners set out with the greatest intentions in the world but there's never much thought for the people that have a real history of living there. As my character says to Jude's, "There's the British library over there, there's King's Cross, there's you, and in the middle is crack village. And you wonder why you get broken into." No one ever thinks about that when they move into a place. People bring a lot of money into an area where there are other people that have no money and they wonder why their cars get robbed. I'm not saying it's right, but there's a reason why.'

If he had any difficulty at all relating to the role he was playing, then it would have to be portraying a policeman who would be as sympathetic and sanguine as his character was. 'It was different from the views that I held about that sort of thing: people break into your house, you naturally want to kill 'em. Then I met a real policeman who was in that situation, who's been working that area, working with these kids for quite a while, trying to get to them. I guess that educated me, in a way, and I started to understand the script a bit more. I know what it's like. I've got three daughters and you can talk to them about the reason why they shouldn't go somewhere, the reason why they shouldn't do something. They say, "Yeah, Dad, you're right," and then they go and do it. Kids take it in and then they just screw it up and throw it away. Human nature, I guess.'

Less than six months after the release of *Breaking and Entering*, while filming John Hillcoat's *Death of a Ladies Man*, written by Nick Cave, and having completed *Fool's Gold* with Matthew McConaughey, Kate Hudson and Donald Sutherland, Ray landed his biggest coup yet, playing

Harrison Ford's friend and foe in the fourth instalment of *Indiana Jones*.

But despite stepping into what is already a well-defined mythos, and all the hype that goes with it, Ray still preferred the company of his old friends to the kind of elaborate celebrity bash that such a blockbuster can bring. As journalist Rebecca Hardy had noted when she caught up with him a few years earlier for a July 2004 feature in the *Daily Mail's Weekender*, if he now feels as comfortable in the acting world as he does in his personal life, and if his success has afforded him a bigger house with a garden for his young daughter to run around in, and, given that his idea of heaven is spending as much time as he can in the garden with his family, then perhaps, that may be the real key to his success. Although Ray makes his living as a TV and movie star, he doesn't have to live his life as one as well.

Notes on *Scum*

S ome more information about *Scum*, including some of the differences between the television and theatrical versions of the film are listed below.

1. The television version was made in 1977 for the BBC who banned the film from being shown due to 'too much incident packed into too short a time and that they doubted the veracity'. The BBC also said that it 'looked too much like a documentary'.

2. Director Alan Clarke and writer Roy Minton got the television version remade as a feature film two years after the television version had been banned.

3. The television version was shot on 16mm film and shown in 1.33:1 aspect ratio and was non-anamorphic.

4. The film version received its British television premiere on Channel 4 in June 1983.

5. The running time of the television version was 75 minutes; the film version was 20 minutes longer.

6. Most of the violence and brutality in the television version, such as punches, slaps or kicks, are muffled.

7. There is a scene with the three new arrivals having a bath in the television version that was not included in the theatrical version. Davis complains about the water being too warm and gets slapped by one of the warders.

8. No strong language was used in the television version.

9. Archer and Carlin talking to each other for the first time differs between the two versions. In the television version, they talk to each other in the laundry whereas, in the theatrical version, their first conversation takes place in a changing room.

10. Banks bullying Davis is slightly different. In the television version, Banks grabs Davis and slaps him and tells him that he is the Daddy here and he has to pay his dues like the rest of the inmates. When Davis says he doesn't smoke, Banks slaps him again. In the theatrical version, he does something similar but kicks Davis as he stood up and shoves him back on to the bench.

11. In the television version, Davis getting bullied again. Richards pours hot tea on him and Mr Sands shouts at Davis for being a slob.

12. The television version omits a scene with Archer talking to the matron about vetos on books.

13. In the television version, Mr Greaves asks Carlin about his bruised face. The theatrical version is similar but Mr Sands asks Carlin about his face.

14. The television version omits Meakin asking the matron when she is going to call them by their first names.

15. Banks's beating by Carlin is similar in both versions. In

the television version, Carlin dunks Banks's head in the sink and hits him a few times and calmly declares himself the new Daddy. He finally kicks him once in the groin. The theatrical is similar but Carlin is more aggressive in his attack.

16. The snooker-ball scene is different in the television version. Carlin places the balls in a sock but conceals them inside his jacket pocket. In the theatrical version he carries them down by his side.

17. Baldy's beating by Carlin is fairly brief. The sound effect when Carlin beats him with the pipe is muffled.

18. Toyne's suicide is deleted in the television version.

19. There is a brief scene with Archer painting 'I am happy' on a wall. This is not in the television version.

20. Carlin's homosexual relationship with another inmate is in the television version only.

21. Davis's rape is brief and non-graphic in the television version compared to the graphic and prolonged film version. His suicide is not as graphic as the theatrical version.

22. After the riots, Carlin is taken to the punishment block and beaten up. The theatrical version is similar but more graphic.

23. The credits has music unlike the theatrical version.

Film Glossary By Charlotte Rasmussen

The following is a guide to definitions frequently used in the technical and creative side of filmmaking which readers may find useful as a glossary to this book.

Ad lib
Improvised dialogue in which the actors make up what they say in real time on the movie set or on stage, when the actors are in the exact situation required by the script and discover that their reaction may benefit with different dialogue. This way the final result can often be much improved. From the Latin phrase *ad libitum*, meaning 'in accordance with desire'.

Agent
Manager responsible for the professional business dealings of an actor, director, screenwriter or other artist. An agent typically negotiates the contracts and often has some part in

selecting or recommending roles for their client. Professional actors usually also have assistants, publicists and other personnel involved in handling their day-to-day schedule and career.

Billing
The placement or display of names of actors, directors and producers for a movie in publicity materials, opening (or closing) film credits, and on theatre marquees. A person's status is indicated by the size, relative position and placement of their name. Generally, higher positions closer to the top with larger and more prominent letters designate higher importance and greater box-office draw, and precede people of lesser importance; the most prominent actor that appears first is said to have top billing, followed by second billing, and so forth.

Boom pole
A person from the sound department operates the boom pole which is a long, special piece of equipment made from light aluminium or carbon fibre that allows precise positioning of the microphone above or below the actors, just out of the camera's frame.

Box office
Measure of the total amount of money paid by moviegoers to view a movie.

B-Roll
Cutaway shots that are used to cover the visual part of an interview or narration. Often made available on the internet or on DVDs as extra material.

FILM GLOSSARY BY CHARLOTTE RASMUSSEN

Blocking
Rehearsal to determine the position and movement of the camera, actors and crew during a particular shot or scene.

Blockbuster
Movie which is a huge financial success, this may be defined as making $100 million or more. The gross of a movie is to some extent a measure of the popularity and talent of its leading actors and can determine whether or not a sequel is economically worthwhile. Often the term *gross profits* is mentioned, referring to 'first dollar gross', this form of compensation entitles an individual to a percentage of every dollar of gross receipts.

Blooper
Funny outtakes and mistakes (either by cast or crew) caught on camera. Bloopers are sometimes included in the end-credits of a movie or in the special-features section of the final DVD, also known as blooper reels or *gag reels*. Causes for bloopers are often uncontrollable laughter, props (falling, breaking or failing to work like expected), forgotten lines or sudden incidents like a bird flying in front of the camera. The term blooper is sometimes also applied to a continuity error that makes it through editing without getting noticed and thus are released in the final product for viewers to see. However, strictly speaking, these are film errors and not bloopers.

Blue screen
Special-effects photography in which a subject (an object or a performer) is photographed in front of a uniformly illuminated blue or green screen. During post-production, the coloured screen is optically or electronically eliminated and a

new background is substituted in its place, allowing images to be combined. Blue is normally used for people (because the human skin has very little blue colour to it) and green for digital shots (because the green colour channel retains more detail and requires less light). Other colours can be used, depending on what technique is used. Often used to achieve the effect of a natural environment such as a forest, beach, prairies, mountains or other landscape in a shot or sequence. Also used to create different sci-fi worlds and environments.

Call back
The follow-up after an audition where the actor in question is called back for a more personal meeting. It gives the director and producers a chance to consider if the actor is appropriate for the role and check if there is the needed chemistry between other members of the cast. At the call back, the actor may discuss the script and character with the director or producer.

Call sheet
The call sheet details what is being filmed on a particular day, in scene order. It details the same information that is in the liner shooting schedule, plus each character name, what extras are needed and what time each actor is to be picked up, when they are required to go into makeup/hair and on to set. Also crew and special requirements for each scene is noted.

Cameo appearance
Small part played by a famous actor who would ordinarily not take such an insignificant part. Often big Hollywood stars choose to do cameo appearances in indies (independent

films) in order to support and maybe draw attention to the specific movie (its theme, co-stars or director).

Camera dolly
The camera can be mounted on top of this little moveable car. During shooting, it is often placed on tracks to ensure stability.

Cast
The actors in the play or film.

CD
The first generation of optical media with a storage capacity of up to 700MB. They are mostly used for music, data and images, but some CDs are designed specifically for video (like VCD or SVCD).

CGI
Computer Generated Image used in a film to create special effects.

Character
Any personified entity appearing in a film or a play.

Composite video
The format of analogue television before it is combined with audio, composed by three signals called Y (luminance), U and V (both carrying colour information).

Credits
Opening credits: On-screen text describing the most important people involved in the making of a movie.
Ending credits: Rolling list at the end of the movie where

everybody involved (cast, crew, studio, producers etc.) are named or thanked.

Cutting room

A location where film rolls or tapes are edited by cutting out unwanted parts.

Dailies

First positive prints made from the negatives photographed on the previous day. Watching the dailies often determines which scenes need to be reshot or changed.

Director

In a stage play, the individual responsible for staging (i.e. placing in the space or 'blocking') the actors, sculpting and coordinating their performances, and making sure they fit with the design elements into a coherent vision of the play. In a musical, there will typically be a separate musical director responsible for the musical elements of the show. In a Dramatists Guild contract, the playwright has approval over the choice of director (and the cast and designers). In film, the director carries out the duties of a stage director and then some (e.g. choosing the shoot list), with considerably more say-so over the final product.

Casting director: An important part of pre-production is selecting the cast. It usually involves auditions and if hundreds or thousands of candidates come in to perform it requires special staff in charge of this process.

Distributor

Organisation responsible for coordinating the distribution of the finished movie to exhibitors, as well as the sale of videos, DVDs, laserdiscs and other media versions of movies.

Dubbing

Dubbing or *looping* is the process of recording voices that match the exact mouth-movements of the actors on screen. Often used to replace the original language with another (i.e. Spanish voice track over an American movie). Dubbing or ADR (Additional Dialogue Recording or *post-synchronisation*) is also used to re-record the lines by the same actors that originally spoke them. This is often the case when the original sound on set was interrupted by unwanted or uncontrolled noise such as traffic or is unclear. The actors are then called into a sound-studio. While watching the film on video they perform their lines again, which are recorded by a sound technician.

DVD

DVD is short for Digital Versatile Disc or Digital Video Disc. A DVD is an optical media like a CD, but has much higher density. There are many different types of DVDs (DVD-R, DVD+R, DVD, DVD-RW, DVD+RW) and they are used for video, audio and data storage. Most DVDs used for movies are 12cm in diameter and their usual sizes are 4.7 GB (single layer) or 8.5 GB (dual layer) – both types can be double sided. Dual-layer DVDs have a semi-transparent layer on top which the red laser shines through to reach the layer at the bottom. Switching from one layer to another may cause a noticeable pause in some DVD players. A newer type of high-density disc is the *High Definition DVD* (HD DVD) which can store three times as much data as the standard DVD format. The *Blu-ray disc* (BD) offers storage capacity up to 25 GB (single layer). The Blu-ray format uses a blue-violet laser (with a shorter wavelength than the typical red laser) that enables a Blu-ray disc to be packed more tightly.

Extras
Individuals who appear in a movie where a non-specific, non-speaking character is required, usually as part of a crowd or in the background of a scene. Often family members of the cast or crew (who hang around the set anyway) are used.

Feature film
A movie made primarily for distribution in theatres that is at least 60 minutes long or has a script at least 90 pages long. Other movies may be made for TV or produced to be distributed on video or DVD.

Foley
Art of recreating incidental sound effects (such as footsteps) in synchronisation with the visual component of a movie.

Frame
Movies are created by taking a rapid sequence of pictures (frames) of action and by displaying these frames at the same rate at which they were recorded, thus creating the illusion of motion. In the US film equals 24 frames per second (NTSC) and video equals 30 frames per second (NTSC). In Europe most film equals 25 frames per second (PAL). In France and fractions of Europe, Africa and the former USSR another standard called SECAM is used.

Franchise
A media franchise (literature, film, videogame, TV programme) is a property involving characters, settings, trademarks etc. Media franchises tend to cross over from their original media to other forms (for example, from books to films). Generally a whole series is made in a particular

medium along with merchandise. Some franchises are planned in advance, some happen by accident because of a sudden profitable success.

Freebie

Promotional samples like tickets, clothing, gadgets, promo DVDs, books or whatever the production or distributing company chooses to give. Some may be signed by the cast or are otherwise unique merchandise or bonus material.

Gate

The film gate is an opening in front of the camera where the film is exposed to light. Sometimes the film celluloid can break off, giving debris called *hair* that can create a dark line on the edge of the film frame. Such a hair can only be removed by painting it out digitally in post-production, which is a time-consuming and costly affair. Several factors influence the frequency of hairs: environment, humidity, camera position, type of film etc. When the director feels he has got a particular shot, he calls out to the crew to 'check the gate'. A clean shot is replied with 'gate is good'. Note: This problem does not exist when shooting digitally.

Grip

Trained lighting and rigging technicians.

Hook

A term borrowed from songwriting that describes that thing (or line) that catches the public's attention and keeps them interested in the flow of a story.

Independent films

Films also known as *indies* that are financed by a smaller production company independent of a (major) film studio, often producing small, interesting movies on low budget which sometimes never get further than recognition at film festivals that may be released in a limited number of theatres.

Laserdisc

The first type of commercial optical disc (LD) with a common size of 30cm in diameter. Also 18cm and 12cm discs were published. Analogue video combined with digital audio. Laserdiscs were recorded in 3 different formats: CAV, CLV and CAA. Mostly caught on in North America and Japan and were quickly replaced by the more popular and smaller DVDs when they were introduced.

Location

A site where part (or all) of a film is shot, as opposed to the *set* or *soundstage*. If the story is based on authentic events, that doesn't necessarily mean the exact same location where the action happened in real life.

Method acting

Sometimes referred to as 'the method'. Style of acting formalised by Konstantin Stanislavsky which requires actors to draw experiences from their own personal lives that correlate to the character they are playing.

Miniatures

Small landscapes, towns or buildings can be built in miniature (usually to scale) to make effects that are impossible to achieve otherwise (either because it is too expensive or too dangerous to do in reality).

Option
Agreement of renting the rights to a script for a specific period of time.

Padding
Material added to clothing or shoes in order to enhance an actor's physical appearance or to protect a stuntman by preventing unnecessary injuries.

Plot
The ordering of events in a story. The main plot is called A-plot. Typical plot structure includes: A) beginning/initial situation; B) conflict/problem which has to be achieved/solved; C) complications to overcome; D) climax; E) suspense; F) resolution after the conflict/problem has been solved (or not!); G) conclusion/end. Simplified, the dramatic structure of a story can be divided into five acts: 1. exposition; 2. rising action; 3. climax (turning point); 4. falling action; 5. resolution (*denouement*, meaning unravelling or untying of the plot). This is also known as Freytag's pyramid: _/_

Producer
The person or entity financially responsible for a stage or film production. The chief of a movie production in all matters save the creative efforts of the director; raising funding, hiring key personnel and arranging for distributors.
Executive producer: Producer who is not involved in any technical aspects of the filmmaking process, but who is still

responsible for the overall production usually handling business and legal issues.

Production company: Company headed by a producer, director, actor/actress or writer for the purpose of creating general entertainment products such as motion pictures, television shows, infomercials, commercials and multimedia.

Production

Pre-production: The stage during the creation of the movie where the producers get everything ready to shoot: hiring actors through *casting*, picking directors and the rest of the crew, making costumes, finding locations, editing the script, constructing sets, doing rehearsals etc.

Production: Actual shooting of the movie (also known as *principal photography*).

Post-production: Shooting extra scenes or alternative versions, editing and cutting of the movie, creating CGI special effects, adding sound effects and composing the music score and generally making promotion (press conferences, trailer shows, billboards etc.) before the premiere.

Prop

A prop is any object held, manipulated or carried by a performer during a theatrical performance either on stage or film, for example a stage gun, mock glassware etc.

Rating

In the USA *The Motion Picture Association of America* and the *National Association of Theatre Owners* operate a rating system for movies: *G* (General audience, all ages admitted), PG (Parental guidance suggested, some material may not be suitable for children), *PG-13* (Parents strongly cautioned, some material may be inappropriate for children under 13), *R* (Restricted, under 17 requires accompanying parent or adult guardian), *NC-17* (No one 17 and under admitted). The rating for a particular movie is decided by a board of parents. They also define an informational warning for the particular movie along with the rating (i.e. for strong language, violence, nudity, drug abuse etc.). In the UK the *British Board of Film Classification* classifies films and videos. The rating system differs from the American system: U (Suitable for audiences aged 4 years and over, movies classified Uc are particularly suitable for pre-school children), PG (General viewing, but some scenes may be unsuitable for young children), *12* (No-one younger than 12 may rent or buy the movie, movies classified 12A may not be seen by children younger than 12 in the cinema unless accompanied by an adult), *15* (Suitable only for *15* years and over, no-one younger may buy, rent or see a movie in a cinema), 18 (Suitable only for adults, no-one younger may buy, rent or see a movie in a cinema). Movies classified *R18* is a special and legally restricted classification: movies are to be shown only in specially licensed cinemas and movies may only be supplied in licensed shops (never by mail order).

Red Carpet

A red carpet is a strip of carpet in the colour red, which is laid out in front of a building to welcome VIPs such as dignitaries and celebrities at formal events such as premieres, special screenings, press conferences etc.

Region encoding

To prevent the newest movie releases on DVD (usually released first in the United States) from being played in other parts of the world before they have shown in the theatres there, a DVD region locking system is used to control which type of DVDs can be played on DVD players. Currently, there are 9 regions (0–8). The Blu-ray movie region codes are different from DVDs, currently there are three (A/1, B/2, C/3).

Rehearsal
A preparatory event in music and theatre. A form of practice to ensure professionalism and elimination of mistakes by working on details without performing in public or on camera. At a *dress rehearsal*, the ensemble tries out their wardrobe for the first time: The different outfits and costumes are fitted to match their exact size.

Reshoot
Sometimes it is necessary to shoot a scene again. It may be obvious in post-production that some scenes don't fit each other very well or the story doesn't come together as intended. Sometimes actors are called back to reshoot scenes months after the final wrap.

Scene
Continuous block of storytelling either set in a single location or following a particular character.

Score
Any printed version of a musical arrangement for opera, film or other musical work in notational form. May include lyrics or supplemental text.

Screening
The showing of a film for test audiences and/or people involved

in the making of the movie. Often several different cuts of a movie are produced. This is why sometimes a DVD refers to the term 'director's cut' which differs from the final version seen in theatres, which is usually a collaboration between the director, editors, producers and by the studio executives.

Script

The blueprint or roadmap that outlines a movie story through visual descriptions, actions of characters and their dialogue.

Lined script: copy of the shooting script which is prepared by the script supervisor during production to indicate, via notations and vertical lines drawn directly onto the script pages, exactly what coverage has been shot.

Production script: a script that has been prepared to be put into production.

Shooting script: changes made to the script after the initial circulation of the *production script* are called *revised pages*, which are different in colour and incorporated into the shooting script without displacing or rearranging the original, unrevised pages.

Unsolicited script: a method of script submission in which the writer sends the script, without prior contact, to the theatre or production company.

Sequel

A second creative work (book, movie, play) set in the same universe as the first but later in time. Often using elements (characters, settings, plot) of the original story. Opposed to *prequel* that is set before the original story. Prequels suffer from the disadvantage that the audience know what the outcome is going to be.

Set

The physical elements that are constructed or arranged to create a sense of place. Usually there is a *set designer/art director* (as well as other professional designers whose job it is to envision any costumes, sets, lights, sound or properties).

Sitcom

Also known as a 'situation comedy'. Usually (in the US) sitcoms are 30-minute comedic television shows revolving around funny situations for the main characters.

Soap opera

Dramas which are often shown on TV during the day. So called because in the USA they were often originally sponsored by the makers of laundry detergent in the early days of television.

Soundstage

Large studio area where elaborate sets may be constructed. Usually a soundproof, hangar-like building.

Spoiler

A summary or description that relates plot elements not revealed early in the narrative itself. Moreover, because enjoyment of a narrative sometimes depends upon the dramatic tension and suspense, this early revelation of plot elements can 'spoil' the enjoyment otherwise experienced. The term spoiler is often associated with special Internet sites and newsgroup postings. Usually, the spoiling information is preceded by a warning.

FILM GLOSSARY BY CHARLOTTE RASMUSSEN

Stills
Static photographs taken from a movie used for advertising purposes.

Storyboard
An organised set of graphics used to illustrate and visualise the sequence of filming. Looks like a comic and is used early in the filming process to experiment and move scenes around. Newer moviemakers often make computerised animations.

Stunts
Often done by a team of professional stunt men and – women by use of a *stunt double* (not to be confused with a *body/photo double* which is a lookalike used in scenes where the actor is unavailable or during nudity shots). Trained stunt personnel are used in dangerous situations to avoid exposing the cast to any risk or for acts requiring special skills (for instance diving, falling or a car crash).

Subtitles
Subtitles are also known as Closed Captions (CC). Closed means they are only visible when activated (i.e. extra features on a DVD), as opposed to open captioning so that viewers see the captions all the time (used for some TV programmes). They are used to translate foreign-languages movies, programmes and movies for hearing impaired.

Syndication
The sale of the right to broadcast radio shows and television shows to multiple individual stations, without going through a broadcast network. It is common in countries where television is organized around networks with local affiliates,

notably the United States. Shows can also be syndicated internationally.

Table-read

When the writer (or writing team) is finished with the script, it's time for the table-read. During this process, the entire cast of actors, all of the writers, producers and other interested parties meet and act out the script. This is very important, because it lets the writers hear how their words sound when spoken out loud. They pay close attention to the audience's reaction and take notes on what works (such as seeing whether people get the jokes and laugh – or not) and what doesn't. Afterwards, the writers (and sometimes producers) discuss the problems and explore ways to improve the script.

Tape marks

Usually, the exact spot where the actors are supposed to be standing is marked with tape on the floor (off-camera), since it's important for the camera-man and the rest of the cast to know where everybody is positioned.

Teaser/Trailer

Teaser: A set of scenes used for promotional purposes, appearing on television and in theatres before other films. Used to 'tease' the audience and grab their attention

Trailer: Like the teaser, a short edited montage of selected scenes to be used as an advertisement for the film, or a preview of coming attractions. Running times can vary from 15 seconds to three minutes. Not everything in the trailer is in the final film, since the trailer is often produced early in the filming process. A trailer is sometimes used as a selling tool to raise funding for a feature film. Originally trailers were shown at the end of a film (hence the term 'trailer'), but people often left the theatre before seeing them so now they are shown before the main feature.

Trailer

A mobile home for the actors when filming on location or in a studio. Trailers can be a midsized RV (recreational vehicle). They can be elaborately equipped with bedroom, bathroom and small kitchen, since the actors sometimes spend a lot of hours there, preparing their work, having meetings, relaxing, spending time with their family or just hanging out and waiting in between takes. Some trailers are made into schoolrooms, dressing rooms or hair and makeup trailers where the cast is fixed up before the shoot. For temporary stays like a movie set, the trailers do not become as personalised as for larger productions like ongoing television shows where the actors tend to decorate their home-away-from-home.

Two-shot

A close-up camera shot of two people in the foreground (often in dialogue with each other to indicate relationship information), framed from the chest up. Likewise *three-shot* etc.

VHS

The Video Home System is a recording and playing standard for analogue video cassette recorders (VCR). The recording medium is magnetic tape. Several variations exists (VHS-C, Super-VHS and others), each also dependent on the type of signal (SECAM, PAL or NTSC).

Voice over
Also known as 'V.O.' or off-camera commentary in which a speaker narrates the action on screen.

Wide-angle shot
A shot filmed with a lens that is able to take in a wider field of view (to capture more of the scene's elements or objects) than a regular or normal lens.

Widescreen
Widescreen refers to projection systems in which the aspect ratio is wider than the 1.33:1 ratio that dominated sound film before the 1950s; in the 1950s, many widescreen processes were introduced (to combat the growing popularity of television), such as CinemaScope (an anamorphic system), VistaVision (a non-anamorphic production technique in which the film is run horizontally through the camera instead of vertically), and Todd-AO and Super Panavision (that both used wider-gauge film). Also known as 'letterboxing'.

Wrap
Term used to finish shooting, either for the day or the entire production. Short for Wind Roll And Print. Often associated with 'wrap party' where cast, crew, producers, studio executives and other associates get together at the last day of filming to celebrate.

Filmography

Feature Films

That Summer (1979)
Directed by Harley Cokeliss. Screenplay by Tony Attard and Jane Preger. Released by Columbia Pictures. Cast: Ray Winstone, Tony London, Emily Moore, June Shipley, Jon Morrison, Andrew Byatt, Ewan Stewart, David Daker.

Scum (1979)
Directed by Alan Clarke, Screenplay by Roy Minton. Released by GTO Films. Cast: Ray Winstone, Mick Ford, Julian Firth, John Blundell, Phil Daniels, John Judd, Philip Jackson, Peter Howell, John Grillo, Ray Burdis.

Quadrophenia (1979)
Directed by Franc Roddam. Screenplay by Dave Humphries

and Franc Roddam. Released by Brent Walker Film Distributing. Cast: Phil Daniels, Leslie Ash, Philip Davis, Mark Wingett, Sting, Ray Winstone, Garry Cooper, Gary Shail, Toyah Willcox, Trevor Laird, Kate Williams, Michael Elphick, Kim Neve, Benjamin Whitrow.

Ladies and Gentlemen, The Fabulous Stains (1981)

Directed by Lou Adler. Screenplay by Jonathan Demme and Nancy Dowd. Released by Paramount Pictures. Cast: Diane Lane, Ray Winstone, Peter Donat, David Clennon, Laura Dern, John Lehne, Cynthia Sykes, Martin Kantar, Fee Waybill.

Number One (1985)

Directed by Les Blair. Screenplay by G.F. Newman. Cast: Bob Geldof, Mel Smith, Alison Steadman, P.H. Moriarty, Phil Daniels, Alfred Molina, James Marcus, David Howey, Ian Dury, David Squire, Ron Cook, Alun Armstrong, Tony Scott, Kate Hardie, Ray Winstone.

Tank Malling (1989)

Directed and written by James Marcus. Cast: Ray Winstone, Jason Connery, Amanda Donohoe, Glen Murphy, Marsha A. Hunt, Peter Wyngarde, Rupert Baker, Jimmy Batten, Nick Berry, John Brett, Jess Conrad, Nick Brimble, Craig Fairbrass.

Ladybird, Ladybird (1994)

Directed by Ken Roach. Screenplay by Rona Munro. Released by Hallmark Home Entertainment/Samuel Goldwyn Company. Cast: Crissy Rock, Vladimir Vega, Sandie Lavelle, Mauricio Venegas, Ray Winstone, Claire Perkins, Jason Stracey, Luke Brown, Lilly Farrell, Scottie Moore, Linda Ross.

Masculine Mescaline (1996)
Directed by Gary Love. Screenplay by Dorian Healy and Gary Love. Released by Jane Balfour Films. Cast: Stephen Breaks, Ewen Bremner, Thomas Elison, Emily Lloyd, Neil Stuke, John Thaw, Ray Winstone.

Yellow (1996)
Directed and written by Simon Beaufoy and Billie Eltringham. Released by BFI. Cast: Ray Winstone, Tracey Wilkinson, Nicola Bland.

Nil By Mouth (1997)
Directed and written by Gary Oldman. Released by Twentieth Century Fox. Cast: Ray Winstone, Kathy Burke, Charlie Creed-Miles, Laila Morse, Edna Dore, Chrissie Cotterill, Jon Morrison, Jamie Foreman, Steve Sweeney, Terry Rowley, Sam Miller.

Face (1997)
Directed by Antonia Bird. Screenplay by Ronan Bennett. Released by UIP. Cast: Robert Carlyle, Ray Winstone, Phil Davis, Steve Sweeney, Gerry Conlon, Leon Black, David Boateng, Lena Headey, Eddie Nestor, Steve Waddington, Christine Tremarco.

The Sea Change (1998)
Directed by Michael Bray. Screenplay by Michael Bray and Billy Hurman. Released by Highlight Video. Cast: Maryam d'Abo, Sean Chapman, Ray Winstone, Andree Bernard, Amparo Moreno, German Montaner, Stephen Bateman, Adrian Beaumont.

Martha, Meet Frank, Daniel and Laurence (1998)
Directed by Nick Hamm. Screenplay by Peter Morgan.

Released by Channel Four Films. Cast: Monica Potter, Rufus Sewell, Tom Hollander, Joseph Fiennes, Ray Winstone, Debora Weston, Jan Pearson, Steve O'Donnell, Rebecca Craig, Paul Bigley, Geoffrey McGivern, Hamish Clerk, Lorelei King, Steven Spiers, Rob Brydon.

Woundings (1998)

Directed by Roberta Hanley. Screenplay by Roberta Hanley and Jeff Noon. Released by UAV Entertainment. Cast: Julia Cox, Sammi Davis, Emily Lloyd, Charlie Creed-Miles, Guy Pearce, Sarah-Jane Potts, Johnathon Schaech, Noah Taylor, Ray Winstone, Twiggy, James Bannon, Benedick Bates, Kristian Taylor-Wood.

Tube Tales (Sky, 1999)

'My Father the Liar' segment. Directed by Bob Hoskins. Screenplay by Paul Fraser. Cast: Edna Dore, Frank Harper, William Hoyland, Tom Watson, Ray Winstone.

Final Cut (1999)

Directed and written by Dominic Anciano and Ray Burdis. Released by Downtown Pictures. Cast: Ray Winstone, Jude Law, Sadie Frost, John Bennett, William Scully, Mark Burdis, Perry Benson, Lisa Marsh, Ray Burdis, Dominic Anciano.

Five Seconds To Spare (1999)

Directed by Tom Connolly. Screenplay by Jonathan Coe and Tom Connolly. Released by ContentFilm International. Cast: Max Beesley, Valentina Servi, Gary Condes, Anastasia Hille, James Hooton, Ronny Jhutti, Kris Marshall, John Peel, Sarah-Jane Potts, Lee Ross, Andy Serkis, Ray Winstone.

The War Zone (1999)

Directed by Tim Roth. Screenplay by Alexander Stuart. Released by Channel Four Films. Cast: Ray Winstone, Lara Belmont, Freddie Cunliffe, Tilda Swinton, Colin Farrell, Aisling O'Sullivan, Kate Ashfield, Megan Thorpe, Kim Wall.

Agnes Browne (1999)

Directed by Anjelica Houston. Screenplay by John Goldsmith and Brendan O'Carroll. Released by UIP. Cast: Anjelica Houston, Marion O'Dwyer, Niall O'Shea, Ciaran Owens, Roxanna Williams, Carl Power, Mark Power, Gareth O'Connor, James Lappin, Ray Winstone, Arno Chevrier, Gerard McSorley, Tom Jones, June Rodgers.

Darkness Falls (1999)

Directed by Gerry Lively. Screenplay by N.J. Crisp and John Howlett. Released by Downtown Pictures. Cast: Sherilyn Fenn, Ray Winstone, Tim Dutton, Anita Dobson, Bryan Pringle, Robin McCaffrey, Michael Praed, Olivia Tobias, Andrew Dixon, Rebecca De-Yoxall, Harry Crossley, Denny Cain, Helen Torlesse, Tara Morass.

Fanny and Elvis (1999)

Directed and written by Kay Mellor. Released by UIP. Cast: Kerry Fox, Ray Winstone, Ben Daniels, David Morrissey, Jennifer Saunders, Colin Salmon, Gaynor Faye, William Ash, Gareth Tudor Price, Bridget Forsythe, Eileen O'Brien, Nicholas Lane, Richard Moore, Sarah Parks, Ron Blass.

There's Only One Jimmy Grimble (2000)

Directed by John Hay. Screenplay by Rik Carmichael and John Hay. Released by Pathe Pictures International. Cast: Lewis

McKenzie, Jane Lapotaire, Gina McKee, Ben Miller, Wayne Galtrey, Ciaran Griffiths, Bobby Power, Robert Carlyle, Samia Smith, Antony Marsh, Sean Delaney, Charles Denton, Azmier Ahmed, John McArdle, Ann Aris, Richard Heap, John Henshaw, Michael J. Jackson, Ray Winstone, Jim Whelan, Jacqueline Leonard, Samantha Cunningham, Chris Carson.

Sexy Beast (2000)

Directed by Jonathan Glazer. Screenplay by Louis Mellis and David Scinto. Released by FilmFour. Cast: Ray Winstone, Ben Kingsley, Ian McShane, Amanda Redman, James Fox, Cavan Kendall, Julianne White, Álvaro Monje, Robert Atiko.

Love, Honour and Obey (2000)

Directed and written by Dominic Anciano and Ray Burdis. Released by Universal. Cast: Sadie Frost, Jonny Lee Miller, Jude Law, Ray Winstone, Kathy Burke, Sean Pertwee, Denise Van Outen, Rhys Ifans, Dominic Aniano, Ray Burdis, John Beckett, Trevor Laird, William Scully, Perry Benson, Mark Burdis.

Last Orders (2001)

Directed by Fred Schepisi. Screenplay by Graham Swift and Fred Schepisi. Released by Columbia Tristar. Cast: Michael Caine, Tom Courtenay, David Hemmings, Bob Hoskins, Helen Mirren, Ray Winstone, JJ Feild, Cameron Fitch, Nolan Hemmings, Anatol Yusef, Kelly Reilly, Stephen McCole, George Innes, Laura Morelli.

The Martins (2001)

Directed and written by Tony Grounds. Released by Icon Film Distribution. Cast: Ray Winstone, Lee Evans, Kathy Burke, Linda Bassett, Eric Byrne, Terry Dumont, Frank

Finlay, Lennie James, Jack Shepherd, Mark Strong, Lloyd Harvey, Tameka Empson, Paddy Considine, Ronnie Fox, Alison Egan, Owen Brenman.

Ripley's Game (2002)

Directed by Liliana Cavani. Screenplay by Liliana Cavani and Patricia Highsmith. Released by Entertainment Film Distributors. Cast: Ray Winstone, John Malkovich, Uwe Mansshardt, Hanns Zischler, Paolo Paoloni, Maurizio Luca, Dougray Scott, Evelina Meghangi, Chiara Caselli, Lena Headey, Sam Blitz, Emidio La Vella, Lutz Winde, Nikolaus Deutsch, Wilfred Zander.

Bouncer (2002)

Directed by Michael Baig-Clifford. Screenplay by Geoff Thompson. Cast: Paddy Considine, Paul Dore, Ronnie Fox, Chris Kenyon, Jo Marriott, Liam Moyhihan, Shaun Parkes, Ray Winstone.

Cold Mountain (2004)

Directed by Anthony Minghella. Screenplay by Charles Frazier and Anthony Minghella. Released by Miramax Films. Cast: Jude Law, Nicole Kidman, Renee Zellweger, Eileen Atkins, Brendan Gleeson, Philip Seymour Hoffman, Natalie Portman, Giovanni Ribisi, Donald Sutherland, Ray Winstone, Kathy Baker, James Gammon

Old Street (2004)

Directed by Angus Jackson. Screenplay by Patrick Marber. Cast: Victor Romero Evans, David Tennant, Ray Winstone.

Everything (2004)
Directed and written by Richard Hawkins. Cast: Ray Winstone, Jan Graveson, Katherine Clisby, Ed Deedigan, Lindy Sellars, Lois Winstone.

King Arthur (2004)
Directed by Antoine Fuqua. Screenplay by David Franzoni. Released by Buena Vista International. Cast: Clive Owen, Ioan Gruffudd, Mads Mikkelsen, Joel Edgerton, Hugh Dancy, Ray Winstone, Ray Stevenson, Keira Knightley, Stephen Dillane, Stellan Skarsgard, Til Schweiger, Sean Gilder, Pat Kinevane, Ivano Marescotti.

The Magic Roundabout (2005)
Directed by David Borthwick. Screenplay by Paul Bassett. Released by Pathe. Cast: Tom Baker, Jim Broadbent, Lee Evans, Joanne Lumley, Ian McKellen, Kylie Minogue, Bill Nighy, Robbie Williams, Ray Winstone, Daniella Loftus, Ediz Mahmut, Jimmy Hibbert, Michel Galabru, Dany Boon, Valerie Lemercier.

The Proposition (2005)
Directed by John Hillcoat. Screenplay by Nick Cave. Released by Columbia Tristar. Cast: Richard Wilson, Noah Taylor, Jeremy Madrona, Jae Mamuyac, Guy Pearce, Mick Roughan, Shane Watt, Ray Winstone, Robert Morgan, David Gulpilil, Bryan Probets, Oliver Ackland, Danny Houston, David Vallon, Daniel Parker.

The Chronicles of Narnia: The Lion, The Witch and The Wardrobe (2005)
Directed by Andrew Adamson. Screenplay by Anna Peacock

and Andrew Adamson. Released by Buena Vista International. Cast: Georgie Henley, Skandar Keynes, William Moseley, Anna Popplewell, Tilda Swinton, James McAvoy, Jim Broadbent, Kiran Shah, James Cosmo, Judy McIntosh, Elizabeth Hawthorne, Patrick Kake, Shane Rangi, Brandon Cook, Rachael Henley, Mark Wells, Noah Huntley, Sophie Winkelman, Liam Neeson, Ray Winstone, Dawn French, Rupert Everett, Cameron Rhodes, Philip Steuer, Jim May, Sim Evan-Jones.

Breaking and Entering (2006)

Directed and written by Anthony Minghella. Released by Miramax Films. Cast: Romi Aboulifia, Kwesi Asiedu-Mansah, Helen Baker, Mark Benton, Juliette Binoche, Daon Broni, Emma Buckley, Anna Chancellor, Caroline Chikezie, O.T. Fagbenle, Vera Farmiga, Martin Freeman, Rafi Gavron, Ting-Ting Hu, Dado Jehan, Eddie Joseph, Branka Katic, Lisa Kay, Jude Law, Rad Lazar, Eleanor Mastuura, Roberto Purvis, Poppy Rogers, Michael Schaeffer, Michael Smiley, Serge Soric, Juliet Stevenson, Ellen Thomas, Velebor Topic, Ed Westwick, Ray Winstone, Robin Wright Penn.

The Departed (2006)

Directed by Martin Scorsese. Screenplay by William Monahan and Siu Fai Mak. Released by Warner Bros. Cast: Leonardo DiCaprio, Matt Damon, Jack Nicholson, Martin Sheen, Vera Farmiga, Mark Wahlberg, Ray Winstone, Alec Baldwin.

Beowulf (2007)

Directed by Robert Zemeckis. Screenplay by Neil Gaiman and Roger Avary. Released by Warner Bros. Cast: Sharisse Baker-Bernard, Richard Burns, Chris Coppola, Sahy Duffin, Greg

Ellis, Brendan Gleeson, Crispin Glover, Leslie Harter Zemeckis, Anthony Hopkins, Nick Jameson, Emily Johnson, Angelina Jolie, Dominic Keating, John Littlefield, Alison Lohman, Chris Mala, John Malkovich, Alan Ritchson, Sebastian Roche, Charlotte Salt, Woody Schultz, Randy Shelly, Tyler Steelman, Nadina Stenovich, Aaron Stevens, Tim Trobec, Jared Weber, Tom West, Ray Winstone, Robin Wright Penn, Rick Young.

Fool's Gold (2008)
Directed by Andy Tennant. Screenplay by John Claflin, Daniel Zelman and Andy Tennant. Released by Warner Bros. Cast: Matthew McConaughey, Kate Hudson, Donald Sutherland, Alexis Dziena.

Indiana Jones and the Kingdom of the Crystal Skull (2008)
Directed by Steven Spielberg. Screenplay by David Koepp. Released by Paramount Pictures. Cast: Harrison Ford, Karen Allen, Cate Blanchett, Shia Labeouf, John Hurt, Ray Winstone, Jim Broadbent.

Television

Play For Today: Sunshine in Brixton (ITV, 1976)
Directed by Les Blair. Screenplay by Brian Glover. Cast: Elvis Payne, Jessie Ball, Jill Gasgoine, Anthony Langdon, Sean Clarke, Ray Winstone, Dave Woods, Richard Ireson, Simon Howe, Peter Hugo-Daly, Herbert Norville, Richard Willis, Colin Raven.

Scum (BBC, 1977)
Directed by Alan Clarke. Screenplay by Roy Minton. Cast:

Ray Winstone, David Threlfall, Martin Philips, Davidson Knight, John Blundell, Phil Daniels, Ray Burdis, Patrick Murray, Ian Sharrock, Tony London, Peter Kinley, Peter Francis, Sheridan Earl Russell, Colin Mayes, Trevor Butler.

Fox (ITV, 1980)
Directed by Jim Goddard. Screenplay by Trevor Preston. Cast: Peter Vaughan, Elizabeth Spriggs, Ray Winstone, Larry Lamb, Bernard Hill, Derrick O'Connor, Eamon Boland, Rosemary Martin, Richard Weinbaum, Cindy O'Callaghan, Margaret Nolan, Yvette Dotrice.

Play For Today: The Factory (BBC, 1981)
Season 12, Episode 9. Directed by Gerald Blake. Screenplay by David Hopkins. Cast: Leonard Rossiter, Benjamin Whitrow, Ray Winstone.

Theatre Box (ITV, 1981)
Episode: Death Angel. Directed by Peter Smith. Screenplay by Brian Glover. Cast: Bill Maynard, Christian Childs, Claudia Curran, Gary Beadle, Malcolm Storry, Ray Winstone.

Love Story: Mr Right (BBC, 1983)
Directed by Peter Smith. Screenplay by Peter Prince. Cast: Carolyn Pickles, David Hayman, Liz Smith, Ray Winstone, Gwyneth Strong, Joan Scott, Sally Watkins, Janet Davies, Jeanne Doree, Joe Kaye, Peter Schofield, Betty Alberge, Barbara Hyslop, Larry Drew, Roger Brierley.

Robin of Sherwood (ITV Series, 1984–86)
Pilot Episode (*Robin Hood And the Sorcerer*), Season 1, Episodes 1–5, Season 2, Episodes 1–6, Season 3, Episodes

1–13. Directed by James Allen, Alex Kirby, Gerry Mill, Sid Roberson, Ian Sharp, Robert Young. Screenplay by Richard Carpenter, John Flanagan, Anthony Horowitz, Andrew McCulloch. Cast: Michael Praed, Jason Connery, Nikolas Grace, Judi Trott, Clive Mantle, Peter Llewellyn Williams, Robert Addie, Ray Winstone, Phil Rose, John Abineri, Mark Ryan, Philip Jackson, Jeremy Bulloch, Claire Toeman, Stuart Linden.

Francis Matthew's Daughter (BBC Series, 1987)

Directed by David Askey. Screenplay by Charlotte Bingham and Terry Brady. Cast: James Bolam, Samantha Hurst, Gabrielle Lloyd, Ray Winstone.

Blore M.P. (BBC, 1989)

Directed by Robert Young. Cast: Maggie O'Neill, Timothy West, Alexei Jawdokimov, Sergei Rousakov, Oscar Quitak, James Warwick, Edward Lyon, Jennie Goossens, Paul Daneman, Rowena Cooper, Jill Baker, Serena Harragin, John Duval, James Holland, Antonia Loyd, Susie Blake, Barry Jackson, Ronald Russell, Rosemary Martin, Peggy Ann Wood, Stephen Moore, Edward Cast, Shelley Pielou, Anna Capaldi, Ray Winstone, Joan Bakewell, Kaleem Janjua, Clyde Pollitt, Mary Duddy, Luke Kelly, Alex Knight, John Badeley, Alan Halley, Steve Hervieu, James Walker.

Palmer (LWT, 1991)

Directed by Keith Washington. Screenplay by Tony Hoare. Cast: Ray Winstone, Gerard Horan, Lesley Duff, Dora Bryan, Barry Jackson, Louise Plowright, Garrie J. Lammin, Vicki Murdock, Carol Holmes, Diana Kent, Wendy Allnutt, Richard Kane.

FILMOGRAPHY

Absolute Hell (1991)

Directed by Anthony Page. Screenplay by Rodney Ackland. Cast: Judi Dench, Francesca Annis, Sylvia Barer, Paul Birchard, Susan Brown, Anthony Calf, Gary Fairhall, Gregory Floy, Moyra Fraser, Sheelagh Fraser, Mark Gillis, Charles Gray, Barbara Hicks, Betty Marsden, Sussanah Morley, Bill Nighy, William Osborne, Eileen Page, Nathaniel Parker, Suzanne Parrett, Ronald Pickup, Cordelia Roche, Pip Torrens, Ray Winstone.

Black and Blue (1992)

Directed by David Hayman. Screenplay by Gordon Frank Newman. Cast: Sidney Cole, Tommy Flanagan, Iain Glen, Christopher John Hall, Don Henderson, Boris Isarov, Rowena King, Bill Leadbitter, David Morrissey, Cynthia Powell, Martin Shaw, James Smith, Sunshine, David Thewlis, Andrew Wilde, Ray Winstone.

Get Back (BBC Series, 1992)

Directed by Graeme Harper and Terry Kinane. Screenplay by Maurice Gran, Laurence Marks, Gary Lawson and John Phelps. Cast: Ray Winstone, Carol Harrison, Larry Lamb, Jane Booker, John Bardon, Kate Winslet, Michelle Cattini, G.B. Zoot Money, Shirley Stelfox.

Underbelly (BBC, 1992)

Directed by Nicholas Renton. Screenplay by Peter Ransley based on the novel by Frank Kippax. Cast: Charon Bourke, Neil Conrich, Trevor Cooper, Pip Donaghy, Penny Downie, Michael Feast, Robbie Gee, Jaye Griffiths, David Hayman, Dorian Healy, Douglas Henshall, Christine Kavanagh, David Keyes, Bill Leadbitter, John McArdle, Lee Nicolls, Michael

Packer, Fred Pearson, Edward Peel, Tim Potter, David Quilter, Ken Robertson, Michael Snelders, Frederick Treves, Simon Tyrrell, Michael Wardle, Martin Wenner, Tom Wilkinson, Ray Winstone, Marjorie Yates.

The Negotiator (BBC, 1994)
Directed by Mary McMurray. Screenplay by Trevor Preston. Cast: Brian Cox, Maurice Roeves, Robin Ellis, Russell Hunter, Paul Higgins, Ray Winstone, Michael Siberry, Fiona Chalmers, Morag Fullarton, Tam White, Jon Morrison.

The Ghostbusters of East Finchley (BBC Series, 1995)
Season 1, Episodes 1–6. Directed by Jim Gillespie. Screenplay by Tony Grounds. Cast: Paul Reynolds, Jan Francis, Ray Winstone, Catherine Holman, Bill Paterson, Carol MacReady, Joe Melia, Sheila Reid, Christopher Fulford, Jane Cox.

Macbeth on the Estate (1997)
Directed by Penny Woolcock. Cast: Ray Winstone, David Harewood, Andrew Tiernan, Graham Bryan, Jonathan Dow, James Frain, Susan Vidler.

Our Boy (BBC, 1997)
Directed by David Evans. Screenplay by Tony Grounds. Cast: Ray Winstone, Pauline Quirke, Neil Dudgeon, Philip Jackson, Perry Fenwick, Rowena Cooper, Scott Thompson Baker, James Bannon, Philip Bond, Simon Bowen, Richard Claxton, Nicola Duffett, Frank Dunn, Annette Ekblom, Jamie Foreman, Tony Grounds.

Birth, Marriages and Deaths (BBC, 1999)
Directed by Adrian Shergold. Screenplay by Tony Grounds.

Cast: Ray Winstone, Mark Strong, Philip Davis, Maggie O'Neill, Michelle Fairley, Tessa Peake-Jones, Frances Shergold, Emily Corrie.

Last Christmas (BBC, 2000)

Directed by Adrian Shergold. Screenplay by Tony Grounds. Cast: Matt Bardock, Mark Benton, Ahsen Bhatti, Suzanne Burden, Ella Daniels, Phil Daniels, Philip Dowling, Donna Ewin, Tony Grounds, Pauline Quirke, Ray Winstone.

Tough Love (ITV, 2000)

Directed by David Drury. Screenplay by Edward Canfor-Dumas. Cast: Ray Winstone, Adrian Dunbar, Ruth Adams, Doug Allen, George Anton, Annabelle Apsion, Sacha Bennett, Samantha Billington, Kelly Brailsford, Bruce Byron, William Chubb, Rebecca Clay, Josh Cole, Peter Coney, Sally Dexter, Amanda Drew, Jeillo Edwards, Hazel Ellerby, Giles Fagan, Andrew French, Vincent Friell, Josephine Gibson.

The Fear (BBC Series, 2001)

Directed by Blake Bedford and Luke Watson. Story by Arthur Conan Doyle and Edgar Allan Poe. Storyteller Cast: Jason Flemyng, Anna Friel, Sadie Frost, Neve McIntosh, Nick Moran, Sean Pertwee, Ray Winstone.

Lenny Blue (ITV, 2002)

Directed by Andy Wilson. Screenplay by Stephen Butchard. Cast: Desmond Bayliss, Neil Bell, Kelly Brailsford, Karen Bryson, Charlie Creed-Miles, Hazel Ellerby, David Hemmings, Mark Lewis Jones, Ivan Kaye, Emma Lowndes, Francis Magee, Elizabeth Rider, Sam Riley, David Scott Roberts, Emma Rydal, Ray Winstone, Jake Wood.

Henry VIII (ITV, 2003)

Directed by Pete Travis. Screenplay by Peter Morgan. Cast: Ray Winstone, Joss Ackland, Sid Mitchell, Charles Dance, Mark Strong, Assumpta Serna, Thomas Lockyer, William Houston, Danny Webb, Guy Flanagan, David Suchet, Scott Handy, Helena Bonham Carter, Benjamin Whitrow, Stephen Noonan, John Higgins, Michael Maloney, Edward Kelsey, Jeremy Child, William Hoyland, Lara Belmont, Emma Darwell-Smith, Emma Buckley, Edward Tudor-Pole, Christopher Good, Emilia Fox, Sean Bean, Simon Meacock, James Hoare, Joseph Morgan, David Gwillim, Tina Malone, Marsha Fitzalan, Terence Harvey, Kelly Hunter, Pia Girard, Britta Becker, Catrin Rhys, Emily Blunt, Tom Turner, Ryan Winsley, Daniel Betts, Clare Holman.

She's Gone (ITV, 2004)

Directed by Adrian Shergold. Screenplay by Simon Tyrrell. Cast: Ray Winstone, Lindsey Coulson, Gary Lucy, Emily Corrie, Haluk Bilginer, David Westhead, Dimitri Andreas, Freddie Annobil-Dodoo, James Barron, Hulya Bilen, David Chircop, Rebecca Clarke, Mem Ferda, Anastasia Griffith, Mercedes Grower, Gihan Kallian, Marit Velle Kile, Murat Kiran, Kayvan Novak, Owen Oakeshott, Celia Robertson, Tina Tutkova.

Vincent (ITV, 2005)

Season 1, Episodes 1–4. Directed by Roger Gartland, Peter Lydon, Terry McDonough. Screenplay by Stephen Butchard. Cast: Ray Winstone, Suranne Jones, Joe Absolom, Joe Beattie, Emma Catherwood, Angel Coulby, Michael Dixon, Rupert Frazer, Philip Glenister, Jonathan Guy Lewis, Paul Opacic, Eva Pope, Ian Puleston-Davies, Adam Rayner.

Sweeney Todd (BBC, 2006)

Directed by David Moore. Screenplay by Joshua St Johnston. Cast: David Bradley, Zoltan Butuc, Paul Currier, Jessie Davis, David Foxxe, Roger Frost, Tom Hardy, Jessica Hooker, Radu Andrei Micu, Anthony O'Donnell, Gabriel Spahiu, Ben Walker, David Warner, Ray Winstone.

All In The Game (Channel Four, 2006)

Directed by Jim O'Hanlon. Screenplay by Tony Grounds. Cast: Danny Dyer, Ray Winstone, Ike Hamilton, Gerald Kyd, Claire Perkins, Nicola Stephenson, Roy Marsden, Oscar Grounds, Idris Elba, Louis Mahoney, Daniel Anderson, Julia Hills, Nigel Boyle, Alexis Rodney, Sarah Manners.

Vincent (ITV, 2006)

Season 2, Episodes 1–4. Directed by Roger Gartland, Peter Lydon, Terry McDonough. Screenplay by Stephen Butchard. Cast: Ray Winstone, Suranne Jones, Joe Absolom, Joe Beattie, Emma Catherwood, Angel Coulby, Michael Dixon, Rupert Frazer, Philip Glenister, Jonathan Guy Lewis, Paul Opacic, Eva Pope, Ian Puleston-Davies, Adam Rayner.

Miscellaneous Television Appearances

The Sweeney (1975)

Role in episode: 'Loving Arms'

Bergerac (1983)

Role in episode: 'Ninety Per Cent Proof'

Fairly Secret Army (1984)

Role in 3 episodes:

'Eight Bods, Need More', 'The Pulses Quicken' and 'When The Talking Had To Stop'

Auf Wiedersehen Pet (1984)
Role in Episode: 'The Fugitive'

Minder (1984)
Role in 3 episodes:
'A Number of Old Wives Tales', 'Goodbye Sailor' and 'The Car Lot Baggers'

C.A.T.S. Eyes (1986)
Role in episode: 'One Away'

Ever Decreasing Circles (1986)
Role in episode: 'Manure'

Boon (1987)
Role in episode 'A Ride On The Wild Side'

Pulaski (1987)
Role in 2 episodes:
'Ten By Eight Glossy' and 'And The Killer of Rose Amelia Bonner'

Home To Roost (1990)
Role in episode: 'High Noon'

Birds of a Feather (1991)
Role in 2 episodes:
'We'll Always Have Majorca' and 'Poetic Justice'

FILMOGRAPHY

Between the Lines (1992)
Role in episode: 'A Watch and Chains of Course'

Murder Most Horrid (1994)
Role in episode: 'Smashing Bird'

Casualty (1995)
Role in Episode: 'Heartbreak Hotel'

Space Precinct (1995)
Role in episode: 'Two Against The Rock'

The Bill (1995)
Role in 2 episodes: 'Mitigating Circumstances'
and 'Innocence'

Sharman (1996)
Role in episode # 1.3

Thief Takers (1996)
Role in episode: 'Remember Me'

Kavanagh QC (1996)
Role in episode: 'The Burning Deck'

One Foot In The Grave (1997)
Role in episode: 'Starbound'

It's The Daddy (2001)
Advertising commercial for Holsten Pils

At Home With The Braithwaites (2002)
Cameo in episode # 3.6

Irish Film and Television Awards (2003)
Presenter

The BAFTA TV Awards (2004)
Presenter

Who Wants To Be A Millionaire –
Celebrity Easter Special (2004)
Contestant

Optivita (2006)
Advertising commercial for Kellogg's breakfast cereal

Theatre

What A Crazy World We're Living In (1975)
Theatre Workshop, Theatre Royal, Stratford.
Written by Alan Klein, music and lyrics by Alan Klein.
Directed by Larry Dann.
Not Quite Jerusalem (1980)

QR's & A1's Clearly State
King's Head, Islington.
Directed by Jimmy Marcus.

Hinkerman (1988)
Old Red Lion, Islington.
Directed by Roland Jaquarello

Mr Thomas (1990)
Old Red Lion, Islington.
Directed by Kathy Burke.

Some Voices (1994)
The Royal Court Theatre, London.
Directed by Ian Rickson.

Dealer's Choice (1995)
Royal National Theatre & Vaudeville Theatre.
Directed by Patrick Marber.

Pale Horse (1995)
The Royal Court Theatre, London.
Directed by Ian Rickson.

This Is A Chair (1997)
The Royal Court Theatre, London.
Written by Caryl Churchill.

To The Green Fields Beyond (2000)
The Donmar Warehouse, Earlham Street, London. Written by Nick Whitby. Directed by Sam Mendes. Designed by Anthony Ward. Lighting by Howard Harrison. Music by Stephen Warbeck. Cast: Ray Winstone, Dougray Scott, Danny Babington, Finbar Lynch, Danny Sapani, Adrian Scarborough, Hugh Dancy, Nitin Ganatra.

The Night Heron (2002)
The Jerwood Theatre Downstairs, The Royal Court Theatre, London. Written by Jez Butterworth. Directed by Ian Rickson. Designed by Ultz. Lighting by Mick Hughes. Music

by Stephen Warbeck. Cast: Ray Winstone, with Geoffrey Church, Karl Johnson, Roger Morlidge, Paul Ritter, Finlay Robertson, Jessica Stevenson.

Executive Producer Credits

Brown Paper Bag (2003)
She's Gone (2004)
Sweeney Todd (2006)

Music

'Hound Dog' (1999)
Fanny and Elvis
Soundtrack

'Love Me Tender' (1999)
Fanny and Elvis
Soundtrack

'The Harder They Come' (2000)
Love, Honour and Obey
Soundtrack

'I Wish My Baby Was Born' (2003)
Cold Mountain
Soundtrack

Awards and Nominations

1980
BAFTA
That Summer
Nominated for Most Promising Newcomer to Leading Film Role

1998
BRITISH INDEPENDENT FILM AWARDS
Nil By Mouth
Nominated for Best performance by a British Actor in an Independent Film
Winner

BAFTA
Nil By Mouth
Nominated for Best performance by an Actor in a Leading Role

1999
RTS TELEVISION AWARDS
Our Boy
Nominated for Best Actor
Winner

BRITISH INDEPENDENT FILM AWARDS
The War Zone
Nominated for Best Actor

EUROPEAN FILM AWARDS
The War Zone
Nominated for Best Actor

2001
NATIONAL BOARD OF REVIEW (USA)
Last Orders
Nominated for Best Acting by an Ensemble
Shared with Michael Caine, Bob Hoskins, Tom Courtenay,
David Hemmings, Helen Mirren
Winner

EUROPEAN FILM AWARDS
Last Orders
Nominated for Best Actor
Shared with Michael Caine, Bob Hoskins, Tom Courtenay,
David Hemmings, Helen Mirren

BRITISH INDEPENDENT FILM AWARDS
Sexy Beast
Nominated for Best Actor

AWARDS AND NOMINATIONS

2005
AUSTRALIAN FILM INSTITUTE (AFI AWARD)
The Proposition
Nominated for Best Lead Actor

2006
INTERNATIONAL EMMY AWARDS
Vincent
Nominated for Best Performance by an Actor
Winner

NATIONAL BOARD OF REVIEW (USA)
The Departed
Nominated for Best Acting by an Ensemble
Shared with Leonardo DiCaprio, Matt Damon, Jack Nicholson, Mark Wahlberg, Martin Sheen, Vera Farmiga, Alec Baldwin, Anthony Anderson, James Badge Dale
Winner

SAN DIEGO FILM CRITIC FILM SOCIETY AWARDS
The Proposition
Nominated for Best Supporting Actor
Winner

MAGNOLIA AWARDS (SHANGHIA INTERNATIONAL FILM FESTIVAL)
Sweeney Todd
Nominated for Best Actor
Winner

2007
BRITISH INDEPENDENT FILM AWARDS
Nominated for the Richard Harris Award
Winner

CHLOTRUDIS AWARDS
The Proposition
Nominated for Best Actor

SCREEN ACTORS GUILD
The Departed
Nominated for Outstanding Performance by a Cast in a
Motion Picture
Shared with Anthony Anderson, Alec Baldwin, Matt
Damon, Leonardo DiCaprio, Vera Farmiga, Jack Nicholson,
Martin Sheen, Mark Wahlberg